Life Unlocked

Life Unlocked

7 Revolutionary Lessons to Overcome Fear

Srinivasan S. Pillay, MD

Rodale books may be purchased for business or promotional use or for special sales.
For information, please write to:

Special Markets Department, Rodale Inc., 733 Third Avenue, New York, NY 10017

Printed in the United States of America

Rodale Inc. makes every effort to use acid-free ♾, recycled paper ♲.

Book design by Joanna Williams

Library of Congress Cataloging-in-Publication Data

Pillay, Srinivasan S.
Life unlocked : 7 revolutionary lessons to overcome fear / Srinivasan S. Pillay.
p. cm.
ISBN-13: 978-1-60529-852-8 hardcover
ISBN-10: 1-60529-852-2 hardcover
1. Fear. 2. Anxiety. I. Title.
BF575.F2P55 2010
152.4'6—dc22 2010020172

Distributed to the trade by Macmillan

2 4 6 8 10 9 7 5 3 1 hardcover

We inspire and enable people to improve their lives and the world around them

For more of our products visit **rodalestore.com** or call 800-848-4735

To my parents, Raz and Sava, and brother, Rajan,
whose astonishing and unflinching love and dedication
have inspired in me the need to reach out to the world
with the gesture that this book represents.

[contents]

[acknowledgments]

I would like to acknowledge the work of all the great scientists who have made this book possible. Without their curious and contentious ways, we would be much poorer for solutions to overcome the fears that trap us in the cages of our everyday lives.

I would also like to acknowledge Jonathan O. Cole, MD; Leston Havens, MD; Shervert Frazier, MD; and all of my mentors through the years—including Deborah Yurgelun-Todd, PhD; Bruce Cohen, MD, PhD; and Scott Rauch, MD—who have been guiding lights that have helped me understand my place and movement in the world.

Last but not least, to all those who love me and to those who afford me the gift of loving them—I thank you with all my heart and pass on the love through this book to those whose lives may be touched by the place where the human spirit finds its metaphor and meaning in science.

[1]

What You Don't Know Can Hurt You

Moving Beyond Unconscious Fear

Death is not the biggest fear we have; our biggest fear is taking the risk to be alive—the risk to be alive and express what we really are.

—Don Miguel Ruiz

The human condition is a vulnerable but powerful one, based on the primitive brain forces of animals lower in the evolutionary chain yet surrounded by a shell of magnificent brain tissue that gives us our unique abilities to think, speak, and express ourselves as we do. These primitive forces of the unconscious brain crouch on all fours as they scour our surroundings for signs of imminent danger. The unconscious brain is never truly silent, always purring in the background, bathing its thinking counterpart with vigilant warnings—"Watch out!" "Don't go there!" "Be careful!" Kindled by a constant flow of electrons, which slide down one neuron and into another in milliseconds, the unconscious brain lights up at the mere hint of danger.

The conscious brain picks up this heat and relies on it in the way that we rely on the sun for our survival. Yet this "giving" of the unconscious is a double-edged sword, as is much of human nature. This same heat that protects us can also burn us when it is not regulated. And cooling down the dubious gift of fear is no easy feat. This tension between the conscious and the unconscious brain, the latter with its suffocating diligence and overprotectiveness, is in many ways responsible for much of our daily ambivalence.

No wonder, then, that recent research has shown that we are consistently unable to recognize the things that will make us happy. Given a few choices, we almost always make the choice that leads us into trouble. So, many of us blame ourselves for not making the right choices in our lives without realizing that in many situations, our choices are beyond our immediate control. They are locked up in the invisible cage of fear that is the unconscious. To unlock this cage, we have to first see it. But "seeing" fear requires much more than just recognizing our inner tremblings. It requires a special kind of attention and knowledge that a vast body of scientific research permits us to employ. In this chapter, we will explore some of this knowledge, with the goal of gaining a deeper understanding of the inner workings of fear—so that we can do something about it.

Every day, people tell me the stories of their lives: people who want to move in one direction, but instead find themselves moving in another; people who claim to be trying, but repeatedly find themselves failing; people who are bored and stuck, yet are unable to make the changes they know they want to make; and parents who worry that their children are depressed, have learning disabilities, or suffer from attentional problems that just aren't improving despite intervention and treatment. If we know what we want, why are we unable to act on it? Why are we unable to follow the directions given by our conscious minds and reach our goals unimpeded? And when we do try to do the right things, why are we unsuccessful? For many, this is a source of much heartache. Whether it is a tortured relationship or a difficult job situation, we often feel regretful after we realize we've made the wrong choice. Why do we continue to make these choices, and what steers us toward them in the first place?

If we are consciously doing our best and yet not getting to where we want to go, something outside of our consciousness must be driving us in another direction without our knowledge or consent. I call this the rip current of human nature. A rip current is a very powerful surface flow of water that is returning to the sea from close to the shore. It can turn an eerily calm-looking body of water into something extremely dangerous that has the power to drag swimmers out to sea. Many people caught in rip currents eventually drown due to the sheer exhaustion of trying to swim against the current.

The unconscious is the rip current of the mind. From a distance, it's calm, barely noticeable, and difficult to anticipate. And at its core lies the threatening force of fear. Much like a rip current is helpful to surfers who rely on its force to pull them away from shore, fear may be helpful if it urges you forward toward your goal. But like the unpredictable rip current, fear can also drag you away from your goals and destinations.

When Sigmund Freud, the father of psychoanalysis, listened to his patients relate their lives as they lay on his couch, he concluded that their behavior was motivated by factors outside of their immediate awareness. Though mysterious and somewhat unsettling, this idea was appealing enough that it formed the basis of psychoanalytic therapy for many decades. The fundamental idea was this: We are capable of doing things that may be the exact opposite of what we actually *want* for ourselves because our unconscious motivations conflict with our conscious intentions. When Freud told the world that human suffering could be alleviated by understanding the unconscious, many people supported this theory. Yet, for those who required hard evidence—for those who could not heal themselves with abstractions—there remained a void and a strong suspicion that Freud's conjecture was unfounded and had no basis in reality.

In this chapter, we will come to understand the many ways in which Freud was correct about our unconscious motivations, as well as the other important insights into human behavior that have since been brought forth. We will also come to understand how this powerful, unconscious fear keeps us from living our fullest lives—and what we can do to transcend it.

Brain Imaging:
The Foray into an Unknown World

In order for scientists to prove that human behavior is influenced by unconscious phenomena, they needed to examine the brain. For centuries, our ability to do this was limited. X-rays were not of much help, because they weren't sensitive enough to pick up the subtle changes that would indicate different brain functions. Measuring brain waves using EEG (electroencephalography) proved to be of some help, but because the EEG leads were attached to the scalp, this usually showed only surface brain activity. With the advent of MRI (magnetic resonance imaging), the entire landscape of understanding brain structure and function began to change.

Still, within these limits, not much could really be learned about how the brain functions. Then in 1990 came the advent of functional brain imaging, also called functional MRI or fMRI. At last, scientists and doctors could actually observe the changes in brain blood flow that coincided with the arising of different emotional states. Though it was first used only for clinical applications in neurology, researchers soon began to use this technology to understand how fear affects brain function. What they saw profoundly changed our understanding of the science of fear.

Your Brain Is Bombarded by Fear Even If You Don't See It:
Scientific Evidence That the Blind Can See

Our brains are made up of nerve tissue, including neurons, other specialized cells, and matter surrounding the cells. Nerve tissue is alive. Like an electrical cord, if you plug this nerve tissue into a power source, current begins to flow. If you plug an electrical cord into a battery, which produces direct current (DC), direct current will run through the cord. If you plug the cord into a wall outlet, which transmits alternating current (AC) from a power plant, alternating current will run through the cord. The nature of the power generated by the source determines how the current flows.

For nerve tissue in the brain, events in the world are literally power sources. And like an electrical current, the nature of the power (a physical sensation or emotion) generated by the source (an event) will determine the nature of the current. An electrical cord receives current simply by virtue of being plugged in, and this is also the case for the human brain. From the time you are born, you are plugged into events whether you are asleep or awake. And because you are plugged in, current is always flowing in your brain. Like the electrical current, the nature of the power reaching your brain determines what kind of current will flow within it.

When this power is fear, the current flows in your fear circuits, even when you can't see what is making you afraid. This has been scientifically proven. In one famous case, Patient G.Y. had had a stroke that damaged tissue in the striate cortex, the part of the brain that processes nerve signals from the retina of the eye. As a result, he had a condition called cortical blindness—for all intents and purposes, he could not see. Though there was nothing wrong with his eyes, his brain couldn't process what they saw. When he walked down the street, he bumped into objects in his path. If you placed an object in front of him, he was unable to describe it.

What was odd, however, was that when a photograph of a person wearing a fearful facial expression was presented to G.Y. as if he could see it, he accurately detected the expression of fear over and over again. The researchers examined this phenomenon until they were able to prove that chance could not account for how frequently G.Y. was correct. This finding rocked the world of fear science.

How could a blind person "sense" a visually communicated emotion? If we accept the idea that we are plugged into the world from birth, then it follows that this man's fear circuitry somehow detected that something fearful was before him. Scientists could only conclude that, because his brain damage prevented him from "seeing" the fear visually, G.Y.'s brain was taking the signals from his retinas and sending them via another route to make him conscious of it.

Given your own life experiences, this must sound at least somewhat plausible. Most people believe that they can sense things, whether or not this can be proven. But how can your brain sense fear when you see nothing fearful—or, in fact, if you see nothing at all? And if this is possible, what are the implications for your everyday life?

Even if you are "blind" to fear, your brain still picks up the danger cues that surround you and runs that current through its fear circuits. This is similar to what G.Y. experienced, which scientists call blindsight—the unconscious recognition of visual information by a person with damage in the striate cortex of the brain. For a long time, the idea of blindsight was mere conjecture, until a group of brain imaging researchers designed an experiment to test it. Below is the theory that prompted that experiment.

How Long Does Your Brain Need to Be Exposed to Fear Before Current Runs in the Fear Circuit?

If something fearful is happening around you, your brain will pick it up. But just as one millisecond is not enough to generate current through an entire electrical cord (electricity moves about as fast as the minute hand on a clock), having fear-inducing events happening around you for one millisecond is not enough to turn on your fear circuits, either.

When your brain is plugged into something fearful, electrons start to flow through your fear circuits. But your brain needs at least ten milliseconds of fear exposure before it can hold on to that fear. It takes between ten and thirty milliseconds for your unconscious brain to process fear, and after that, conscious processing starts to occur.

"Processing" means that the wheels are spinning; the brain is engaged and starting to get some traction. It is like an antiskid device. A car equipped with an antilock braking system (ABS) will automatically try to slow itself down when the brakes are applied as it skids on ice. Fear engages the ABS of the brain after just ten milliseconds of exposure, and it signals the brain that it needs to slow down. And after thirty milliseconds, your brain starts to "know" that it has become gripped by fear, which is causing it to skid. By the time four hundred milliseconds have passed, the brain knows most of what it needs to know about the nature of the fear, and the fear can be called to consciousness quite easily.

Imagine how your brain is applying its brakes on the road of your life every time it senses this unconscious fear. Without your knowing it, your journey toward your goal may be slowed down due to this constant braking in the face of unconscious fear. To take control back from this automatic braking system in the brain, you would have to understand your unconscious fears better and somehow instruct your brain not to respond by trying to slow down. It's a profound thought, but it was mere conjecture until a group of researchers designed an experiment to test whether this "unconscious" processing actually takes place, and where in the brain conscious and unconscious processing occur.

To do this, researchers devised a process called backward masking. Essentially, a photo of a fearful face was presented to subjects too quickly for the conscious mind to register it and then immediately replaced with a photo of a neutral face, or "mask," that was shown for long enough that the subjects were conscious of having seen it; in other words, although they actually saw two pictures, they thought they saw only one. The image of the fearful face was presented for more than ten but less than thirty milliseconds—long enough to activate the brain's fear current, but not long enough to provoke the conscious brain. If this stimulus did not activate anything in the brain, then the researchers would conclude that fear sensing was not occurring. What they found was that the conscious brain could not pick up a fearful expression if it was presented for less than thirty milliseconds.

What Senses Fear in the Human Brain?

The subjects in all of these experiments had been diagnosed with anxiety disorders, but Paul Whalen, PhD, and his colleagues at Harvard carried out a similar study in a group of individuals who did not meet any criteria for psychiatric diagnoses. They showed them the fearful face very quickly, and then showed them the mask for a longer time—167 milliseconds—so that consciously, they "saw" only the mask and had no idea that the fearful face had also been shown to them. The experiment was done while the participants were lying down in an MRI scanner, so the researchers were able to see any areas in the brain where the blood flow (and thereby the electrical current!) increased when the fearful face was shown.

What they found elegantly explained how G.Y. had sensed fear. At the time that the subjects were shown the fearful face, the blood flow to a brain structure called the amygdala increased even though the subjects had no conscious knowledge or memory of seeing the face. If this were you or me, we too would have denied having seen an image of fear. Yet our brains would say otherwise, for the wheels of our amygdalae would have begun churning at the moment we were exposed to fear.

What this discovery tells us about the role of fear in our lives is profound: It implies that you and I could be completely unaware of many things that create fear in us, even though they generate current that flows through our brains. Think of all the things you encounter on a daily basis as you take the subway, drive a car, or step into an office building. Even if you don't consciously see a person who looks as if he or she is feeling fear, your amygdala is very aware that fear is all around you.

To understand the implications of this, let's look again at what happens when current runs through a wire. If the current is one that the wire can handle, it will be fine. But if there is too much current, the circuit won't be able to handle it and the system will shut down. Unconscious fear has a similar effect on your brain. It starts to run current through the amygdala, but if there is too much, your amygdala will either malfunction or stop functioning altogether.

Moreover, the amygdala is not isolated within the brain. Located at the center of the brain, it is connected to the conscious brain by one of the brain's main freeways. Signals travel between it and the conscious brain all the time. So the current—the emotion or sensation—you send through it can affect your conscious functioning and thinking as well.

This danger detector may in fact be the switch that gets turned on every time we try to do something that our brains perceive as risky. In his book *Money Success and You,* John Kehoe, who writes about mind power, argues that making money becomes less complicated when you understand that negative thoughts can prevent you from attaining financial success. He advises that we face and banish negative thoughts from our minds in order to make more money. Although this may sound like a simple concept, it is not an easy one to put into action. But the Whalen experiment may help us figure out how.

If, for example, you decided that you want to make more money, your cortex would need to be well organized for its mission; like a ship, it would start at point A and travel to reach point B, where the money would be made. But the story is not that simple. As Kehoe suggests, unconscious negative ideas you have about money may disrupt the cortex, and going from A to B might require some forceful and careful navigation in the winds of these fears. That is to say, if the thought of money activates feelings of fear, it will cause your amygdala to activate. This amygdala activation will spread to the cortex and disrupt the synchrony your brain needs for your cortex (in this case, the frontal cortex) to organize your efforts toward this goal. If your amygdala isn't disrupted by fear, your efforts will be well executed and synchronized. When your amygdala disrupts this action, even if you aren't aware of the disruption, your efforts to make money will be swept along by the rip current, pulling you in the opposite direction and away from your goals.

Every day in my clinical practice, I encounter people who fall prey to this very phenomenon. They think that they are doing everything they should be doing and can't understand why they aren't getting any closer to their goals.

The effect of the amygdala is even more dramatic than that of a rip current, because you never know for certain that it is exerting an influence. But you *can* infer that it is always in surveillance mode, always responding to any fears you have, and always spreading this disruption to your cortex. And it needs only ten milliseconds to register fear. These amygdala ripples are constantly affecting your brain, and your life.

The Unconscious Brain:
Where Does Unconscious Fear Live?

The structure and function of the unconscious brain is vast and complex. Through the years, we have evolved from our predecessors by developing a more advanced outer layer of brain cell connections called the cortex. Yet we have preserved some of the important parts of the brains of our predecessors, including the parts that make up the fast-detecting, fast-acting unconscious. In our predecessors, the fast-processing unconscious brain (which some people call the subconscious) quickly assessed the circumstances for danger, allowing the creatures to protect themselves.

The amygdala is one of these vital structures that we inherited from our ancestors. This almond-shaped mass of nerve cell bodies (*amygdale* is the Greek word for *almond*) alerts us to danger in our environment within tens of milliseconds of detecting it.

The amygdala buzzes with electrical activity whenever danger looms, even when we are not aware of its presence. Joseph LeDoux, PhD, a renowned fear researcher, has referred to the amygdala as the guard dog of the human brain. It is small, sensitive, and very reactive, and it is the focus of modern inquiries into the brain mechanisms underlying fear.

There are various types and sizes of nerve cells in the amygdala, and they are arranged into pathways that have specific functions. After performing extensive brain mapping research, scientists confirmed the existence of two important pathways related to fear. One pathway is more direct and produces a more immediate response, but it is also less accurate. For example, if you see a coiled rope in a dark corridor, you may jump back in fear because your brain perceives it as a snake. In this case, information travels from the thalamus (the brain part that first senses danger) directly to the amygdala, which then instructs your body to jump away from the danger (circuit 1 → 2 → 3 → 4 in the diagram showing the direct pathway). However, shortly thereafter, the thalamus also relays a message to the cortex. Because the cortex takes longer to process the visual information, its assessment is more accurate than the amygdala's. When the cortex recognizes that the object in the corridor is a rope rather than a snake, it calms down the amygdala and turns off the body's fear response (circuit 1 → 2 → 3 → 4 → 5 in the indirect pathway diagram).

Direct Pathway (The Brain's First Response)

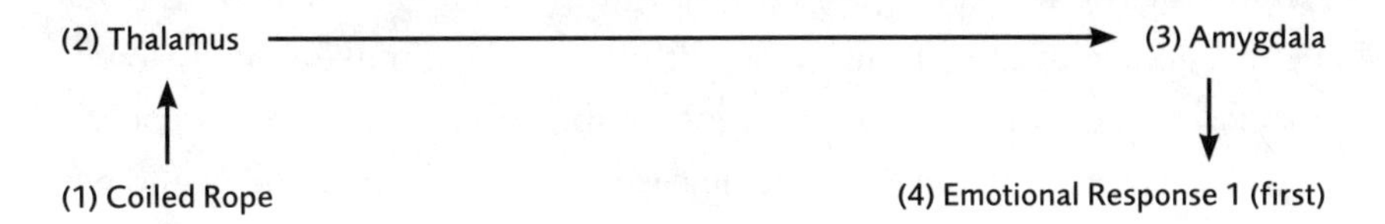

Indirect Pathway (The Brain's Eventual Response)

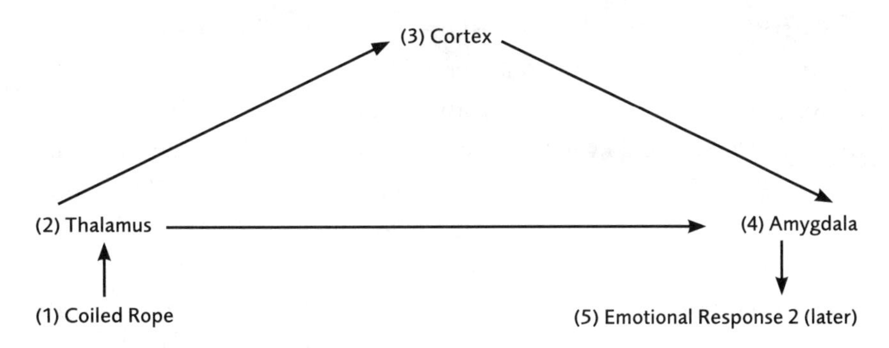

Fear can easily register in the amygdala (having traveled the short route) without being passed on to the cortex (the long route), preventing you from knowing that you have been exposed to something fearful. To have an emotional response, you do not have to know about the fear; it only needs to be registered by the unconscious brain. Since the amygdala has extensive connections with the rest of your brain, your emotions and behavior could be deeply and extensively affected without your knowledge of it.

The Story of Brian:
Is Panic the Result of Mixed Messages to the Amygdala?

Brian was a successful, forty-eight-year-old senior corporate executive at a prominent firm. He came to me because he was suffering from disturbing panic attacks. He had used medication, but this helped only up to a point. The attacks persisted.

Over time I came to understand that Brian was a good-natured person, but he hated his job. He had always wanted to be an entrepreneur, but he was afraid that he wouldn't be able to make it on his own. He had thought about leaving his job on many occasions over the previous twenty years, but every time he came close to doing it, he would get promoted. He felt the corporate claws grabbing him, digging in deeper and deeper.

On one hand, Brian knew that life was short and that the longer he procrastinated, the harder it would be to leave. On the other hand, he wondered how he could leave a secure job when he had a wife and children to support. What if people thought he was making a terrible mistake? What if he failed? As he talked more and more about this, he realized that he had even more fears. He uncovered his fear of dying, and also his fear of living. Somehow, living required a sense of faith that was all about being in the moment and looking forward. Brian was not used to living without looking over his shoulder.

Now imagine what was going on in Brian's brain. All of these fears had been causing an emotional earthquake in his amygdala, and it wasn't until he started to talk about this that he even realized that they were there. We can infer from the Whalen experiment that this amygdala activity was probably disrupting the efforts his cortex made to get him to move on with his life. These two parts of his brain were sending contradictory messages to the "action center" (the motor cortex) of his brain, the part that gets things done. When his brain's action center received these contradictory messages, it didn't know what to do. The cortex wanted to help him organize his departure, while his amygdala sent panic signals to his cortex to tell it to stop doing this because Brian was in danger.

No wonder, then, that Brian suffered from recurrent panic attacks. They would come on suddenly and without warning. The older he got, the more intense the conflict grew between his hatred for his job and his desire for the life he wanted. And the more intense this conflict became, the more severe his panic attacks became.

We now know that panic attacks are associated with increased amygdala activation that likely disrupts the functioning of the cortex and, in particular, of the part called the anterior cingulate cortex (ACC). The ACC is important in attention and usually monitors decisions and actions for errors and conflicts. It has a direct connection to the amygdala. From a psychological viewpoint, Brian's panic attacks resulted from his conflicting feelings about the security and familiarity of his job versus the frustration of not being an entrepreneur. From a neurological perspective, whenever his cortex tried to move him toward his goal, the riptide generated by his overactive amygdala disrupted his cortical intentions, dragging him further away. But on a daily basis, these fears buzzing around in his amygdala were invisible to Brian. We will revisit Brian later in the chapter to see how he ended up dealing with this.

A Little Fear Goes a Long Way

Brian was obviously struggling with a lot of fear. But how much fear does one need to be exposed to before the amygdala becomes active? Whalen and his colleagues addressed this question by examining how the size of the eye whites, called the sclerae, affects amygdala activation in a person looking at them. They wondered if the amygdala required exposure to a full facial expression to read it as fear, or just to the critical components that signal fear, such as wide-open eyes. And if the amygdala did react to just the critical components, would its reaction be the same as it was when the subject saw an entire face that expressed fear?

So Whalen and his colleagues again used backward masking, but this time they showed participants images of only eyes instead of whole faces. That is, they exposed their subjects to pictures of eyes that showed varying amounts of the sclerae of the eyes. They were able to show that the amygdala is more responsive to larger eye whites (indicating fear) than to the smallest eye whites (indicating happiness), even when the subjects saw these images too briefly to be aware of having seen them. This extended their findings that the amygdala is indeed sensitive to fear stimuli, and even to excerpts of fear stimuli. The eyes of a fearful person communicate much of the fear independently of the rest of the face and are enough to cause the amygdala to activate. A frightening stimulus does not have to take the form of an earthquake or a lion to engender fear. Even subtle stimuli can significantly activate the amygdala. Imagine the buzz created in your amygdala by all of the little things you confront each day. How can the frontal lobe do its job with all this disruption in the background?

The evidence that even small amounts of fear can activate the amygdala made scientists realize that it does not need a complete set of information to react: The amygdala responds to even the most subtle whiff of fear.

Where There's Smoke, There's Fire:
What Happens If You Trip the Amygdala Switch?

The amygdala is made up of nerve cells like the one shown below.

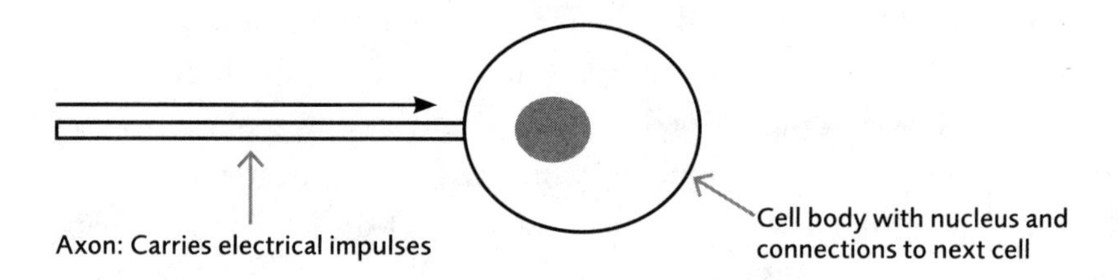

The axons transmit electrical current. Since they have a defined size, they can transmit only a certain amount of current. Like a house's electrical circuit, if you overload it, it will blow a fuse or trip the breaker. Have you ever felt like you were having an emotional meltdown or that you were extremely tired but couldn't quite account for it? Have you felt that after you get home from work, all you want to do is watch television and space out? Do you feel guilty about being tired after a day of taking care of your kids? Or, perhaps, do you feel guilty because you have help with the kids, but you still feel exhausted by the end of the day?

Well, an overloaded amygdala can help explain your fatigue. Your conscious brain may think that you have no reason to be so tired. But we now know that your unconscious brain may be absorbing the stress and fears of your daily life. Absorbing this stress takes energy, so much that it may eat up most of your energy stores, leaving less energy available for your body to do other things. Also, when the amygdala activates, it sends electrical impulses down the spinal cord to activate the fight-or-flight response so that your heart, lungs, and other organs work overtime as well. The resulting fatigue affects your entire body.

Think of your amygdala as the engine of a car. If you accidentally leave the lights on, eventually the battery will die. When your fear is unconscious, it's like not being aware that you've left the lights on in your car. When fear is outside of your conscious awareness, it begins to drain your battery life. Oftentimes, you may not recognize this until you have nothing left—your car has stalled. Without warning, the amygdala activation reaches a peak and you find yourself having to go to extreme measures to recalibrate your emotions.

In general, it is safe to assume that this is always occurring. It therefore makes a lot of sense to always maintain the amygdala. Servicing the amygdala involves many important steps that we will discuss later in this chapter. Vacations, for example, may be equivalent to amygdala service visits. But for now, it is important to remember that fear you aren't even aware of can overstimulate the amygdala, using up vital energy that you could apply toward doing other things.

When the amygdala overfires, this malfunction spills over into the decision-making centers in the frontal cortex with which it is connected. Furthermore, as we mentioned earlier, if there is too much electrical stimulation, the amygdala may blow a fuse or burn out, so to speak. In such cases, it is possible that it may be unable to perform its protective function, making us inclined to take unnecessary risks. This theory is also sometimes used to explain why thrill seekers do what they do. They start out being unconsciously afraid, do not recognize this, burn out the amygdala, and then truly do not recognize when they *should* be afraid. It also explains why people sometimes seek out damaging relationships. It has been shown that some people who have had amygdala damage due to major life trauma or brain lesions are unable to correctly interpret anger or fear in themselves or in others. As a result, they may be prone to putting themselves in dangerous situations because they don't recognize them as dangerous.

Science is now starting to show us that connecting with this unconscious fear and trying to cool off the amygdala may be important for people who are exposed to too much unconscious fear. We can't let the amygdala go on buzzing just because it is outside of our awareness.

The Story of Ellie:
Can We Choose to Limit Amygdala Activation?

Ellie, a very highly functional woman I was seeing in therapy, reported that she often woke up in the morning trembling or feeling afraid. She had no idea why this was happening. "I feel like I'm losing my mind," she would say. I inquired about the nature of her fear. "I don't know," she would respond. "I just get up, and with absolutely nothing intimidating or frightening in sight, I can feel that something is not right. It's not that my heart is racing. Or that I feel panicked. I even make a deliberate attempt to calm down before I sleep. I drink noncaffeinated tea. I wind down. Nothing seems to help."

When we explored this further, it turned out that her husband, with whom she would watch television in bed in the evening, would continue to watch television long after she had gone to sleep. For about two hours, he would watch crime shows and action dramas that typically involved cars screeching to a halt or gunshots or people screaming, as well as frightening music. They had been married for ten years. When we explored whether this could be affecting her while she slept, she scoffed at the idea. "Believe me," she said, "when I go to sleep, I am out in a second." We know that one second is ample time for the brain to register information consciously. And if you recall the findings of the Whalen experiment, the unconscious brain needs only thirty milliseconds of stimulation. So while Ellie slept, I thought it was likely that she was processing the stimulation outside of her consciousness. She thought that this was, as she put it, "a load of Freudian b.s." until I shared many of the latest brain research studies with her.

I explained that these frightening stimuli do not require an awake state or conscious processing to turn on the amygdala. All that they require is a way in. And if a person with blindsight can see, then a sleeping person might also be able to process auditory stimuli. These stimuli readily entered her brain through her ears. Much like Patient G.Y., I thought, Ellie's brain was registering the stimuli even though she had no conscious awareness of them.

Ellie was still skeptical, but she agreed to conduct an experiment for six months, during which time her husband agreed (not without protest!) that he would not watch television in bed while she slept beside him. Seemingly miraculously, Ellie's morning fear, although still present, decreased significantly over three months and was virtually gone after six months. Ellie became a believer!

We are all exposed to frightening stimuli all the time, whether we are paying attention to them or not. From watching the evening news to hearing car horns scream on the street, to seeing an anxious person on the subway, to being around someone who feels but does not look anxious—the examples are countless. The amygdala processes all of these stimuli automatically. Nobody is immune to these effects. And furthermore, it doesn't matter how many positive things are taking place at the same time: If a threat is presented, your brain is trained by evolution to pay attention to it *above all else.*

The Biology of Bittersweet Experiences

At any one time, there are many positive and negative experiences going on in your life. Why, then, does it often seem that no matter how many positive things you have going on, all you need is one or two stressful situations to put a damper on things?

Your brain can process many emotions at the same time. But evolution has programmed it to preferentially process threat first, and often at the expense of other emotions. It is a bit like listening to AC/DC at top volume while you play Whitney Houston in the background at a lower volume. You would barely be able to hear Whitney's gentle ballad against AC/DC's hammering of drums and screeching of electric guitar.

This is what researchers Patrik Vuilleumier, MD, and Sophie

Schwartz, PhD, found in 2001 when they conducted an experiment to see what would happen if they presented different images to the visual fields of people who, like Patient G.Y., had cortical blindness, although in these cases only one eye had lost its connection in the brain. The visual field is the entire area that a person can see when he or she is looking forward. The blind visual field in a person who has cortical blindness is therefore that same area, but within it the person thinks he or she sees nothing. When the researchers presented one outline drawing of a flower, a spider, or a ring shape—all very similar in shape—to the intact visual field and a different drawing to the blind visual field at the same time, the subjects were able to correctly report that the spider had been shown in the blind visual field more often than when neutral or pleasant drawings were shown in that field. The brain accurately detected spiders more often than neutral or pleasant stimuli. It is as though the unconscious first processes a stimulus that might require a protective response (a threat) before it processes other stimuli. In other experiments, Vuilleumier and colleagues extended these findings by showing that the same principle applies to fearful faces; when presented with images representing fear and other emotions, the brain preferentially attends to fear before it considers other emotions. This is one of the things that was happening in Brian's life. His brain was behaving as all brains do when left to their own devices: It processed fear first. With his priorities determined by his fear, Brian procrastinated his way into doing nothing. His fears canceled out his wishes for a more expansive life and also consumed his positive emotions.

Many times, these conflicts between unconscious fears and conscious events lead to a mysterious kind of numbing. For example, you may be praised for your work but find that you genuinely are unable to feel good about it. Or you may find that having a minor fight with your boss on your birthday consumes your entire mood despite being surrounded by gifts and positive feelings. The brain always chooses to shine its spotlight on fear above other emotions. This phenomenon will be described in more detail in Chapter 2.

Some therapists propose that making your unconscious fears conscious will have the effect of "canceling out" the fear, but this hasn't been proven scientifically. Although it is advisable to try to bring unconscious fears to the level of consciousness (so you can deal with them by using your frontal cortex), it is important not to abandon the process without taking it any further. What you will end up with is fear in both the unconscious *and* the conscious. As described below, your attention to this needs to be dedicated and complete, and your unconscious can do a lot of work on its own, as well. Frightening dreams are a way for the unconscious to deal with fears that may be too great to hold in the conscious brain.

One study examined this interaction of two levels of emotions—one conscious and the other not—occurring at the same time. Several images were presented to a person with hemianopia (a loss of vision in only the right or left half of the visual field). When a fearful face was presented to both the blind and intact visual fields at the same time, activation increased in several brain regions (the amygdala, fusiform gyrus, and pulvinar). Simultaneously seeing and "not seeing" (in the blind field) the fear created twice the amount of activation that simply seeing the fear did. This is not surprising, since we know that a fearful image can make an impression even when the conscious brain doesn't see it. And it makes sense that conscious and unconscious fear add up.

What was surprising, however, was that there was less brain activation when the picture of fear was presented only to the intact visual field than there was when the picture was presented only to the blind field. This suggests that unconscious fear has a greater impact than conscious fear on brain activation. What you don't know activates the amygdala more than what you do know.

When you encounter things that provoke fear at an unconscious level, your sensory perception can be affected in other ways as well. It has been shown that when fearful faces are presented to a subject outside of his or her conscious awareness, the subject's ability to correctly identify emotion in voices is also impacted. If both the image and the voice are threatening, it enhances brain activation, especially if both of the stimuli are outside of the subject's conscious awareness. Thus, fear that is simultaneously heard and seen outside of your conscious awareness has more impact than just seeing the fear does. Remember that in Ellie's case, the sound of danger was enough to dominate her emotional state.

Notably, we still strongly register fear even when we're concurrently presented with an incongruent happy facial expression or voice. If there is some reason to pick up fear, the amygdala will process this. Also, incongruity between a voice and a facial expression activates the brain's "conflict detection" center (the ACC), which then activates the amygdala.

This has important implications for your life. Many people I see are worried by their inability to consciously identify why they are unhappy. These experiments explain why you may not feel happy even when everything around you appears to be fine. Many times, for example, people are concerned because they did not feel happy or they were unable to relax while they were on a vacation. Their spouses complain that they are ungrateful or that they cannot appreciate the positive things in life. These people feel guilty because they know that their spouses are right, and they don't understand why they feel the way they do. I once had a dog that would start to whimper hours in advance of a thunderstorm. While the rest of the family was having a good time, he would crouch, put his head down, and whimper. It was only after I connected this behavior to his sensitivity to the impending thunder that I realized that he was responding to fear. Similarly, some humans are more sensitive to negative stimuli than others are, and their amygdalae may start to activate way in advance of those of other people. Or, these more sensitive people may pick up more of what is going on around them than they need to. This sensitivity may be the result of a combination of genetics and social and environmental influences. Knowing that this may be happening can help to reduce the guilt they feel and provide a context for understanding why they feel bad even though everything appears to be good.

And on the subject of vacations, a study conducted several years ago found that when people rated and tracked their moods, they were actually happier at work than they were on vacation, although their recollection was that they were happier on vacation. Vacations tend to lessen the intense attention (and frontal activation) that work requires. This leaves the amygdala to its own devices, which may actually enhance uncomfortable feelings. The answer here is not to avoid vacations, but to recognize that your own predispositions may differ from what you expect. Some people focus on doing specific activities, like scuba diving or swimming, while they're on vacation to fulfill their need for frontal activation so they can relax their amygdalae during time away from work.

Even after an event that provokes fear in the amygdala ends, the amygdala may remain activated. Mark Williams, PhD, and Jason Mattingley, PhD, found that images of negative emotions presented first to a person's blind visual field (and therefore unconsciously perceived) can affect judgments of emotions presented a little later to the unaffected visual field. This phenomenon is called affective priming. So, leftover negative emotions linger in the brain and affect our outlook on positive events. This may explain why it sometimes takes a few days to fully get into "vacation mode."

Another way to understand this is that unconscious fear tints the lens through which you view life, even after the conscious fear has subsided. The leftover tint affects the way you see and think about things. This is why some people think of the glass as half full and others think of it as half empty. Both are correct, but the people who think of the glass as half empty are seeing it through the tint left by their previous unconscious fear. What we are therefore coming to see is that the amygdala affects the way we view the world. And your brain's fear-tinted lenses often prompt you to avoid pursuing exciting opportunities.

The Story of Sonia:

The Biology of Being on the Rebound

Sonia was an attractive, thirty-six-year-old woman who had been in an abusive relationship that ended in a difficult breakup when she was twenty-eight. Since then, she had been unable to sustain a long-term relationship with any man she dated. Getting dates was not an issue, but every time she grew close to a man, she would find something terribly wrong with him. We talked about this for a long time before she started to see what might be happening.

"All the good ones are already taken," she would sometimes half joke. "I don't know what to say. They always seem so great, but they turn out to be jerks." Sonia did not need any deep psychological insight to understand that her relationship with her ex had something to do with this. "I don't get it," she would say. "As soon as they start to get angry, I flash back to Richard and the abuse I suffered there." This was her conscious fear. But her unconscious fear was a little more precise.

Recognizing that a previous hurtful situation makes you more cynical is not enough. Sonia recognized the leftover amygdala activation she was experiencing, but because she didn't do anything about it, she continued to be disappointed by her inability to find a partner.

Sonia was afraid that she could not face the anger of her potential partners without succumbing to it, as she had when enduring Richard's abuse for five years before he left. Her amygdala was always idling in the background, and even when her partners were genuinely positive, this leftover negative emotion (a constantly buzzing amygdala) was too powerful to allow her to clearly see their positive traits. The men she dated felt unappreciated and confused. They accused her of being cold, and the recurrent breakups made the amygdala activation even worse, further priming it for the next relationship failure. It was only when she consciously started to talk about this with her current boyfriend that he was able to remind her at certain times that he was not Richard. This pattern continued as long as she viewed her relationship through the amygdala-tinted glasses that her relationship with Richard had put on her. It was only when she made a conscious decision to take off those glasses that she began to see things more clearly.

In therapy, Sonia worked on increasing her confidence about handling an abusive situation in a less victimized manner. She learned to break the long-held association that anger always led to abuse, and she learned that she had experienced her ability to leave her boyfriends as a powerful action she took in response to remembering her abuse. Eventually, she also learned that leaving her boyfriends was not a sign of power after all, but rather the result of succumbing to the fear engendered by her conditioning.

Sonia's new glasses afforded her a new vision. But to develop and maintain this vision, she had to dig deep into her unconscious to truly understand the pain that she had blocked off. To block off her pain, she had disconnected her frontal cortex from her amygdala. The amygdala was still running. When she reestablished its connection with her frontal circuits, she was able to use her conscious mind to decrease her amygdala activation and change her lens. Remember the diagram on page 11. The frontal cortex can modulate what is going on in the amygdala, but you have to make contact with the amygdala and the pain that it is reflecting. Shining a light on the amygdala may not be enough. Sometimes, you have to literally go to where all of this feeling lies.

Sonia spent a lot of time exploring her emotions through therapy. She used her relationship with me as a template for connecting with real emotions in a safe environment. She worked through some of her brain's automatic responses to situations, and by becoming more conscious of those reactions, she was able to cool down her overactive amygdala and feed it new, more accurate information.

Sonia has now been in a happy relationship for the past year.

If you have just been rejected or have suffered through a difficult breakup, the unconscious fear of disappointment will intrude upon any new relationships. This is why you hear so many people say that they "need some time" after a difficult breakup before entering a new relationship. The fear remaining from what happened lingers in the amygdala, and any new person barely has a chance. This, then, is the biological reason to avoid relationships on the rebound: The amygdala needs time to quiet down before you can perceive positive things accurately. But it needs more than just time. It needs new connections with your frontal lobe, too.

Is Fear Just About the Amygdala?

It turns out that the amygdala is just one of several parts of the brain that register fear outside of conscious awareness. These structures also respond more quickly to subliminal fear than to other, more positive subliminal emotions. When something dangerous occurs outside of awareness, the conscious brain also reacts to it. One hundred fifty milliseconds after a frightening stimulus is presented subliminally to a person who at that time is being asked to attend to something else, neurons in a conscious part of the frontal lobe of the brain called the ventromedial prefrontal cortex start to fire long before they fire in response to the task to be performed. About five hundred milliseconds after this, other involved brain regions also start to fire.

Thus, your brain prepares you to respond to danger faster than it does other tasks, and it starts to respond to frightening things before you realize they are frightening. In addition, the brain stem (the portion at the base of the brain) may also be affected by subliminal fear. Subliminal fear stimuli have been shown to elicit activity in the brain stem regions of the superior colliculus, the locus coeruleus, and the pulvinar. Also, the front and sides of the brain, which are associated with orienting the body in space, may be affected. These findings suggest that the slightest detection of fear by the brain stem sends an alert to the amygdala and results in a fear reaction. These regions all communicate with each other. Thus, it is not just the amygdala, but also an extensive network of regions that become activated outside of awareness. The buzzing of the amygdala also may result in disruption in other important, connected parts of the brain.

"But Doctor, I can't move forward with my life because . . .": Does It Matter What Fear "Means"?

Nike's advertising slogan—"Just do it"—has become a modern emblem of action. It stands in contrast to what's understood as the purpose of psychotherapy, which, in general, encourages exploring before doing. Exploration allows for more efficient doing in some cases. It is a little like training for a race. You do mental rehearsals, think about the distance, change your diet and your water intake, and gradually add more miles to your runs. You need this time and contemplation before you can win the race. But, eventually, you still have to run it.

In therapy, many people try to avoid running the race. They talk about it, plan for it, explore their fears about it, but have trouble putting one foot in front of the other. The reality is that no matter how carefully you prepare for it, a race still requires action. Standing at the starting line provokes anxiety. But it is a different kind of anxiety than the anxiety you experience while actually running the race.

Brian, Ellie, and Sonia all went back to the starting line several times before they made any headway in their races. But in the end, they realized that they had to act: Brian had to leave his job, Ellie had to ask her husband to watch television in another room, and Sonia had to take a chance on a new relationship. How much psychoanalyzing is enough?

Many therapists would argue that understanding the *meaning* of fear is critical to moving forward. Biologists would argue that understanding the *existence* of fear is enough. But considering only the prolonged psychological narratives attached to fear overlooks some of the automatic narratives the brain generates. In my practice, I have found that embracing both of these perspectives can help people understand but not dwell on fear-based situations.

So how can science help you move forward with your life?

While stories that we attribute to our fears may indeed "explain" the fears we experience, behind these uncomfortable feelings and sudden reactions may simply be too many neurons firing in one area of your brain.

The basic theory is this: Your thoughts result when neurons connect in your brain. Neurons transmit electricity. When light circuits connect, you get light. When sound circuits connect, you get sound. When neuronal circuits connect, you get thoughts. In all cases, electricity flows. Thoughts are therefore the flow of electricity. Thoughts are stored in various parts of your brain as proteins that give rise to electricity. Negative thoughts, including fear and anxiety, are called up from various brain regions and travel as electricity to the amygdala. The electrical energy of a thought can be converted into action if it is directed away from or through the amygdala to an action center in the brain. Thus, reiterating thoughts without connecting them to action closes the circuit before the bulb is turned on—before action occurs.

In human subjects, electrical stimulation of sites within a region called the dorsal periaqueductal gray matter elicits intense anxiety, distress, panic, terror, and feelings of imminent death, while stimulation of sites within the medial hypothalamus elicits anxiety and fear.

Several brain regions, when stimulated by electrical currents, produce feelings or "narratives" of fear. The mere electrical stimulation of these areas results in a story being retrieved. What is this narrative or story, in physiological terms? Most researchers think of it as a stored memory that was activated when the electrical impulse traveled along a brain nerve cell. The electrical impulse is like a double click that opens a saved document. Brain nerve cells transmit this electrical impulse much more quickly than nerve cells outside the brain because they have fewer built-in resistors and are structured to allow the free flow of electricity with little interruption. Without a lot of electricity buzzing through the brain, many individual thoughts are created, and many stories are created from these thoughts. However, the brain is a tricky thing. For example, when it perceives two segments of a line that are situated close enough together, the brain sees it as one continuous line. In the same way, when presented with two closely related thoughts, it combines them to make up a story. Fear stories abound in the human brain. But we must be suspicious of them if we are to have the courage to act at all.

Imagine the chaos that exists both within and outside of consciousness at any given moment. There are billions of neurons and quadrillions of connections, all with flowing electrical impulses that are activating stories. Which ones should you pay attention to? While the answer to this is not yet clear, in my experience, stories that support feeling "stuck" are almost never helpful, whereas stories that acknowledge difficulties but promote movement do help people move forward with their lives.

If you pay endless attention to "but this is so difficult," not much action will occur. If, however, you pay attention to "I will overcome this difficulty," you are still paying attention to the difficulty, but also encouraging electrons to flow to the action centers in your brain that will help you overcome the difficulty. When you come to understand your reasons for being afraid, your conscious brain (arising in the cortex) is in the process of forming new connections with your unconscious brain (situated in the subcortex).

So far we have focused on fearful feelings as though they are products of our own making. But are they always?

The Brain as a Mirror:
Is Unconscious Fear Contagious?

By now, you understand that the amygdala registers unconscious fear. But it's not just danger that causes the amygdala to activate. You also know that showing a picture of a fearful face to someone triggers a reaction of fear in that person. But what if this face were real instead of a picture? Would it still trigger amygdala activation? If so, how does it affect you when fearful people surround you?

Several studies have shown that facial expressions are, in a sense, contagious. First the face is seen; then the facial expression is unconsciously mimicked. This facial mimicry sends signals to the brain, creating the emotion that is consistent with the facial change. How do we know that this is true?

In one experiment, researcher Ulf Dimberg, PhD, measured muscle activity in subjects who were shown photos of people who were smiling or frowning. Within milliseconds of exposure to these images, the subjects' facial muscles showed corresponding activity. This response was specific to the emotions involved—i.e., happy faces evoked increased activity in the zygomatic muscles involved in smiling, and angry faces energized the corrugator muscle used in frowning. Furthermore, happy faces increased the subjects' feelings of happiness, and angry faces increased their feelings of fear. Fearful faces, too, have been shown to engender facial responses related to feelings of fear, such as contraction of the corrugator muscle of the forehead.

This finding had profound implications, because it explained how the brain is wired to mimic expressions in others. This may help explain the adage "Misery loves company." Some people will actually be drawn to those with opposite temperaments, however, because, for example, being around a positive, happy person may help a negative individual experience his or her own positive feelings more acutely. Positive people may charitably seek out negative people in order to help them, but also so that they can enjoy the reward that comes with transforming the misery of the negative person. People who experience a lot of fear will often settle into relationships with emotionally detached people in the hope of picking up this detachment automatically. They feel secure around their calm partners in part because of some of these automatic mimicking processes. That is, if we balance out each other's extremes automatically, by literally affecting the muscle contractions in the other person, each person feels changed or augmented in some way. This may partially explain the theory that opposites attract.

Brain imaging studies corroborate this effect on the brain. People register the emotions of others, consciously and unconsciously, and their brains respond by activating the same circuits to reflect those emotions in themselves.

Biological studies show that subliminal fear and anger elicit muscle and brain responses; thus, while you might not have any reason to be angry, an angry face may cause you to feel angry or fearful; while you may not have anything to fear, seeing a fearful face may cause you to feel afraid. Even if you are feeling happy, seeing fear or anger being expressed can impact your brain. For example, if you've had a good day at work but come home to an angry spouse, his or her anger will elicit the same emotion in you, and you may begin to argue.

Scientists have recently discovered cells in our brains that they have dubbed mirror neurons. When we watch someone move, our brains activate to mimic that movement as if we were making it ourselves. Have you ever noticed how sometimes you and a companion will cross your legs or scratch your arms almost simultaneously? Or how yawning seems to be contagious? In the same way, we are beginning to see that emotions are also mirrored. When someone around us indicates fear or nervousness, we usually choose to move away from him or her because, in part, we've mirrored the expression and do not like the feeling of doing so. (This may also be the reason why dogs pick up fear so easily. Their mirror neurons activate and they start to bark!)

Mirror neurons also enable us to have empathy for others. When you witness something upsetting, the mirror neurons in your frontal lobe (the premotor cortex) and parietal lobe (the inferior parietal cortex) become active. They mirror the situation, causing you to feel sadness and sympathy when you see someone else who is upset. This mechanism also applies to fear. In the presence of danger or fear, our mirror neurons become active, causing us to be afraid as well. It takes a lot of conscious effort to control this response.

Are All Unconscious Brains Equal?

As you might have guessed, the answer is probably not.

Studies have shown that your self-impression and level of anxiety may affect how you process subliminal fear. In one study, subjects were divided into four groups: those who felt highly socially desirable (felt that people loved them), those who felt socially undesirable (felt that people did not take to them easily), those who had a high level of anxiety traits (a long-term predisposition to being anxious), and those who had a low level of anxiety traits. Threatening faces were then presented to these subjects, both within and outside of their conscious awareness. In all of these subjects, skin conductance response (the body's stress response based on sweat production) was measured. The most profound findings occurred in subjects who were presented with the faces subliminally. Skin conductance was low in those who thought of themselves as socially desirable (regardless of their anxiety level) but high in those who had the combination of high trait anxiety and low social desirability.

Thus, when you're faced with danger that registers on an unconscious level, your response will be greater if you are highly anxious by nature or if you normally feel socially undesirable. What is striking is that even if you do not know consciously that you are being threatened, your stress response is greater. These personality characteristics make the amygdala more sensitive.

Another study corroborated this by showing that your anxiety level affects the way that your unconscious brain reacts to fear, but it does not have the same effect on your conscious brain. In people with greater trait anxiety—those who have an innate or long-term history of anxiety as opposed to occasionally feeling anxious—the unconscious brain is activated more easily, and they also react faster to danger. This may be advantageous in situations that are truly dangerous, but it is clearly disadvantageous when no danger is present. The person becomes stuck in a cycle of constant overreaction.

So why can't you simply find a way to feel better about yourself in order to prevent this reaction? In therapy, increasing self-confidence is a tricky issue. Much of the challenge lies in finding a way to decrease the amygdala activation. In psychological terms, this implies finding the right path to the amygdala by precisely identifying the fears that are activating it.

Since self-impression and expression of it affect how you process anxiety, if you lead with your weakness, you will create a weakness mirror response in the other person and probably frighten him or her away. If you lead with your strength, you will activate the other person's strength circuits and probably attract him or her. But you have to be able to believe in your own strengths and truly examine what you value, not just in yourself, but also in others. Your own amygdala can create the identical electrical current in the amygdala of another person—so if you want to have positive social interactions, you have to present yourself positively. Focus on your strengths rather than your weaknesses.

Who's More Afraid, Men or Women?

Does gender have an effect on unconscious emotion? Well, a recent study examined the effects of testosterone on sixteen female volunteers by administering five milligrams of testosterone in a double-blind crossover study (the most rigorous kind in its category) while the participants were exposed to subliminal images of fear.

Testosterone, the primary male sexual hormone, is also produced by women, and it is linked to interest in sexual activity and response to sexual stimulation. Healthy testosterone levels in females are also associated with greater well-being and reduced levels of anxiety and depression.

When they were given a placebo, the subjects showed a vigilant and hyperattentive physiological response to the "invisible" images, but when testosterone was administered, their responses were greatly reduced, despite the fact that they judged themselves to be just as anxious. The researchers concluded that the observed response to fear can differ from the felt response and that testosterone, in diminishing the fear response, probably exerts its effects outside of awareness. Thus, women—whose bodies produce less testosterone than those of men—may be at a specific disadvantage when it comes to dealing with unconscious fear.

We are also learning that cortisol, a hormone long implicated in stress-related conditions, may also have something to do with the response to subliminal fear. When researchers examined the relationship between baseline salivary cortisol levels and ability to identify anger in an image presented first outside of and then within awareness, they discovered that subjects with higher cortisol levels named unconscious but not conscious anger more quickly than subjects with lower levels.

Thus, hormones can affect your baseline reaction to fear.

If It Is Unconscious, How Can You Do Anything About It?

In recent years, glaciers all over the world have been melting. Global temperatures increased steadily during the twentieth century, and the change continues today. On a day-to-day basis, it is not detectable. But melting glaciers provide dramatic evidence of the slowly rising heat. We now know that global warming accounts for this rise in heat. Armed with this knowledge, we can do something about a phenomenon that we cannot see on a day-to-day basis.

The situation is similar to unconscious fear: Inability to make life changes, inattention, boredom, and stuckness are equivalent to melting glaciers. They are negative consequences of an unseen phenomenon. Unconscious fear is equivalent to global warming—it is a powerful force that is outside of our immediate awareness, but it can still be met with changes directed at minimizing the harm it does to our brains and our lives. The science of the unconscious has shown us that just because fear can act outside of awareness does not mean that we cannot reach it.

In the past, the brain was viewed as a mass of tissue that stops developing after adolescence. The adult brain was considered to be a finished product. We now know that this is not true.

This ability of the brain to change is called neuroplasticity, and nerve cells in the conscious and unconscious brain are all susceptible to change. We can influence our brains biologically, psychologically, and socially. And all of these influences can help us reduce the negative impact of fear. When people believed that the brain could not change after adolescence, adults just accepted their lives as they were. Now, studies show that although making changes is easier earlier in life, the brain can change its connections in adulthood as well. Not only medications, but also talk therapy can change the connections in our brains. This potential for change is the basis of this book as well, for if you can introduce some of these exercises into your life, you can target what needs to change in your brain.

Associations that are developed early in life largely form unconscious fear. For example, as a child you might have learned that dark alleys are dangerous. Current research shows that the amygdala is instrumental in forming and retaining these unconscious associations. Any subsequent exposure you might have to darkness may bring up this fear because it activates the learned association held in the amygdala. The key to addressing unconscious fear is to retrain the amygdala; in essence, this involves forming new connections by making new associations. In the human unconscious, this is akin to "unplugging" a neuron and "replugging" it into the right connection, or to adding a dimmer switch so you can control the amount of current flowing to or from the amygdala. Below are some examples of things that can be done to reduce the impact of harmful unconscious fear.

Approaches to Dealing with Unconscious Fear

The MAP-CHANGE Approach

To deal with unconscious fear, there are many things that you can do. In this section, we will review the evidence that supports using an approach that I call MAP-CHANGE: meditation, attentional interventions, and psychological tools derived from the science of fear. This

MAP-CHANGE approach is the same approach we will use to address issues in all subsequent chapters.

Meditation

Two published clinical trials have shown that when a specific protocol is followed, kundalini yoga is an effective treatment for obsessive-compulsive disorder, a syndrome in which people become obsessed with performing certain actions over and over again to calm an underlying fear of what will happen if they do not engage in the ritual.

Studies have shown that when different parts of the brain's frontal lobe act harmoniously—a phenomenon known as frontal coherence—it can prompt a sense of inner calmness and reduce fear. Transcendental meditation (sometimes called simply TM) has been shown to increase frontal coherence. The coordination of frontal function is a strong advantage, since there are extensive connections between the frontal lobe and the amygdala. This effect can be seen as soon as two months after beginning to practice meditation.

When you feel fear coming out of nowhere, take a second look. Realize that you are not losing it; you're merely experiencing your unconscious dominating your conscious mind. If you ride the wave with this knowledge in mind, you will see many positive results. Riding this wave is not easy. You may need assistance in training your mind; meditation, physical exercise, yoga, and psychotherapy are all disciplines that train the mind in different ways.

Some Buddhist meditators practice a kind of meditation called loving-kindness meditation. In studies, Buddhist monks have undergone MRI scans of their brains when they were engaged in meditation, and there is evidence that it increased the monks' capacity for empathy—and caused their amygdalae to become more active. Remember that the amygdala does not just process fear: It processes all emotions, but it defaults to fear because fear is so overwhelming. Well, in a practitioner of loving kindness, the amygdala regards this state of meditative pleasure as more important than unconscious fear. The result: Stand aside, fear; step forward, meditative pleasure.

The more you practice loving-kindness meditation, the more easily and often you can use it to trump unconscious fear. During the practice stages, like anything else, it is difficult to achieve. It may feel forced or be challenging at first, but if you can stick with it over time, the practice becomes automatic, and you will make inroads toward gaining the upper hand over fear.

When you meditate, your attention becomes focused. The brain's attentional system is more like radar than like a telescope. Meditators refer to this as awareness. Conscious attention is distinct from awareness, which is both conscious and unconscious. Meditation steadies attention, and when attention is steadied, there is less radar interference. This lessening of interference alone is pleasurable enough for its benefits to be noted by the conscious mind. Some people refer to this as being in the zone. Basketball great Earvin "Magic" Johnson, NFL quarterback Tom Brady, and Olympic swimmer Michael Phelps all brought meditation into their daily lives to improve their performance by steadying their attention and tapping into the power of the radar.

If loving kindness is not your cup of tea, try focusing your attention on another positive emotion that will compete with the unconscious fear in your amygdala.

Attention

One of the major problems with unconscious fear is that the brain is in a state of constant anticipation of negative things. We use our attention to look for these things since we are expecting them. From an evolutionary perspective, this was meant to protect us, but when unconscious fear grabs hold of the brain, it overprotects. In fact, evidence shows that when fear is moderate, we pay less attention to it, but when it is severe, the activity of the ACC is "captured" by it.

However, more and more studies are showing that the amygdala and the ACC are captured by fear only because it is such a strong emotion. In fact, one study showed that babies' faces were also strongly able to capture attention. Thus, when positive emotions compete with negative emotions, they can take over the amygdala activation.

The idea, then, is to capture attention with positive things. Know, though, that the ACC and the amygdala are very sensitive and will know if you are only pretending to be positive. People often try to fake having a positive attitude, and this will not reduce their unconscious fear. I do, however, think that there is some virtue in trying, because practice in this case does make perfect. A good example of this is the fake smile theory. In his book *Descartes' Error,* Antonio Damasio, MD, points out that when we truly smile, it activates the ACC, but when we fake a smile, the cingulate does not activate. If we repeatedly fake a smile, however, the cingulate cortex does activate, indicating that an attempt to feel positive becomes spontaneous through practice.

Thus, we can reduce unconscious fear by attending to positive things. In fact, I believe that attention only needs to be switched away from the negative; attending to even something neutral will reduce fear.

Psychological Tools

Forming new associations through thinking

One of the most common errors that people make is lumping "impossible" and "difficult" into the same category. As a result, you may find yourself paralyzed when you want to do something about a situation that arouses fear in you.

For example, one of my patients, Nancy, earned $400,000 a year. She had put away enough money to be able to pay for two of her three children's college educations and was able to support herself and her children after her divorce. She became accustomed to this security, but gradually became bored with her job and needed a greater challenge. As the boredom set in, her brain seemed to slow down. Consciously, she was comfortable with her financial security. Unconsciously, her passionate nature found itself in a conflict with this security.

Although there were many signs that she needed to change her job, she ignored them. Instead, she became angrier and angrier and started to want to work on her anger as a primary obstruction in her life. When I drew her attention to the basis of her anger, her thinking started to change. At the root of her anger was fear: fear that if she changed her job, she might not find another; that she already earned more than most people and had no right to expect a better life; that she would be hated for deserting her company; that her third child's college education might not be paid for. The list of fears was endless. But suffice it to say that these fears kept her paralyzed and unable to act, even after she recognized what was lurking in her unconscious. Every time we began a discussion about a potential job change, she became irritable and threatened to leave therapy. Occasionally, she even missed sessions, not realizing how powerfully her conscious brain did not want to face her increasingly restless unconscious.

Nancy was overwhelmed by the number of factors that she thought she had to consider; she did not realize that she could make small changes that would begin to lighten her psychological load. If you are carrying a burden of five hundred logs of fear on your back, every time you lay one log down, your load is one log lighter. Laying down the log is not easy, but it becomes easier and easier once you realize that this is what you have to concentrate on. With five hundred logs of fear on your back, walking seems impossible. As each log is removed, what once seemed impossible will instead seem difficult and, eventually, possible.

After Nancy had removed a few of these logs by talking about her fears, she became less nervous and in time started to make inquiries about new jobs without knowing how she would make up the income she would be forfeiting. By following her passions, she eventually found what she wanted—and also managed to make more money than she had been making. When we listen to our passions, the amygdala stops growling and we are able to find what we need. But when we fight this impulse, the amygdala roars even louder, making it impossible to attract what we want to our lives.

Most people are resigned to enduring their fears because they think they reside in established nerve cell connections that are difficult to change. However, the key word here is *difficult,* which is very different from *impossible.* Forming new associations through thinking involves relearning, which takes time and effort.

Research shows that breaking old patterns of thinking to learn new ones can change amygdala activation. In addition, new learning can also change activation in parts of the brain that are responsible for perception and behavior, such as the medial prefrontal cortex (located at the center front of the brain). New learning is at first conscious, but after several repetitions—some investigators refer to this as the rule of seven, for the seven repetitions that seem generally necessary for learning to occur—the information becomes incorporated into the unconscious brain.

The interpretation of inner happenings is called interoception. When we misinterpret these happenings, we call it faulty interoception. Many studies have shown that faulty interoception can be changed so we develop new understandings of what is happening within us. Cognitive-behavioral therapy (CBT) may be especially helpful in doing this. If we are more conscious of our false associations and distorted thinking, we can relearn things. That is, we can change our interoception.

My experience as a clinician is that for life situations, it takes more than seven repetitions to learn a new way of thinking, and you can't give up after the second try. Some people have already decided that they cannot get what they want, but they go through the motions of trying to change their lives anyway. This is one of the most destructive approaches to life. It is aimed at alleviating the guilt of "not trying" without actually having any intent to succeed. To succeed in overcoming unconscious fear, you have to make a commitment to it.

I call this working with possibility. When you work with possibility, you open the door for things to support that possibility. When you hold on to impossibility, it creates noise in the brain that confuses the "intent" centers in your brain. Every time these intent centers want to direct you toward something, they are uncertain about whether to satisfy your desire to give up or to fulfill your desire to move forward. Our brains are much more cooperative than we think. We just have to give them clear information about what our desires are.

Efforts at reaching the unconscious work only after your commitment to change is clearly articulated in your conscious mind. When

Nancy told her unconscious that change was impossible, all of her efforts at creating new opportunities failed. Only when she came to terms with her fears and made a commitment to change despite them was she able to actually let her unconscious brain know that it needed to rally against the force of fear.

Most of us do not realize how empowered we actually are. The brain will act consciously and unconsciously to respond to our requests. If you give it conflicting messages such as "This is impossible. . . . I want to change my job," the brain will respond as though change is impossible. As a result, hopelessness and failure will set in. If you let your brain know that change is difficult but your fears are irrational, it will cooperate accordingly.

The two processes that are involved here are extinction and imprinting. Extinction is the removal of the learned association, such as the idea that changing your job is impossible. This is discussed in greater detail in later chapters. Imprinting is the process of learning new associations, which establishes new connections between nerve cells in the brain. For example, Sonia changed her learned association from "anger leads to abuse and relationship breakups" to "anger may lead to abuse, but it may also be a sign of health in a relationship." By reiterating this new meaning over and over again, she formed a new memory; eventually, if an electrical impulse stimulates the region where the old memory is held, it will instead call up the newly formed memory. A good example of imprinting is how you find your way home without actually thinking about the route. When you drive or walk the route over and over again, getting home becomes automatic.

A stepwise method for achieving new thinking and cementing new frontal cortex inputs to the amygdala is:

- Recognize what is not happening in your life that you would like to have happen.
- Identify the fears that are associated with it.
- Connect the fears and the failures more overtly; make a list of how each fear contributes to your inability to change.

- Intend to change (change *impossible* to *difficult;* recognize that you do not have to know how to change, you just have to believe that change will happen and not that you have to fight the fear). Work *with,* not against, possibility. Ask, "How can I make this possible?" rather than stating over and over again, "This seems impossible."
- Repeatedly convey this new information (that you will start dating or change your work situation, for example) to yourself to give your frontal cortex new information to convey to the amygdala. Do this regularly either by setting aside time to think it or by writing it down with full emotional investment and belief. This will reset the connections between your frontal lobe and amygdala.
- Perform this self-instruction regularly and frequently. I have found that setting aside ten to twenty minutes a day is helpful. If you cannot devote this time, then recognize that you have not structured your life to make the changes you want. Very often, people come into therapy expecting to get a magic bullet that will change their lives. To stimulate the occurrence of noneffortful opportunities (which the unconscious maneuvers to bring about), you have to match time with effort (from the frontal cortex). That is why people say hard work creates luck. Hard work is frontal activation, and luck is the unconscious process that directs you toward your goal.
- Along the way, recognize it when your unconscious mounts new resistance or you encounter new distractions, and stop them from making the difficult seem impossible.

Forming new associations through feeling

In our society, there are many distorted ideas about feelings. One frequently encountered misconception is that feeling is somehow less intelligent than thinking. Extensive research now shows that not only is feeling a critical component of new learning, it is also essential if thinking is to be effective. Brain research shows that decision making involves a combination of thinking and feeling. Feeling affects the internal environment in which decisions are made. And emotions can affect whether you get the opportunities that you want. For example, research has shown that a smile may make you appear to be more intelligent, and you may therefore become more successful. There are countless examples of feeling allowing you to get what was previously unattainable. Studies show that higher levels of emotional intelligence help people cope more effectively with stress at work and significantly assist them in becoming leaders. Thus, if you can challenge the emotion of fear by enhancing other emotional states, you can change your life significantly. Whereas fear may lead to avoidance of a challenge, that same fear may disappear into the background if another emotion displaces it. As we have seen from the experiments we reviewed, this replacement emotion will need to be very strong and to set in over time. Making a positive effort one time will not suffice to overcome the evolutionary priority the brain gives to fear.

Fear creates anxious feelings that may directly affect behavior without your conscious mind being aware of them. When fear is disruptive and not reality based, there is constant input from the amygdala to other parts of the brain. One reason that connecting with fear and the feelings associated with it is important is that research shows that very frequently, it is the anticipation of fear that makes people spiral out of control or develop ways to avoid it. Surprisingly, most of the unpleasant effects of fear (trembling, palpitations, emotional paralysis) occur when we are at a distance from it. If we approach the pool of our fears and dip our legs in it, we will slowly get accustomed to the idea of swimming in it.

In Brian's case, for example, just the anticipation of being seen as a flake or of not being successful as an entrepreneur was enough to make him avoid the thought of leaving his job. When he did talk about leaving his job, it aroused many fearful and unpleasant feelings. But it also motivated him to get close to the fear and then to dismantle those previously learned associations ("If I think of leaving my job, I will be a failure") so he could make the necessary changes in his life. Feeling the fear over time allowed him to make the changes he needed. The bark of fear is often worse than its bite. In some ways, we have to befriend it until it can eat out of our hands. That is what Brian did whenever he got panic attacks once he understood his fears and the biology of the fear reaction. He would say, "Here goes my amygdala again," and this was a way of touching and understanding his fear without being overwhelmed by it. Writer Ambrose Redmoon said, "Courage is not the absence of fear, but rather the judgment that something else is more important than fear." Taken literally, this means that we can make a conscious decision to take our attention off fear and place it on courage instead.

When this type of exploration is done in therapy, it has to be done carefully and not aversively. When fear feelings are intense, you have to learn how to swim in the shallows before you can dive into the deep end. Paradoxically, the thing that motivates most people to face these unpleasant feelings is realizing that there is hope and a possibility of change for the better. It is only when you are in a position to be hopeful and optimistic that problem solving can occur. In fact, a recent study showed that positive emotions are superior to negative emotions when trying to problem solve. When the problem is fear, understanding the bigger picture is what will most effectively motivate you to dismantle the fear.

Having a greater ability to identify and communicate your emotional state is associated with greater coupling between the ACC and other regions in the frontal lobe of the brain (the prefrontal regions). This association is not present in people with a lesser ability to identify and communicate their emotional states; instead, the coupling between the ACC and the amygdala is accentuated. Thus, having the ability to identify and communicate your fears is critical to optimal brain development and formation of protective connections. Simply put, when your brain works like a well-oiled and synchronized machine, you stand a greater chance of eliminating unconscious fear.

How can you connect with your fear emotionally?

- Find a safe environment where you can let yourself go; this could be a therapist's office or the pages of a locked journal.
- As you explore your feelings, translate your fearful emotions into biological terms, the way that Brian did. You fear is not coming out of *nowhere*—it is coming from your *brain*. The nowhere you sense is your unconscious.
- Realize that when you make contact with your innermost fears, you do not have to run away, even when you are tempted to; this fear is the stream that you have to navigate in order to make it to the other side. Dip your legs in fear before you swim in it. And swim in fear before you dive into it.
- Know that fear never really disappears. But instead experiencing it as a loud tuba in the orchestra of your emotions, you can train your amygdala to lower its volume.
- Develop the habit of challenging your fears by putting yourself in situations that increase your courage and confidence slowly. Start with the thing that you are least afraid of. Then, slowly work your way toward the major issues. In this way, you will increase the emotional forces that you can use to work against your fears.
- If you are an emotional person, recognize that this is a strength. People may tell you that you need to control your emotions, but you will probably be able to closely examine any uncontrolled feelings.
- For many people, doing positive things like listening to music that they love, eating food that they love, and improving their physical health are all things that will slowly boost their confidence and challenge the emotion of fear. Increase these positive facets of your life.

A picture is worth a thousand words

Recent research has shown that visual imagery is more effective at reducing anxiety than words are. Thus, imagining calming things is probably an effective way to change your state of mind. People often respond to a statement of this fact as though it is obvious. Yet, very few people actually take the time to imagine anything at all. When was the last time you spent a half hour imagining calming things? Many people say that this would drive them crazy, because it would feel like they were wasting time. Yet the practice of mental imagery is now becoming understood to be very powerful. One striking example of this is stroke patients who, when they vividly imagine themselves moving, may be saving the brain tissue that surrounds the damaged tissue where blood flow has been compromised. Thus, imagining positive things is not as ineffectual as many skeptics think. It actually is a powerful way (probably more powerful than talking about your feelings) to change the way you feel when you are fearful.

Visualization is not all about inviting magic into your life—it is a potent and scientifically proven method that stimulates the unconscious in powerful ways and directs your brain toward what you want.

You don't have to imagine anything specific. Choose any image that works for you. When you imagine a calming scene, it will activate your brain's visual system, and this emotion will then influence whether the amygdala activates or not. This is a potent way to transform the kind of electricity that is reaching the amygdala.

Steps to take when imagining something include:

- Make sure you are in a place where there are no distractions.
- Reduce any inputs from your other sense organs at first—keep it visual. Turn off any music you may have on so you can practice building your image clearly.
- Eventually, combining calming images with calming sounds may have an additive effect.
- When you imagine something calming, recognize that you are feeding your amygdala calming information.
- Use this technique to prevent or eliminate fear.
- Choose a different image every week to avoid getting bored.
- The most important element is to allow your emotions to flow when you are imagining.

- As you practice these images, increase the level of detail that you imagine every time you practice this technique. For example, you might start by imagining the ocean. Then, see if you can follow the waves at their exact speed. And see if you can add a sailboat floating by. Increasing the specificity increases your absorption in the calmness and is more of a guarantee that this new input will reach the amygdala.
- As with all other techniques, practice makes perfect. Do this repeatedly.

Other ways to access the unconscious

Sometimes it helps to take a lighthearted look at what we are feeling. Life *is* short. Experiences do come and go. And our brains, because their fast, unconscious responses are like barking dogs, are not always barking or frenzied for an actual reason. If we take every physiological sensation and narrative seriously, then we are assuming a certain conscious responsibility that is entirely outside of awareness. So if you are afraid, you might be able to calm yourself by asking yourself, "Now what is my brain up to?" It helps to give yourself this feedback because it can stop the vicious cycle of "Oh my God . . ." that then leads to a greater sense of catastrophe.

Remember, too, that concrete interventions can help. Ask your doctor about testosterone and cortisol, and whether it makes sense to measure your levels of these hormones. It could be every bit as important as self-help, medication, or psychotherapy.

Simple things to remember here are:

- Check with your doctor about hormone levels.
- Contemplate using a therapy such as CBT.
- Choose the type of meditation that suits you. Make your practice as much of a priority as eating and sleeping.
- Exercise frequently.

- Go easy on yourself. When things seem overwhelming, recognize that your brain might have blown the situation out of proportion.
- Use brain analogies that you have learned about in this chapter to help yourself get closer to what is happening.

Conclusion

What you don't know *can* hurt you. Part of life is learning what to accept, and when to let go. If you are feeling limited in your life in any way, examine your life through the lens of "Am I afraid?" even if you do not feel afraid. The exploration will likely be very fruitful. And knowing that fear can turn on your amygdala without your knowledge may help you feel more certain about the need to develop new neuronal connections by using some or all of the tools offered here.

[2]

The Science of Overcoming Dread

How Human Brain Biology Can Support an Attentive, Inspired, and Positive Life

Hope is the thing with feathers
That perches in the soul,
And sings the tune—without the words,
And never stops at all,
And sweetest in the gale is heard;
And sore must be the storm
That could abash the little bird
That kept so many warm.

—**Emily Dickinson**

How can hope be a component of reality when it is seldom based on fact? How can you hope that you will be able to pay your mortgage if you're fearful about not making enough money? How can you hope that you will find a partner in life if being alone for the past five years has made you fearful about never meeting anyone? How can you hope that you will get pregnant if you fear that you are trying and failing? Hope requires believing in a positive outcome, which can be difficult to do if the facts do not support its accomplishment. We choose whether or not to hope based on the facts before us. And we use these facts to justify our fears.

But what if, instead of allowing the facts to justify the fears, we use hope to reveal new facts and remove the fears? What if having hope is as simple as turning off the light that illuminates the fallen tree trunk blocking your hiking path and turning on the light that reveals a new path that allows you to continue on your journey? This is precisely what former South African president Nelson Mandela, world-class athlete and cancer survivor Lance Armstrong, and countless everyday Joes have done: Rather than wait for their fears to disappear or for facts to back up their hope, they used hope to *create* new facts and reach their goals. As Lance Armstrong said, "If children have the ability to ignore all odds and percentages, then maybe we can all learn from them. When you think about it, what other choice is there but to hope? We have two options, medically and emotionally: Give up, or fight like hell."

Now, at this point, you're probably asking, "What if I don't have the stamina to believe? What if I get up every day dreading that I may lose my job, or that I may never change my job, or that I may always be alone? What if I can't persevere like Mandela or Armstrong? How can I use the knowledge of scientific research and brain biology to help myself change?"

In this chapter we will learn how scientific research is increasingly showing us that the burden that we feel in life is less related to the actual load of our troubles and fears than it is to the attention that we give it. In addition, we will learn how to rewire our brains so we can overcome fear and live more positive and productive lives.

Why Hope? The Benefits of Optimism

The power of hope has been demonstrated in a number of settings. A group of researchers, Louis Gottschalk, PhD, and his colleagues, found that terminally ill cancer patients who were hopeful lived longer after receiving irradiation treatment than those who lacked hope. The hopeful cancer patients also made more progress in psychotherapy than patients who were not hopeful. Based on these results, another researcher, Guido Zanni, PhD, concluded that optimism leads individuals to better overall health. Another study—this one conducted with elderly subjects—provided evidence that a low level of optimism may lead to unhealthy behavioral choices and, as a result, an increased risk of cardiovascular death.

But the benefits of optimism aren't limited to improved health. A study of first-year law school students found that those who were optimistic made more money ten years later, suggesting that optimism may affect the quality of our lives in various ways. Thus, there are many situations in which a positive attitude may lead to better health or greater wealth.

Fear can be very damaging to this essential sense of optimism and hope that many of us strive to achieve or maintain. Studies have shown that a subset of mothers whose children were hospitalized for stem cell transplantation had significant fear and, therefore, little optimism about the potential for their children's recovery, and this psychological state had enduring effects on both the mothers and the children. These mothers continued to be more afraid even six months after the transplantation, and this excessive fear could cause continued distress in their children. Also, the mother's fear played a primary role in how she adjusted to her child's transplant procedure, which in turn negatively affected the child's recovery. This connection between fear and decreased optimism has been identified in other groups of people as well, such as those who have had a heart attack; their subsequent optimism is related directly to a lack of fear. Thus, fear can directly compromise hope, leaving many people who want to make life changes without the resources to do so. How can science help us understand the connection between fear, optimism, and pessimism, and how can we use this information to help ourselves move past our fears?

Why Hope Matters in the Human Brain

For different people, achievement means different things. For some, having a child is a symbol of the highest creativity, whereas for others, it is making a million dollars. Regardless of the kind of achievement, in my experience, there is one important principle that distinguishes successful from unsuccessful people: Successful people rely less on the existing facts to get what they want. Instead, they recognize the challenges, and rather than acquiescing to the relative improbability of achieving their goals, they seek out routes that will allow them to achieve them. That is, successful people do not lead statistically sensible lives. Rather than asking questions based on what is probable, successful people ask their brains to focus on what is needed to accomplish the less likely of two options.

If there was an 85 percent chance that an older couple could not give birth to a healthy child, a successful couple would ask themselves and their physicians, "How do we become part of the 15 percent of older people who do have a healthy child?" By pursuing the less likely of two probabilities, this couple asks their brains an entirely different set of questions than a couple that hears this and says, "What else can we do?" When we choose to pursue the less likely of two options because we want it, we are hopeful. And hope is not simply a matter of wishful thinking. It is focusing on achieving something difficult and beginning to search for and find a solution.

Your brain's action centers rely on the instructions that you give them. If you impress upon your brain that something is improbable (by focusing your attention on the improbability), you will likely succeed in convincing it not to pursue your ambition. If you ask your brain how to achieve the improbable, however, it will start to work for you. The former attitude is based on fear; the latter, on hope. Fear-based messages and hope-based messages provide very different directions to the brain.

The brain also uses its energy to process thoughts and feelings in the unconscious. If you feel doubt—or fear—when you are asking your question, the brain will have to use its energy to process this feeling. If you have hope, the brain will use its energy to process hope. Also, doubts, fears, and hope affect the brain's ability to process other information. Fears and doubts are more likely to disrupt your attention, while hope will likely enhance and focus your attention.

For example, what do Roger Bannister, Neil Armstrong, and Sir Edmund Hillary have in common? They were all the first people to do something. Roger Bannister was the first person to run a mile in less than four minutes. Neil Armstrong was the first person on the moon. Sir Edmund Hillary, together with Tenzing Norgay, was the first person to reach the summit of Mount Everest. Prior to each of these feats, numerous attempts to achieve the goal had been made by other people. All of those people had failed. After each of these successes, many more people replicated it. Why is this? When the brain thinks that something is possible, it will sketch out the route for achieving it. Bannister, Armstrong, and Hillary all had to hope against reason. They had to ask their brains to sketch out paths to their goals. The people who followed them used these previous feats to launch their own journeys. Once the brain believes that something is possible, it will chart a path toward your goal that is radically different from the course it would chart without hope. We call these maps motor maps, and they are action plans based on information that we give the brain. They are highly dependent on what we imagine. If we remain fearful, fear will disrupt our imagination. If we focus on our goals instead of on the fear, the brain can use what we imagine as a guide for sketching out motor maps. This imagining is so closely tied to doing that expert athletes can literally make improvements in their performance by first imagining them and then practicing them. We call this motor imagery (or imagery of action), and it precedes actual movement or action. Thus, if you want to make a change in your life, first imagine yourself making the change so your brain can determine the route that will take you to your goal. Hope is necessary for action.

In the first chapter, we saw how we are limited in what we know about fear. Much of this unrecognized "knowledge" and much of what drives us in this world lie in the human unconscious. At first, it seems impossible to know what lies in the unconscious. But if you are skeptical about hope, then perhaps, like any scientist, you might be willing to consider this second perspective: that hope is a hypothesis about the potential of the human unconscious. Stated more simply, hope is not an answer. Rather, as something that stimulates the imagination, hope helps us to pose the right questions, just as a hypothesis helps a scientist design experiments. It provides a way of moving through the world.

The implications of this approach are profound and far-reaching. In this context, hope is what is possible. Can you imagine what most people thought of the likelihood that machines could fly before the invention of the airplane, or of the possibility of replacing human organs before the first successful transplant was performed? Yes, all of these things were developed as part of a logical sequence of events that we can retrospectively point to, but they would not have been possible without hope. To hope is to make the assumption that something is possible. If you think about it, many of the things that you want in life have actually been done before. A partner, money, a child, love—all have been attained in unlikely circumstances before. So the hope that you are being asked to have is based on reason and experience.

Contrary to what many people believe, intuition is not some psychotic, nonfactual brain process. In fact, brain imaging studies show that intuition is a result of the complex processing of information received by the brain. This information is collected from multiple sources and then integrated in parts of the brain called heteromodal association areas in the frontal, temporal, and parietal lobes. This sophisticated processing is what gives rise to the "intuitive sensation." Intuition also activates specific brain regions, including the outer half of the amygdala. Some studies have shown that imagining positive outcomes (having the feeling of hope) increases amygdala and rostral anterior cingulate cortex (ACC) activation. These brain regions are also implicated in fear processing, suggesting that hope and fear wander around in similar brain regions and that hope is often processed outside of conscious awareness. Because hope seems to travel in the same dungeons as fear, it might be a good soldier to employ if we want to meet fear.

Deploying the Soldier of Hope to Fight against Fear: Introduction

So far, we have learned that hope and fear both wander around in the unconscious parts of our brains. They both require amygdala activation, and whichever one is stronger will win the amygdala for its own use. To be processed by the amygdala, emotions have to stand in a queue, with their order determined by their strength—the strongest soldier gets to the front of the line. If fear is strongest, then it will grab the amygdala's power and dominate all of the other soldiers in the line. If hope is stronger, then it will be preferentially processed over fear. In neuroscientific terms, we call this strength valence. In this chapter, I will refer to it as the impact factor. It turns out that we have to develop a strategy to help hope "bulk up" and have an intelligence that supersedes the intelligence of fear. This is not easy because, as we've learned, our brains are structured so that the amygdala processes fear first in order to protect us from danger.

The First Attack Strategy:
Enlisting Attention as a Partner

Attention is one of our most powerful assets as human beings. We have direct access to it. We can enlist it by merely intending to enlist it. Hope and fear compete for our attention, and we can make a conscious decision to partner attention with hope. But why would we want to do this? In his book *Creating Affluence,* Deepak Chopra, MD, suggests that "attention is everything." He claims that if we want something to happen, we have only to attend to it and it will happen. Recent scientific research has shown that attention is a powerful force that has an immense impact on our emotional states. This is because the brain pathways for attention make their way directly to the areas that generate our emotions. In a sense, attention is one road that we can take to reach our emotions. But the traffic flows in both directions: Attention affects emotions, and emotions affect attention. The way we feel can powerfully direct our attention—even in ways we are not always aware of.

For example, people who are anxious are more prone to identifying anxiety-provoking or fearful things than people who are not. Their own anxiety shines a light on other anxious things. Furthermore, they are less likely to see neutral things as benign—anxious people are more prone to misidentifying neutral situations or objects as threatening.

Jeff was a thirty-eight-year-old man who came to see me because of his intense anxiety and panic attacks. What was striking to me was that Jeff spent his entire day anticipating these attacks. He believed that if he kept a vigilant lookout for this anxiety, he could prevent it from becoming unmanageable. What he did not realize was that his constant attention to this anxiety actually helped the anxiety grow, in both his conscious and unconscious brain. As a result of this focus, he would frequently experience bouts of sudden, overwhelming anxiety. The very thing he tried all day to prevent would happen because he was focusing his attention on it.

When I directed the Outpatient Anxiety Disorders Program at McLean Hospital in Belmont, Massachusetts—Harvard's largest psychiatric teaching hospital—I observed this pattern in most of my patients who were extremely anxious or fearful. They spent most of their days worrying about their fear in an effort to prevent it, and to their utter dismay, this worry did nothing to prevent their anxiety.

We call this state of constant worry about fear and anxiety anticipatory anxiety, and in a sense, it is much worse than anxiety itself. A recent clinical and brain imaging study showed that when people worry about a dreaded outcome, they will actually choose to experience the outcome immediately rather than putting it off. The tension of waiting for it is so great that they prefer to get it over with. In one experiment, people were given electric shocks and then asked to wait for the next one, which, they were told, would be of either a greater or lesser voltage. Many people asked to receive the greater shock first just to get it over with. They could not stand anticipating the anxiety any longer. Anxiety is also threatening because it causes people to lose control of their emotions. Choosing the dreaded alternative is a way to regain control.

I've witnessed this phenomenon over and over again in early romances. Many people are so worried that they will lose the relationship that they sabotage their own happiness. Their worry that the relationship may end eventually becomes a reality. People would rather just get the dreaded outcome over with than wait for it to happen. Their constant attention to and anticipation of the worst drives their anxiety level upward and out of control. And rather than reorient their attention toward achieving a positive outcome, they end this dread by inviting the dreaded negative outcome to occur.

What I often tell people is that when they spend their lives in dread, they are writing an invitation to the feared outcome rather than preventing it. Many argue that they are afraid that if they stop worrying, they will be shocked or surprised by something negative happening. Somehow, shock and surprise are worse to them than their dreaded outcomes.

What happens in the brain when we are dreading something? The study I referred to earlier, in which researchers randomly administered electric shocks to study participants, revealed what researchers described as "the cost [of] waiting." The research team found that some people dread negative futures very much while other people do not. In those who did have high degrees of dread, the posterior parts of their brains (which are responsible for attention) activated more. What this means is that, compared to people who don't care as much, people who dread negative outcomes pay more attention to the possibility of a negative outcome, and this is shown by the attention centers of their brains firing more. It wasn't that the people had more fear or anxiety. In fact, in this experiment, the amount of dread people felt was directly related to the amount of attention they paid to the possible negative outcomes. Fear and anxiety themselves probably do play a role, but it is the attending to a feared outcome that most increases one's feeling of dread.

In another experiment on dread, researchers looked at the brains of people who were immersed in a virtual maze, watching a virtual predator chasing them on a computer screen. The creature was able to chase and capture them, and inflict imagined pain. What they found was that as the predator got nearer, brain activity switched from the medial prefrontal cortex, or mPFC, to the periaqueductal gray, or PAG.

When we remember why and how to inhibit fear, mPFC neurons activate. PAG neurons activate with acute anxiety. The dread of being caught by the predator activates the PAG, removing the inhibition of fear. In situations arousing dread, then, it is helpful to be aware that we need to consciously invoke at least some of the previous inhibition to reengage the mPFC. Otherwise, all of our decisions will be determined by the PAG because of our out-of-control anxiety.

The brain circuits that light up when we attend to something have direct connections to those circuits that light up when we are afraid. In one brain imaging study I did, and in numerous other brain imaging studies, it has been shown repeatedly that when people are anxious, it is nearly impossible for them to attend to something; the amygdala, the blood flow to which increases with anxiety, has direct connections to the ACC, which is needed for attention. The amygdala sends electrical current zooming into the ACC, disrupting its ability to do its job.

These two experiments show us that the amount of dread or fear we feel is actually related to the amount of attention we pay to that fear. The same concept relates to positive emotions. When we pay attention to positive emotions, we stimulate the consequences of positive emotions. Attention adds to the impact factor of an emotion and makes it bulk up. Attending to hope will begin the strengthening process.

The Second Attack Strategy:
Changing the Lens through Which You View Life

There are many who would argue that reality is not *what is,* but how we interpret what is. Rather than being a collection of objective phenomena, the nature of reality is colored by our individual perceptions, thoughts, histories, and feelings. One man's bread is another man's poison. What would happen if the lens we viewed life through was hope, and what if this very hope served as the basis for all of our future experiences? In effect, what would happen if you exchanged your fear lens for a hope lens?

For many of us, the lens of hope we are born with gradually loses its clarity as we age. Are the good outcomes and fortunes enjoyed by those who are hopeful a result of their positive outlook on life? William James, the famous nineteenth-century philosopher and writer, addressed this question in an essay called "The Will to Believe." He argued that the reason to hope is that it provides an opportunity to navigate the world with the possibility for discovery. Without hope, all doors are closed and we live in a world where magic is limited by the end of possibility. Contemporary writer Richard Bach once said, "The mark of your ignorance is the depth of your belief in injustice and tragedy; what the caterpillar calls the end of the world, the master calls a butterfly." As inspiring as these words are, how many of us can make butterflies from the caterpillars of our human endeavors? And are we wired to have this ability?

In my practice and day-to-day encounters, I see many people who recognize that hope makes them feel better, but they often feel that there is no external sign that hope makes any sense; in fact, rather than viewing hope as a harbinger of reality, they see a hopeful outlook as an impossibility or something that signals desperation and the wish to avoid the real. People will say, "Have you taken a look at the gas prices recently? Do you see where this country is going?" News broadcasts spell out the doom and gloom of the future, starving our hopes and feeding our fears. As our fears grow, it becomes even more difficult to be optimistic. But we would have more of a choice in this matter if we just gave up the idea that we are what we are, immutable. Not only is this an inflexible attitude, it also completely ignores the fact that we have conscious control over our beliefs and actions, and that *our brains can change if we train them to change.* This is a biological fact.

Many of the inspirational leaders of our time—Deepak Chopra, MD; Wayne Dyer, PhD; and Eckhart Tolle—have espoused the importance of focusing on the here and now and being relentlessly dedicated to positive thinking. *The Secret,* by Rhonda Byrne, has inspired millions of people to think positive rather than negative thoughts. Yet, inspired though people may be by these uplifting ideas, they often find themselves with secret doubts and questions about how exactly this so-called positive energy works. Is it metaphysical, is it all hype, or is it scientifically sound? Someone I met recently said that he, following the tutelage of positive thinkers, had written numerous million-dollar checks to himself in the hope that the universe would sense his intention and send some money his way—but nothing seemed to be happening. What was he doing wrong? Or was there any sense to this effort at all?

In his book *Money Success and You,* John Kehoe writes that making money requires having faith that you are going to make money regardless of how difficult things are. He argues that the optimist and pessimist are both correct in their half-full–half-empty views of life. He says that, with practice, we have a conscious ability to change the lens we view life through. This is true not just from a philosophical perspective, but from a biological perspective as well. Changing your lens is equivalent to shifting your attention, which is partly within your voluntary control, and within the realm of the brain's capability to learn.

The Biology of the Life Lens

When we view life, there are two biological processes going on: a passive one, in which our memories, innate predispositions, and social circumstances impact the way we see things; and another, more active process, in which we get to choose what we see and how we see it. When we choose to see the brighter side of things, we are actively choosing to attend to it. Attention is within our voluntary control, but it is not as easy as it might sound to switch your attention from the negative to the positive.

Attention is the thinking process of selectively focusing on one aspect of an object or life circumstance. It is the human spotlight that roves over the world according to the dictates of other brain forces, such as the need for vigilance and constant surveillance in a dangerous world. In the human brain, attention is a complicated process requiring sophisticated coordination between the frontal and parietal lobes. These two brain regions work nonstop to satisfy our daily attentional needs in the midst of competing forces that threaten to distract us. The human life lens is thus the frontoparietal cortex. It is this part of the brain that actually brings you into the realm of hope, out of the realm of fear. The first step in this process requires you to partner hope with the frontoparietal cortex (in a sense, like a realtor, you show hope to this part of your brain), and the second step involves moving yourself out of your previous house of fear and into the house of hope.

To move into the house of hope, the relationship between the life lens and attention has to be cemented. This requires practice.

When the frontal and parietal lobes are brilliantly coordinated with each other, attention has the quality of fingers racing up and down a piano keyboard, producing a sweet and captivating sound that leads to an inner feeling of rest and well-being. We call this being in the zone, and it can be *seen,* not just in the Dalai Lama and other spiritual teachers, but also in the eyes of golfer Tiger Woods, gymnast Nadia Comaneci, and figure skater Michelle Kwan. But when the frontal and parietal lobes of the brain are not coordinated, it is like a huge boulder falling on the piano keyboard, emitting sudden cacophony in the midst of the melody. Fear is one of the boulders that disrupt the music of attention and frontoparietal coordination.

The amygdala has a direct input into the centers of attention. Nerve cells in the amygdala form various chains of connection until they reach the frontal cortex, allowing fear impulses to freely and easily plop into the serene pool of attention whenever they want to. To keep the pool serene—or the music playing, as it were—many people will try to close the gates to the frontal cortex in the hope of stopping the amygdala impulses from reaching the attention centers. But this is about as effective as putting your finger in a hole in a dike to prevent a flood. It may work for a while, but it can't be done forever. Besides, the unconscious nature of fear will eventually overcome any forceful exclusion from the frontal cortex. So, biologically, how can we make sense of what to do about this?

If we go back to our original thesis, optimism is the selective focusing on the positive aspects of an object or situation. But I would like to extend the definition by referring to the quote of Ambrose Redmoon's that I mentioned earlier: "Courage is not the absence of fear, but rather the judgment that something else is more important than fear."

It's not that the aforementioned sports stars don't have fear, but rather that they've trained their brains to focus on their mission even in the presence of fear. They replace their brains' predisposition to focus on fear with an authentic predisposition to focus on another mission.

When we allow our attention to be captured by fear, our level of fear grows. But if we swing our attentional spotlight to focus on something else, our brains will respond in kind.

Thus, we can tame the amygdala if we exercise the frontoparietal cortex, and at the end of this chapter, we will explore some ways in which to do this. But tapping into the frontoparietal cortex is not as easy as it seems. And when we want the amygdala to stop processing fear, we need to give it a suitable alternative.

Resilience and Resistance to Fear:
The Role of Hope

When we fear things, we face the challenge of being resilient. What does it mean to be resilient? In this context, it means resisting fear, or finding a way to deal with fear that promotes survival and an improved quality of life rather than the fragile and depleted sense of self that fear will give us. Using our knowledge of scientific research, how can we remain resilient in the face of fear?

In a recent review article, one group of researchers emphasized how resilience in the face of adversity results from shifting the *focus* of attention to positive rather than negative things. The researchers concluded that true resilience is dependent on "commitment, dynamism, humor in the face of adversity, patience, optimism, faith, and altruism." All of these characteristics are also fundamental to hope. Thus, hope is akin to a wind that swings the flashlight of attention toward positive things and away from fear. When it becomes a commitment—that is, when you are dedicated to manifesting hope in your life—this also affects the way in which your brain works.

Being committed means that you are able to access nerve circuits in the prefrontal cortex, parietal lobes, and basal ganglia, all of which are critical for processing attention and acting on beliefs. When there is no commitment, these regions are underactivated. So even if we cannot directly attend to positive things because fear prevents it, indirectly activating these regions through intuitive positivity can stimulate them to improve our ability to focus on positive things and decrease fear.

Fear likes to be the frontrunner in the Grand Prix of life. But in the face of hope, it loses steam, especially when hope invites allies like focused attention, mindfulness, and inspiration to the racetrack as well.

The Impact Factor

Different emotions affect our brains differently. Fear, probably for evolutionary reasons, dominates in terms of its impact factor. One of the few ways in which we can change this instinctive response is to develop an emotionally resonant, positive mission that is authentic and has a high impact factor.

For example, would you cross a raging river that threatened to wash you downstream over the edge of a waterfall? Probably not. But would you cross this same river if doing so meant you could save the life of your child? That answer requires more contemplation, and, for most, if this were the only option, the answer would be yes. In other words, fear can be overcome by an alternative priority of greater significance to you. Rather than trying to overcome the powerful nerve impulses from the amygdala, you can instead offer it a higher-impact, positive, and constructive emotion.

A recent study that looked at subjects' brain waves after positive and negative stimuli were presented found that both positive and negative stimuli can capture attention. But for attention to be captured by a positive stimulus, the positive stimulus has to have a greater impact factor than the negative stimulus.

Swinging your brain's spotlight from negative to positive is possible because we do have voluntary control over the frontoparietal circuits. Note that exerting this control is not *easy*. That is why exercises are important. Tiger Woods and Michelle Kwan did not develop such high levels of concentration and focus without any training. They spend time training their minds to focus on their higher-impact goals. Rather than focusing their attention on being afraid to win, they focus their attention on improving their speed, accuracy, and force. At the end of this chapter, you will find some exercises that you can use to train your frontoparietal cortex. The good news, then, is that we can access our attention circuits. The bad news is that it takes work. But with this work, fear can be eased out of focus and replaced by something of greater importance in your life. Fear does not have to go away, it just has to be less important than something positive. Richard Branson, a self-made billionaire, once said, "Everyone needs something to aim for. You can call it a challenge, or you can call it a goal. It is what makes us human. It was challenges that took us from being cavemen to reaching for the stars." Biologically, he is talking about creating an authentic partner for attention that is more attractive than fear.

Beyond Focused Attention:
The Biology of Being in the Zone

We started out understanding attention as a biological process of selectively focusing on an object or situation. But there is another important component to attention, and that is *depth*. You can look for days at material that you are supposed to work on without actually attending to it deeply. You may argue that you have been attending to this book for days, and that may be true, but have you attended to it deeply for days?

Actually, being in the zone requires depth in addition to focus. Although practicing how to focus attention can be effortful (like playing scales endlessly on the piano before you play an actual piece), the result, when it is most successful, is not. Any successful musician will tell you that at jam sessions, they let go of the focused attention and just let something happen. In fact, focusing the attention can actually obstruct playing good music.

I remember playing one of my own musical compositions on the piano at a school concert. I had practiced very hard for days, and on the day of the concert, as I took my seat after the introductory applause, I saw my music teacher in the front row. I started to play and things were going very well. The music flowed smoothly and my fingers raced across the keyboard without any strain, taking advantage of the automaticity that practice confers. Suddenly, for a reason unbeknownst to me, I started to have this perverse thought that I did not know what I was doing. I started to wonder where my fingers should go next, and I realized that I might not remember. I started to panic. For a few bars, it was touch and go. I thought I might have to give up and walk out, but just in time, I looked up at my piano teacher, aghast with terror that I was not going to remember what to play. She smiled at me and closed her eyes, gently chopping the air above her lap with her palm downward, signaling that I should just lose myself in the music. So I did, and all of a sudden, my fingers found themselves and I could play again.

Much later in life I came to understand what happened that day: I had practiced the piece so much that it had become automatic. And I could play it well, as long as I let it be automatic. Starting to think disrupted the automatic brain processes and started to engage the slower thinking processes. This had worked when I was practicing, but wouldn't when I was playing. This was one of the most startling realizations that I had ever had—that fear can disrupt the automatic processes of daily living and throw us into a paralysis of thinking that can stop the music of our lives. Moreover, fear can result from making what has become automatic deliberate once again.

In this case, knowing what to do comes from extensive practice, and suddenly losing this reasonable faith in automaticity disrupts performance. This is the intrusion of "what if," and it signifies a less than completely trained sequence. Similarly, when you try the exercises at the end of this chapter, remember that being able to perform them expertly is just one step toward developing the weapon of attention that will enable you to thwart the obstructions of fear.

Thus, the first step in developing positive thinking and reducing dread is to engage the frontoparietal cortex in focusing on a positive goal. The second step is to develop a deep focus on that goal. With repeated practice, this will become automatic. When it does, allow the automatic process to take you to your goal. Many creative possibilities emerge when you do this.

Replicating in a performance what has been learned with extensive practice is only one level of proficiency. Having the ability to improvise—to be spontaneous—has a joyfulness about it that characterizes the absence of fear. One study that looked at what happened in the brains of six improvisational jazz performers when they played alone or improvised to prerecorded music relates to much of what we are talking about. Researchers compared functional MRI scans of the performers' brains when they were improvising and showing spontaneous creativity to scans of their brains when they were playing learned musical sequences. What they found was that parts of the prefrontal cortex worked differently during improvisation than when performing the practiced piece of music. In contrast to what was seen in the brain during improvisation, the sides of the frontal lobe did not activate when the musicians played the practiced piece, whereas the middle parts did. Amazingly, the researchers also found that limbic structures (parts of the brain, such as the amygdala, that are involved with emotion) deactivated during improvisation, suggesting that emotions—such as fear—had been converted into expertise and focus.

Did this absence of amygdala activation represent a renouncement of fear? It requires practice, but I have worked with people who, instead of attending to and giving power to their fear, declaw it with a different narrative in their heads. They dismiss the brain's automatic response to fear—"Oh my God!"—and change their narrative to something more like "Here we go again—whatever." Taking this kind of attitude has permitted them to try more things and to push *through* their fears instead of getting rid of them.

Revisiting the Science of Emotion

So we know that fear is an electrical current running through several structures in the brain—the amygdala, in particular—that sometimes disrupts other structures, such as the frontoparietal cortex, that are important in attention. Think for a moment about the implications of this.

Fear is an electrical current. What can an electrical current do? It can help you cook something in a microwave, start a car, turn on a light, and amplify an electric guitar. It can also run through your body and kill you if you are struck by lightning during a storm. Because fear is electricity running through a certain part of the brain, it is probable that we can redirect this electrical energy to run through other parts of the brain that *do not* elicit fear. This is partly what the experiment on improvisation showed. And the message in this to you is that there are two important biological realities that give us hope for overcoming fear: First, nerve cells can change (we call this property neuroplasticity), and second, fear, as electricity, can be rechanneled through other circuits. We will examine how to do this later on in this chapter.

Extensive practice and improvisation both deepen attention. Extensive practice leads to the ability to replicate learned sequences, whereas improvising involves experimentation. Both of these exercises turn off the fear circuits.

The Science of Spirituality

Another aspect of attentional depth is captured in spiritual literature. Many faiths all over the world extol the virtues of stilling the mind. Focused attention has the power to do this, and after extensive practice, the nature of the reality that one experiences changes. Most people think of reality as being that which meets their immediate perception: What we see, think, feel, hear, and smell make up what we believe to be reality. But think about this for a minute. If this is true, then why do our eyes lie to us with a mirage? What we *see* is interpreted by the brain before we know that we see it. Our visual sense of a thing is not the first information that we encounter. The first information comes from jerky eye movements that would make us nauseated if the brain did not correct them. Why are we unable to hear sounds at the high frequencies that dogs hear? Why do some cheeses smell terrible but taste good? Imagine the repercussions that would arise if we believed in mirages, did not believe that dog whistles produced sound, and responded to the initial smell of cheese. Clearly, perception is not as accurate a reality detector as we would like to think. That is why spiritual paths prescribe looking inward.

Looking inward is difficult to practice because it is an abstract concept. We can start to know what is internal, however, when we focus our attention on external things, because attention stills the mind and the constant movement of thoughts. When the mind is still, a sense of our selves, often one that is filled with peace, becomes available. This state of being is a state beyond fear. It is also a state that is beyond our perceptions. When we attend to our thoughts, we fix our attention, insulating ourselves from distractions. When we are afraid, our attention wanders all over the place, and vice versa: When our attention is scattered, it can activate fear as well.

Fixing your attention stops the frontal cortex from randomly provoking the amygdala. The frontal cortex is like an electrode that can buzz the amygdala, but if we occupy it with other thoughts, it will not randomly shoot current toward the amygdala. If your attention is scattered and chaotic, though, the frontal electrode will randomly activate the amygdala and cause fear. Harnessing attention allows the amygdala to react to other high-impact positive and negative emotions, and in the absence of fear, even negative emotions can feel less unpleasant. Similarly, fear can make even positive emotions feel overwrought or too activated, and we often come to regret these states of forced happiness.

Thus, attentional depth is critical to overcoming fear. One way to develop this depth is by using the power of intention.

Intention and Attention:
The Scientific Connection

In his powerful and inspiring book *The Power of Intention,* Wayne Dyer explains how understanding intentions—strongly held desires or plans—can lead us to our goals in life, especially if we remain committed to our intentions as we proceed toward our goals. Intention in this context is not just a need that we have recognized in ourselves, but also the deeper drive to accomplish our goals. What is remarkable about this is that intention is more connected to hope and belief than to desperation, and that, as much as it is connected with a heartfelt desire to achieve what we want to, it also requires less forceful action and greater use of the power that we have available to us. One way to understand this is if I asked you to move your car from Minnesota to San Francisco. You could push it (with heartfelt intention to succeed, but lots of sore muscles) or you could drive it, using the power of the car's engine to get you there. This highlights the importance of harnessing our power, rather than forcing our power, but this is easier said than done. When I mentioned this to a client on one occasion, she said, "You try using your power when all your mind can come up with is negative thoughts."

A mind with negative thoughts is like a car that is idling. She was right: You can't get anywhere in a car that is idling. You have to change gears and step on the gas to start moving, and then you have to be constantly aware of your destination. "But how do I change gears?" she asked. "How do I shift the gear from park to drive?"

This is where *attention* comes in. Studies have shown that mindfulness (the awareness of one's thoughts, actions, and motivations) leads to the manifestation of intention. Generally, certain behaviors automatically lead to other behaviors. When people binge drink, for example, they are likely to have hangovers, feel fatigued and lethargic, and not be very motivated to exercise—clearly, these are deleterious effects. In one study, however, people who were characterized as more mindful were able to continue to honor their intentions to be physically active, while those who were not mindful were not.

Thus, attending to what you feel or having a deep understanding of what is important to you can definitely lead to the fulfillment of your desires. But how do we develop this *understanding* of your desires? I call the process of coming to understand them the savoring effect.

When you eat a piece of chocolate, you can throw it into your mouth and devour it. You will satisfy your sugar craving that way, but you haven't really tasted it. If, on the other hand, you take a piece of fine Belgian chocolate and place it on your tongue, letting it slowly melt as you savor the taste, you will have a completely different experience. You will develop a heightened sense of appreciation for this chocolate, and your understanding of it will be very different from the understanding you would arrive at if you gulped it down. This quality of sustained attention and allowing your taste buds to savor the chocolate is akin to developing an understanding of ourselves. If we take our time and practice mindfulness, we begin to develop a true appreciation of the complexity and nuance of our own thoughts.

Thus, mindfulness in this context refers to your awareness of your own thoughts; it is internal attention that focuses on what is happening within us. The crucial variable here is *happening:* That is, mindfulness is about bringing your attention away from the past and future and into the present to focus on not what has happened or what is going to happen, but what is happening. Thus, while mindfulness is absolutely necessary for intention to manifest, attention to the present is essential for mindfulness to occur.

Brain imaging studies have shown that the brain areas responsible for attention and intention are closely related anatomically and functionally, especially the portions located in the parietal cortex. Scientists refer to intentions as motor plans; that is, they believe that the brain sketches out plans of action that we then attend to in order to execute them. The parietal cortex is located at the top and just behind the very front of the brain. It has many connections to parts of the frontal lobe such as the anterior cingulate cortex, which is known to also be involved in attention. One of the ways in which current can flow in the human brain is from the attention centers in the frontal lobe to the intention centers in the parietal lobes. Attention is intricately related to intention. This works both ways. In addition to attention helping to convert our intentions into actions, intentions can also tell us what to attend to.

So, one way for us to make sense of the power of intention is to view our intentions as deep desires that we must savor as we might a piece of chocolate. These intentions are plans that our brains have already sketched out. To access these plans, we need to be mindful. That is, we need to focus our attention on the present and on the plans—and we can, because the brain circuits for attention and intention are connected. Thus, intention is very powerful because it is the plan that the brain makes for you to execute. For an action to occur, for you to actually reach or "attract" your goals, you must connect with the intention deeply.

Understanding intention deeply helps to put you within close proximity of your goal—which will make it appear that you attracted this goal. For example, I have a deep desire to alleviate human suffering on a large scale. And it was only when I connected with this intention that I put myself in the position to write this book, get an agent, find a publisher, and now, reach you, a reader.

Some other things have also happened to seal the deal, however. The book had to be written, published, and distributed to you. This reveals another question to explore before we delve into the role of fear in positive thinking: What is the connection between intention and action? And what do we know about the science of this?

From Intention to Action

One of the most powerful attributes of the human brain is its capacity for choice: We can choose or choose not to do something and thereby control our own destinies. We know without a doubt that our brains are adapted for making choices in life, however overwhelming they may at first seem. Doing something requires the participation of a part of the frontal cortex called the medial frontal cortex (MFC). This part of the brain does three things: (1) It assesses the value (reward versus cost) of an action, (2) it registers information obtained through exploratory actions, and (3) it processes conflict and tells the movement centers in the brain what action to perform. Essentially, it acts as the brain's accountant.

For example, I once saw a client, Catherine, who came from an established and well-known social circle, but her father had limited her spending and she didn't know how to move forward in her life. She decided that having sex with men for money would be the way she would survive. We talked about the dangers of this before she acted on the decision, but her intellectual understanding of the risks did not impact her actions. She began to prostitute herself. After several months of doing this, her MFC told her that the personal cost to her self-esteem and psyche was not worth the reward of the money. The MFC learned this from her exploratory actions. And once she started being mindful of how this conflicted with her long-term goals, she stopped the activity, went to school, and then got a job.

Now, to most people this course might have been the obvious solution all along. But Catherine had to connect deeply with her intentions to understand how prostitution stood in the way of what she wanted in life. What we consciously *think* are our intentions may not in fact be the whole story. In fact, a brain imaging study showed that we may devise what we think are our intentions after we set out upon a course of action. For example, when I asked Catherine how she understood her prostitution, her initial response was that it was a way for her to make money. Over time, she came to understand how the sexual abuse she had suffered as a child impacted her sense of her own body—she blamed herself for the abuse. As a result, she felt obligated to pleasure others in a way that alleviated her guilt. This time, though, she was asking to be paid for it. But she realized that this was not in itself sufficient recompense. Our reasons for doing things usually involve multiple conscious and unconscious reasons, and when we initially think that we understand our intentions, we should think again, because it is likely that we are creating a reason retrospectively.

Patrick Haggard, PhD, has shown that the conscious experience of intending to act arises from the preparation for action that occurs in the frontal and parietal lobes—a process that intricately involves attention, as mentioned earlier. Intentional actions also involve a strong sense of agency—the sense of controlling events in the external world. This latter capacity is critical to actually attaining our goals. If we don't have a sense that we can change things in the external world, no amount of attention or intention will lead to action. From my clinical experience, I've concluded that most people have some intention to change their lives, and they have a reasonable ability to attend to this intention. What they lack is the belief that they are actually capable of changing their lives, that they have any control at all.

When Megan, a patient of mine, told me that she needed to be more creative and have a more fulfilling job, she said that such a career was impossible because she needed to stay at her secure, reliable job to put her kids through school. Now, although it was in fact true that leaving her job would mean initially that she would not be able to support herself, it was also true that she could get another job that she might enjoy more that would also allow her to meet her financial needs. It was true that it would be difficult to get such a job. But there was no hope of getting one as long as her intention and attention did not match her sense of agency. She knew what she wanted, but she wasn't able to tolerate the anxiety of leaving her secure job. As a result of not believing that a solution was possible, she never took on the challenge of finding one.

A contrasting example is found in the life of David Whyte, a writer who left the corporate world to honor his love of poetry. Most people thought that he had made an insane choice. But David followed his passion. He had an intention. He paid attention to it. And he had the critical sense of agency that he could make this change and affect his own world and the world of others in a more meaningful way.

When I talk to my clients about this, a protest that I frequently hear is "But I'm afraid to make that move. How do I overcome that fear?" And when I hear these protests, I recall that wonderful Redmoon quote: "Courage is not the absence of fear, but rather the judgment that something else is more important than fear."

Harnessing Fear to Confront Dread:
The Science of Positive Thinking

The MAP-CHANGE Approach

Using the MAP-CHANGE approach, we can learn to make the necessary changes to decrease dread and increase positivity.

Meditation

Several studies have shown that meditation is associated with a better quality of life, and that positive thinking is one of the factors that it enhances. Furthermore, studies have shown that mindfulness can be cultivated and that it also leads to positive outcomes. If you are uncomfortable with closing your eyes and repeating a mantra, then merely observe your thoughts. These techniques have been shown to benefit people who are suffering from cancer and HIV infection. Even in such difficult circumstances, meditation can help people feel more positive. Also, practicing mindfulness does not mean just relaxing or doing nothing. Although both relaxation and mindfulness produce positive mood states, mindfulness is unique in reducing distracting thoughts and harnessing your attention.

How does the science of meditation relate to the science of positive thinking? For positive thinking to be successful, the brain's attentional spotlight has to swing from the negative to the positive. Meditation paves the way for the spotlight so that when it swings, it is as deeply connected with the positive as it was with the negative. Meditation does this through several scientifically proven mechanisms—it "holds" the chaos that arises from fearful attention, quieting down the amygdala and allowing you to become less fearful. The result of this is that your action centers are suddenly able to see your intentions more clearly, because they are no longer obscured by the murky chaos of fear. Your action centers are then able to act on the clear intentions. Any kind of meditation that appeals to you would likely be helpful.

People often object to the idea of meditating because they think they won't be able to sit still or keep their eyes closed for twenty minutes; they think they are just too internally restless. I tell them that in the first few moments of meditation, you are not expected to achieve a thoughtless state. Although you are aiming for a clear, undisturbed consciousness, it takes time to clear out the murky thoughts that cover up your real intentions. Expect it to take a while for your thoughts to come under your control. The brain can change, but it does not do this instantly. It needs time.

If you feel you cannot manage twenty minutes of meditation, start with five minutes a day for a few weeks. Even five minutes of this practice will start to tame the chaos arising between your frontal lobes and amygdala.

Attention

Any exercise that truly grabs your attention will quiet down the amygdala. Have you ever wondered why it is that when you are absorbed in your work, you feel lost to the world and can even have a very positive feeling that is very different from the dread you may have experienced when you were anticipating doing the task? Anticipation activates the amygdala and disrupts your attention. It is like trying to get your sailboat going. Until the sails are up and the course is properly charted, the boat rocks. It is only when the sails are up and the direction has been determined that you can start to relax.

Whenever you start a task that you dread doing, realize that the dread has already blown through the attention centers in your brain. Dread is a strong gust of wind that challenges your ability to sail your boat. As you start to get into your work, you begin to focus your attention and to tame the gust of dread into a soft breeze.

This occurs because the attention centers of your brain are the reins that harness the amygdala, and when you choose to focus, no matter how difficult it is, you are putting your hands on the reins. With practice, you will gain control over the reins of attention, and thereby of the amygdala. But this control is an art: It has to be learned, and attentional exercises can help you do this.

What are attentional exercises? I have found that anything that holds your attention can start to help you learn to do this. Games like sudoku, for example, provide an alternate focus that swings your attention centers to a different kind of challenge.

Earlier we mentioned that the amygdala processes fear above all other emotions, but if a new challenge whose impact exceeds that of the fear is presented, the amygdala will give up the fear. This is because the new challenge distracts your attention away from the fear and because your amygdala now has new information to process from the attention centers in your brain.

What other exercises can you perform? For many people, playing video games in moderation is calming because the fear that lurks unconsciously is replaced with a conscious task that demands attention.

In reality, any task that you do can help you develop your attention and reduce your fear. If you find that your fears disrupt your task execution, don't lose faith. Think of attentional training like weight reduction. It is difficult, but doable. And sticking to your program will help you enhance your ability to attend to positive things. A great technique that Wayne Dyer says he uses to kick-start himself whenever he has a negative thought is to say to himself, "Next."

What this does is force your frontoparietal (attentional) processing to change its object. As a result, you do not nourish the negative thought, you starve it and turn your attention to helping positive ideas grow in your life.

Some of my clients have argued that this feels like denial; they say that just ignoring your fear, anger, or sadness invites unconscious rebellion because you are not working out the problems. In part, they are correct. Completely ignoring your fears and negative thoughts is not optimal. But in my experience, people tend to get addicted to attending to their negative ideas because keeping an eye on them calms them down; they feel as though they're watching over a potential disaster. This is akin to the captain of an army focusing only on the enemy instead of also on his own soldiers' strength. Both are necessary.

When facing fear and uncertainty, it is challenging to shift your focus to the positive while not simultaneously feeding the negative with your attention. That is why directing yourself to go on to the "next" thing works well in transferring the nourishment of attention from the negative to the positive.

Psychological Tools

For something to have a greater impact than fear, it has to genuinely attract our attention. It has to be a powerful and meaningful intention. This is not the same as saying, "I want to make lots of money" or "I want to be in a relationship." These are just expressed wishes. An intention is a deep-seated desire that resonates to your very core.

To maintain positive thinking in the face of fear, the positive thought has to have a higher energy level than fear does. That is, the literal electrical energy representing the positive thought in your brain has to dominate your attention in order to quiet down the amygdala's processing of fear. Essentially, two strong emotions—positive (such as hope) and negative (such as fear)—cannot exist at the same volume at the same time in your brain. The one that has more electricity will be louder.

Here is a striking example: Leona was a forty-five-year-old doctor who left the workforce for ten years to raise her two children. When they both were old enough to go to school, she wanted to rejoin the workforce. However, she feared that she had been out of the workplace for too long and began having periods of anxiety in which she fixated on her fears of never being able to work again. When she applied for jobs, despite her Ivy League background and her excellent interpersonal skills, people questioned whether she could do the job at the level of energy that it required. This made her reconsider whether she actually wanted to go back to practicing medicine.

Then she came up with what sounded like a great idea. She started to talk about wanting to do something that made her feel that she was giving back to society. I questioned whether this was a heartfelt idea or one that she felt she should have. I had no doubt that she was a humanitarian at heart, but for some reason it didn't seem to me that she was recognizing a passion. She explored all sorts of humanitarian options, ranging from working with underserved populations to joining Greenpeace missions. She was unable to sustain any interest in these options, and when she did start a job, she would leave within a few months for any reason she could concoct other than not feeling fully invested in the job. We continued to talk about what truly moved her, and she eventually came to the understanding that what moved her was art. But then she found herself in a quandary, because she couldn't think of any jobs that could incorporate this passion. I encouraged her to take one step closer to her passion, to recognize that this valence or impact was real, and to get closer to what she actually wanted to do. She took a step closer and found that she was profoundly interested in studying art history. After realizing this, she felt even worse because she had now moved from making a difference to what felt like a self-serving concentration on education, which she already had plenty of.

Throughout this process, I was confident that Leona would be able to let go of a deeper anxiety when she resolved her anxiety about this career choice. To make a long story short, she followed her heart. And before she graduated with a degree in art history, she connected with numerous philanthropic causes that, to this day, are still thriving and related to her passion for art. She became much more comfortable with her life, and less afraid.

But even if she was prone to being afraid, genetic studies of anxiety tell us that, while genes play a major role in childhood anxiety, for adults, environmental modification can significantly decrease it. Leona was able to develop a new focus on her much-loved interests, and, in doing so, she gave her amygdala new and impactful material to process instead of her fear. None of her talk of personal service had done this.

The following are some principles that will increase the impact of positive thoughts.

- First, focus on something that is of importance to you.
- Do not respond to your guilt about "service"; the benefit it gives to others will arise on its own when you pursue your passion.
- If you are unable to find your passion, as most people feel is the case, do not despair. Doing so only adds another level of despair or fear to an already existing fear.
- Even if your passion makes no practical sense at first, slowly move deeper into it. Nothing in the world is impractical; business and money will come from any idea or action once you connect with it deeply.

The Savoring Effect

Earlier in this chapter, I spoke about the savoring effect—the ability to be mindful about your desires and intentions so that your attention guides your brain in the right direction. Scientific research has shown us that mindfulness increases attention, decreases fear, and allows us to focus on the positive. Just as melting a piece of chocolate slowly in your mouth or swirling a taste of wine on your tongue allows you to fully appreciate the flavor, so too does contemplating your desires help you to understand what you want.

Now, here is a subtle but very important point: We taste chocolate or wine in order to understand, but our eventual understanding and appreciation of them are not due just to taste. In the human brain, smell and taste are closely connected, and these sensations evoke memories that are then intertwined with the present, and it is this amalgamation of sensations and memories that produces your experience of tasting the chocolate or wine. For your desires or intentions to lead to actions and help you overcome your fears, you have to move beyond thinking and the senses. This requires a staunch commitment to your essential feeling, whether or not you can "justify it." Methods for creating an environment to stimulate mindfulness are:

- Spend ten to twenty minutes alone each day (after the kids have gone to sleep or after your evening rituals) preventing yourself from thinking. Allow your thoughts to flow, but when you become aware of them, consciously stop them. They will arise again, but when they do, become an observer of them. You will notice that as you change from being an *experiencer* of your thoughts to an *observer* of your thoughts, you start to engage the attention circuits that will quiet down your amygdala. When you attend to your thoughts, however, do not judge or conclude anything about them. Let each thought go gently, and if it arises shortly afterward, repeat the process.
- Repetition is key to learning in the human brain. I call this mining your consciousness. The real jewels of consciousness are found deep down, beyond your senses and your thoughts. To mine your consciousness, use attention as a drill. Ramana Maharshi, a Hindu sage of the early twentieth century, used to say that the mechanism for doing this is to ask at every juncture of thinking, "Who am I?" He did not recommend answering this question in words. He recommended repeatedly using the question as a drill and an attentional focus to help you go deeper and deeper to unveil your deepest intentions. At the deepest levels, your desires are connected to their outcomes. You will not need to *do* anything. What you end up doing will be fueled by

inspiration. Rather than just using the horsepower of effort, you will be able to lubricate your efforts with the complexity of your consciousness, allowing complex actions to flow. Biologically, this sensation of inspiration is thought to be due to the simultaneous integration of different mental faculties, seen as synchrony in the electrical activity in various brain regions.

The Balance Sheet Perspective:
Paying the Cost to Be the Boss

The brain is not as closed a system as it may seem. Although it is securely housed in the skull and body, it connects to the universe via your sense organs and excretory and sexual orifices. It is continuous with the universe. Whatever is going on in your brain can be seen as a series of molecular events that are in equilibrium with the universe. Your brain is made up of atoms that emit energy through vibration. We know that what is going on outside of you affects you, so it follows that the energy from outside affects the energy inside. Whenever we are out of equilibrium with the universe, fear and distress become more prominent and positive thinking becomes more difficult.

This same concept of being in equilibrium applies to what is going on inside the brain. If your amygdala is firing out of control and your frontoparietal circuits have not established control over it, there is no sense of equilibrium. This internal chaos makes it difficult to focus on positive ideas that will reduce fear and anxiety. Fear becomes your boss when chaos is the rule. The cost attached to this is dread.

When you allow fear to take over your life, dread and anxiety result, accompanied by an inability to materialize what you want. This is on the expense side of the balance sheet. If you see fear as the cost of being alive and careful, then you will unconsciously seek to accentuate this dread by constantly feeling the need to be afraid. That is, fear can be within your control if you pay the price necessary to buy out the fear. The price you pay is not in dollars; it is in *attention.*

Fear is the cost; you pay attention to be the boss. That means that you have to have enough attention in your attention bank account to pay off fear so it gets lost. Fear never completely leaves us. But when it is starved of attention, as we have seen happen in the experiments showing how attention to fear and pain accentuates the sensation of fear, we can see how paying attention to positive things over a lifetime can become habitual for your frontoparietal cortex. We are lucky enough to be able to train attention to starve fear.

As an exercise, try out the following:

- The next time you find yourself distracted by fear, write down five positive things in your life and repeat this daily for a month. When the fear arises again, realize that you will have trained your attentional circuits to focus on something more important and impressive than fear.
- Many inspirational writers advise us that we will attract negative things if we focus on negative things. Why is this? When you focus on negative things, your whole way of interacting with the universe occurs within this framework. The goal is to avoid negative thinking. But rather than using any effort to stop doing this, simply focus on the positive. Actively avoiding the negative often results in the negative happening because you are attending to it.
- The next time you are confronted by the memory of a previous failure, train yourself to retell the story. For example, change "I am afraid that I have not been able to get what I want" to "I have learned from my failures that focus is key to getting what I want, so I will focus on that."

I learned this lesson from my father when I sprinted competitively. I consistently came in second, and I grew very frustrated by this. One day, my father, who attended all of my athletic events, said to me, "I've been watching you as you run, and you are ahead for more than 75 percent of the race. But just as you are about to win, you look over your shoulder and someone overtakes you. The next time you run, focus on getting to the end. Forget what is happening behind you. Leaders can't be afraid that they are alone."

His words have stayed with me to this day. After I won the next race I ran, I turned to the crowd and saw him stand and throw up his hands to acknowledge my victory. To this day, I have found this principle to always hold true. My dad did not realize it, but he was telling me that by looking over my shoulder, I was switching my attention from the positive goal of winning to the possibility of someone overtaking me. When my attentional circuits swung toward this fear, it affected my amygdala, and together they slowed me down by affecting my motor circuits. When I learned to focus on breaking the tape rather than outrunning the challengers behind me, I was telling my attentional circuits to steady my amygdala and maintain my pace. I no longer got information on who was behind me, but I gained the possibility of victory by staying focused on the goal.

The brain is really a very cooperative organ. If you tell it to win, it will strive to do this. If you tell it to win and to look over your shoulder, it will try to do both things, and then the noise of the looking-over-the-shoulder circuit (your fear) will impede your chances of winning.

The point is: Reframe the fear story. Brain imaging studies tell us that when we reframe a fear story, we become less fearful of it. It is not fear itself that causes anxiety, but rather fear of fear. When we replace fear of fear with attention to fear, we succeed in overcoming a critical component in what obstructs movement in life. Brain imaging studies have shown that when this is done, amygdala activation decreases.

Conclusion

Dread, as a feeling state, is more related to what you attend to than what you are feeling. If you train your mind to shift the location and depth of its focus, you can reduce the amount of dread and anticipatory anxiety in your life.

[3]

Fear of Success

The Biology of Understanding and Transcending the Largest Fear Paradox

Our deepest fear is not that we are inadequate. Our deepest fear is that we are powerful beyond measure. . . . As we are liberated from our own fear, our presence automatically liberates others.

—Marianne Williamson

Perhaps the greatest sadness that we can burden ourselves with is the vulgarity of mediocrity, for mediocrity is an unnatural and untenable condition. In my opinion, it is a theoretical perversity that has been synthesized from man-made fears as a lowly alternative to suffering in the phenomenal world of intense desire. To be mediocre is to deny the essence of the greatest offerings of which you are capable and to collude with the masses that tend to identify with the social ideal of "normal."

When clients enter my office, I work to ensure that their identities are not absorbed by medical terminology that highlights their vulnerabilities. I will not rest upon the labels of *depression* and *anxiety*. Nor will I encourage human beings suffering from the consequences of being human to explain the meaning of their emotional difficulties in ways that conform with foolish diagnostic standards. Every human being is an individual. And the capacity for greatness that lies in any one of us is a product of the complex flavor of our complete selves. But why are we so afraid of this power of greatness? And what is it in our biology that directs us to avoid it?

The idea of avoiding the very thing we search for in our lives—this magnificent power, this opportunity to be and give our greatest—is a cruel twist played by the brain under the dictatorship of fear. Fear of success is a blatant reality. We are no less valuable for having this fear, nor should we choose to listen to its lamentations wrapped in a shroud of shame.

Too often, our best faces are seen only after they've been laid to rest in a casket. Why wait until this inevitable moment to reveal your best face? Show your essence like a lion. Strut the streets with longing, if this is what it takes to unleash your roar. The cries of our success cause inner trembling, and it behooves us to understand the biology of this madness so we can see the beauty clearly enough to transcend it.

This chapter describes the psychology and biology that underlie our fear of success. In the pages that follow, you will learn how your brain biology sets up your fear of success and what you can do about this by using that very same brain in a different way.

Fear of Success:

How Brain Biology Sets Up the Psychology of This Paradox

Fear of success is an alluring concept that seems at first glance to be based on nothing. After all, why would we fear the very thing that we desire? Many people have wondered whether this is just a recasting of our fear of failure within a positive framework. To address this suspicion, researchers began examining the validity of this psychological construct as early as the 1950s, and since then we have learned much about why it is that we fear accomplishing the very goals that we set out to achieve. Although the earliest studies found that fear of success was more common among women than among men in the United States (suggesting that it was the fear of departing from traditional gender roles that fostered a fear of success), later studies in the United Kingdom and the United States found that this syndrome was just as likely to occur in men. Researchers concluded that personality characteristics and social opinions—not gender—influence the likelihood of developing this fear.

As a therapist and coach, I have been astounded by how common this particular fear is. The only thing more shocking than its prevalence is how blind people are to their fear of success. When I reflected on some of the causes of this fear among my clients, I identified what are probably the major psychological underpinnings of the fear of success. Now, with the advent of functional MRI, we can begin to understand how each of these fears is explained by the ways in which our brains work.

So, why exactly do people fear success?

Reason 1—The loneliness of success: The goal of being successful is tricky because success puts you at the top or in front of the pack, so you have nobody to follow and nowhere to go. I once had a client who always flew first-class. One day, he mentioned that he hated the first row and always selected a seat in the second row instead. I assumed that he did not like having to place his hand luggage in the overhead compartment during takeoff and landing, and he agreed that this was one of the reasons, but when we delved into it more deeply, he realized that he hated not having anyone to look at in front of him. Row 1 was extremely lonely for him, as it is for anyone who is in the lead. Even though he wanted to fly first-class, he could not tolerate being out in front. This is a powerful metaphor for how people view success.

Ask any CEO how it feels to sit alone in the big corner office with the great view. The story will likely be different than you imagine. Day after day, many executives sit in their penthouse offices feeling isolated by their power. Furthermore, whether or not you are a CEO, success often requires spending a large portion of the day keeping your feelings contained. Cultivating the necessary focus to expertly match the task at hand is an opportunity for embarking on an inward journey that most people would rather avoid because it requires attending less to things outside of oneself, and thus feeling apart from the world. Inward journeys involve delving deeply into your own thought processes and plans and maintaining the motivation and energy to do this. Doing well at an academic task requires memorizing and following your own thoughts. Planning a successful career involves being able to imagine alternatives—and perhaps even waiting for options to show up as ideas. Processes like memorizing, imagining, and generating ideas require negotiating the internal landscape of one's own mind and tolerating many unknowns. As a result, the paradox of fear of success is often accompanied by the paradox of fear of this inward journey, for it is only this inward journey that can truly help you feel connected to the outside world.

Champions of all kinds spend time sharpening their focus and being inside themselves. When it is time to perform, they let go of this disciplined practice, and the art of what they have learned takes over. The long practice hours, however, can be very lonely, and that is often what distracts people from developing expertise. When we avoid developing our skills to a degree that enables us to achieve success, we remain novices at endeavors we might actually want to be good at. The fear of loneliness is one of the reasons that we are nervous about becoming experts.

In my practice, I have noticed that high-achieving people always find ways to enjoy themselves—that is, they literally enjoy being with themselves, and rather than focusing on loneliness, they focus on how their success will attract people to them. Simply put, becoming an expert requires practice, and practice requires spending time alone. Note, though, that *aloneness* is different from *loneliness,* and that the reward for the initial sacrifice of being alone is that your expertise will eventually make you a people magnet. When you have given yourself over to the spontaneous practice of your ability and the practice becomes ingrained in your brain, you will become magnetic to others. This naturalness is extremely attractive, and you will be sought after as a result.

Traveling the biological road to achieving the automatic or spontaneous level of performance is a two-step process: There is the somewhat tedious practice or novice phase, and then there is the more exciting and freeing expert phase. In novice golfers, for example, the preshot routine is associated with activation in brain regions that do not activate at all in experts. These regions are the posterior cingulate, the amygdala-forebrain complex, and the basal ganglia—all of which are involved in emotional stimulation and information filtering. This indicates that novice golfers experience interference from emotional intrusions, doubts, uncertainties, and other fear-based thoughts and emotions. Although first being a novice is essential to learning to refine expertise, it will not result in expert performance. We need to practice in order to be able to moderate the effects of these emotions and ideas, but as we practice, we must learn to change our brain response. Initially, we can learn in groups, but ultimately we have to step out into the lonely terrain of self-learning in order to reach the next step.

In the expert phase, the superior parietal lobule, the dorsal lateral premotor area, and the occipital area—regions responsible for vision, attention, and motor planning—become activated. The brain has already taken in the emotional information from the novice phase, integrated it, developed a filtering system through practice, and sharpened the attention. Eventually, the brain economizes its use of energy for optimal performance and completing necessary actions—in the case of golfers, putting a ball into a hole. Although they spend much time alone learning their craft, why is it that experts do not suffer from the aftereffects of loneliness? Because they have practiced integrating their emotions, and their focus is on the joy they derive from their success.

To internalize a practice, a state of aloneness in which the information learned in the practice phase is consolidated is essential. This can feel lonely despite our best attempts to identify it as solitude. Loneliness is what we experience as a sacrifice in order to succeed. If we fear loneliness, we fear our own success. After we overcome this fear of success, we engage our brains more automatically and spontaneously. In so doing, we come to feel that other people will want to be with us. Rather than fearing how expert we are compared to others, our success gives us an opportunity to include others as well.

Think of how you feel when you watch an expert musician or tennis player show off his or her skill. The time he or she spent alone learning translates into an ability to attract you and other people across the world. By looking inward and overcoming their fears of loneliness, experts set the stage for enjoying themselves with other people and for other people enjoying them. In contrast are huge stars like Michael Jackson, who often spoke of his talent and success as the source of his isolation. This sense of stardom as a responsibility can take a toll on a person's life unless the artist, for example, is willing to agree that he or she is not alone in creating magic, that talent is more about opening him- or herself to the world than it is an innate, exclusive gift. In this sense, taking responsibility for actual creation is a formula for loneliness.

Reason 2—The disorientation of success: Marathon front-runners will attest to the fact that in the early stages of a race, it's best to stay in the leading pack so you pace yourself rather than breaking away. Pacing yourself requires someone being in front of or close by you, and it provides some external orientation as to where you are. Success, at its peak, takes away this orientation. You have nobody to follow but yourself. A leader has to eventually commit to being a visionary, and, by virtue of the leader's position itself, he or she is forced to take on the sensibility of a herding sheepdog (but with a biologically much more extensive thinking cortex—not an easy challenge!). Fears about leading the pack and of being wrong and potentially misleading an entire group of people often result.

Leading in this context means that you have to have faith in the path you are following. Faith is not a rational state of mind. It is not necessarily irrational either. It is just nonrational. There are many worthwhile nonrational experiences, love and accurate gut instinct being two of them.

Some people are afraid that they cannot be successful visionaries because they have no evidence to justify advocating the paths they choose. This is because the successful paths of visionaries are unconscious. And once these leaders learn to trust the unconscious process, they learn to lead without asking where the information is coming from. Trusting the process involves believing, but we often dismiss this essential form of thinking as silly or ungrounded in reality.

Scientists are beginning to examine this phenomenon from multiple perspectives, one of which they have termed preemptive perception. Preemptive perception is essentially what the brain figures out on its own (unconsciously) before you consciously register that you have perceived something. As we develop this sense and learn to trust it (and we can do this because we know that the brain is working very hard before we even perceive anything), we can begin to lead because we stop feeling that we need to follow others.

Studies conducted on expert golfers and musicians illustrate how spontaneity is key to success and how intention can actually impair performance. To be spontaneous (like a musician who is improvising or a soccer goalie who dives to save the ball), we have to learn to detach from our rational brain systems. This is frightening, and the path of success, especially when you are gliding along, friction free, on it, can be very intimidating for this reason. In imaging studies that have been done on improvisational musicians, the activated brain regions included the right dorsolateral prefrontal cortex, the presupplementary motor area, the rostral portion of the dorsal premotor cortex, and the left posterior part of the superior temporal gyrus. These are similar to the regions activated in expert golfers, suggesting that spontaneity arises from learned sequences that are recalled *after* practice and indicating that success can be practiced and that practice can help people overcome their fears.

When the fear of success is based on being afraid of leading, we need only to realize that the guiding light of those in front of us can be replaced by the guiding light within us. This guiding light is that biological phenomenon called preemptive perception, and it is often a largely unconscious process. When you are in the lead, realize that you got there through a combination of rational and nonrational processes. If you suddenly don't understand how you got to a certain level of success, do not become anxious or self-conscious about it. Realize that if you did understand all of it, you probably would not have been successful. Part of overcoming the fear of success is submitting to the unconscious.

Reason 3—The responsibility of success: The herding sheepdog has more responsibilities than just being an orienting force. The dog has to carry an awareness of the needs of the herd at all times.

Being successful is therefore as selfless as it can be selfish. It is relentlessly dedicating yourself to the needs of others by consistently attending to your own strengths. This can lead to a fear of scrutiny. People may fear that if they are successful, they will be scrutinized and criticized for their imperfections. They conceive of success as a blinding spotlight that shows the imperfections under their makeup. This is one way in which thoughts of success can lead to guilt and embarrassment, which in turn can prevent you from pursuing success because you fear guilt or embarrassment under scrutiny.

Thus, biologically, the ability to be successful requires having the ability to concentrate on the task at hand, which, when the task involves others, requires filtering out the awareness of others despite being responsible for them. A successful person has to have integrated the needs of others into his or her practice prior to serving them. As seen in the examples of the brains of experts, this requires the expert to trust that he or she has learned this information, sometimes without knowing this consciously. In fact, thinking about what others will think may prevent you from achieving success because it prevents inspired and successful action.

To overcome the fear of success, you have to embrace the concept of having practice periods and active periods in your life. During the practice periods, you can engage your brain's capacity to change by directing its deliberate, rational thoughts. If you fear responsibility, for example, you can focus on the needs of others and think about how you can best serve them. During the active period, you put this learned information into action. As in learning a dance sequence, you may have to focus intently on which foot to put in front of the other at first, but eventually you will be able to let go and let the unconscious take care of the rest.

Spend time understanding what your responsibilities are, then allow yourself to do them. Entertaining obsessive fears that you are not satisfying every person you know does not enhance success, it distracts you from it.

Reason 4—Fear of the unknown: The environment that will surround us in success often is different from the environment we inhabit prior to our success. Although we may hate aspects of our current stations in life, we know these stations well. People often live out the adage "Better the devil you know than the one you don't know." Success is a future goal; it is an unknown, and the vagueness of this projection may be intimidating to anyone who has begun to chart a course different from the one conferred by the biology of automatic brain processes and familiarity.

That is to say, choosing to be successful means that you are choosing the unknown. Choosing the unknown requires being attentive to the present and not being in a constant state of anticipatory anxiety. Anticipatory anxiety activates the anterior cingulate cortex (ACC) to continually monitor for error and uncertainty. In fact, brain imaging studies have shown that uncertainty activates the ACC and decreases activation in the basal ganglia. The basal ganglia filter information before we act on it, and they are also involved in taking action. Thus, uncertainty keeps the thinking variables online without sending directions to an action center, and eventually it overloads the online resources. This prevents success.

In order to be successful in the face of uncertainty, we have to make a judgment at every step along the way about whether we believe a path is worth taking. Compared to uncertainty, both *believing* and *not believing* are more definitive ways of acting that increase basal ganglia activation, increasing the chances that you'll actually pursue success rather than just think about it.

What this indicates is that we have a greater chance of acting in ways that will secure future success if we can overcome the fear of uncertainty. Contrary to what we often think, small actions go a long way toward helping us believe or disbelieve as opposed to remaining uncertain. This makes it more likely that we will pursue our ideas about success.

Reason 5—Fear of being unable to maintain the success: Every time a champion takes center stage, all eyes are on him or her to see whether previous successes are repeated or, perhaps, even bettered. How, then, can we avoid fearing that if we are successful once, we might have to be successful again? In my experience, the way success is first achieved is almost never truly known. We can chart out our course as carefully as possible, but it is usually the ineffable parts that are crucial. A brilliant man I once saw in therapy, Karl, had reached the heights of success in conventional terms: He had a wonderful family, a jet-setting lifestyle, a huge home, an idyllic vacation home, and continued creativity and success with business enterprises. He once said that he thought it funny that the business students he gave lectures to carefully wrote down everything he said, because he knew that the reason for his success was that it was his individual process and not something that could be copied. Much of how we succeed is unconscious. And we have to be practiced in the art of going along with this to be successful over and over again.

The fear of not being able to maintain success is a doubt that engages the rational brain, thereby removing you from the unconscious brain state necessary for success to continue. Once again, uncertainty will cause the brain to stall until a decision is made. It engages the conscious and unconscious brain in a conflict and prevents the free flow of information to action centers. Uncertainty also decreases basal ganglia activation. Since the basal ganglia provide feedback to the action centers, the brain will not be able to move forward until doubt has been resolved.

When I took my first cross-country skiing lesson, I got off to a magnificent start. I found my natural rhythm quickly and wound my way around trees, bending to the right and left as I did. I was enthralled for a while until I started to wonder how long this was going to last. As I began to feel afraid, I called out to my instructor, "How will I be able to stop when I want to?" He called right back, "If you're starting to think this, you'll find out soon enough." At the very next moment, I found myself falling forward, to the side and off the main track. When he joined me, he laughed, and, after seeing that I had no major injuries, he asked me why my sudden success had been so threatening to me.

At the time, I didn't know that the sudden doubt threw my brain out of the state of movement and into a state of uncertainty. All of a sudden, I had stopped the flow of information to my movement centers and effectively sent a signal that I had to stop. Worrying about stopping effectively shifted my brain into a state of fear that instructed my movement centers to stop activating immediately. That is why I crashed.

People fear the sudden openness of success. It makes them feel as if they can't grasp or control anything. When rational thinking leaves your side in the midst of success, you have two reasonable choices: You can connect with it again at your next practice session, or you can just go with the flow. Calling it to your side to quell fear will cause your brain to stall on its mission toward success.

Reason 6—Fear that once success is reached, the drive to succeed will be lost: For those who strive to fulfill a purpose in life, the very act of striving becomes a purpose. Many young adults filled with a sense of purpose to become medical students go to college for four years to enable themselves to go to graduate school. Then, their goal to become doctors sustains them through years of med school and residency, and they then achieve this. And then their purpose expands to becoming a specialist—and this, too, is reached as a goal. And then, suddenly, the very drive that created this advancement—the drive that made the unnatural sleep schedules and overwhelming amount of work okay—is gone. The challenge of *being* starts to erode the achievement of *becoming.* Disillusionment ensues. Increasingly as a society, we are creating this creature. The structure and protection provided by striving for a goal are thwarted by reaching it. Again, we have to look deeply inside ourselves to keep the fires burning.

It is important to remember that when you reach a goal, it's just one step in the context of your whole life, no matter how great the goal is. You can always build new goals upon reached goals. For many people, a goal is like a beacon or guiding light. It is counterintuitive for them to give up this light, because it provides orientation and allows them to feel as though they are being pulled by something. Attaining a goal can be very disorienting. It suddenly forces you to ask difficult but important questions: "Now that I am here, what will I do with this? How will I use this? What if this is less enchanting than I thought it would be?" I have yet to meet anyone who sustained the level of happiness and enchantment he or she felt in striving for a goal once it was reached. People are usually happy for a while, but then they lose the excitement of attaining their goal unless they are able to find in it a sense of continued meaning. This partly explains the high divorce rate in our society, because the goal for many people is simply to get married.

Here is where we enter a subjective and difficult zone. Over my nineteen years as a physician, I have come to understand that having a goal is at its most basic a way to control the vagaries of the mind. It is a mental exercise that quiets and trains the mind. Under this training schedule, the real *meaning* of life starts to reveal itself. It is not in words or thoughts or ideas, but rather in a subjective sensation of the possibility of bliss that often arises during states of intense concentration. This bliss (which meditation can also eventually provide access to) is the unrestricted state of human consciousness with its infinite potential to create and manifest the tangible from the intangible. The deeper the concentration in this state is, the deeper the attention, and the more magical the goal. Scientists call this awareness. Once we reach our goals, this magic slips out from beneath us and we find ourselves having to deal with our unruly minds again. ACC activation increases, stirring up emotional systems (the amygdala, primarily) and creating a new level of chaos for which we have to find a new goal, a new level of training.

We are beginning to understand some of this from our studies on meditation. These studies show that Buddhist meditational techniques activate the brain's attention centers. In fact, mindfulness (the awareness of one's thoughts, actions, and motivations) has been shown to decrease amygdala activation and increase activation in the prefrontal cortex. As we said earlier, this improves motor planning and the actions that result from it.

Thus, when fear of success involves fear of reaching a goal, it is based on the fear that we will no longer have our guiding light and will need to find a new one. Having alternative guiding lights and practices (such as meditation, reading, and critical thinking) can be helpful in stalling this fear until a new goal is established. Also, it is important to understand that the real and most fulfilling goal is not one that we consciously set for ourselves, but the one that reveals itself as we train our attention to respond to the gap between where we are and where our goals will take us. After all, our goals are ultimately aimed at attaining happiness. The happiness of reaching a goal is subtly but importantly distinct from the bliss that emerges from the brain state of attentional control utilized during the process of striving for the goal.

Reason 7—Fear that success will attract opportunistic people who will prey upon us: Many lottery winners lose their windfalls and end up back where they started before winning the money. Why would this be? One possible reason relates to what we learned in Chapter 2. Since there is tremendous fear of losing something after acquiring it, this very fear can attract the feared outcome. Attention becomes focused on loss, and the most feared outcome comes to pass. Thus, paradoxically, when people anticipate success, they simultaneously feel threatened by how they will maintain this success.

As I have mentioned many times, we attract what we fear because our brains register fear as a warning that must be processed. One hypothesis about this is that when our brains register fear that another person will do something negative, for example, the activation of our own fear centers in turn will activate the other person's fear centers through the action of the mirror neurons. In this way, you attract or create fear in those around you. In a similar way, when you fear these emotional "vultures," it is possible that you activate vulture circuits in people around you, thereby attracting what you fear. In addition, when you feel vulnerable and helpless, you act vulnerable and helpless, and, as they say of the animal world, creatures of prey can sense fear. The same principle applies to humans. Act like a victim, and you will increase your odds of becoming a victim.

Reason 8—Fear of losing our identity: We often fear that success will change who we are and cause us to forget where we came from. People often project, based on their experiences of others who have become successful, that success will change them in ways that they may not like. Sometimes, they hold on to their old lifestyle as though it is a sign of integrity. Why are we so addicted to "being the same" when we know that our brains change over time, whether we like it or not? Why do we focus on the fear of being greedy if we are successful, rather than on the possibility of being generous? Why do we focus on the fear of being egotistical when we can focus on the reality of sharing the wealth?

We have been taught that we have to declare that we are *something* if we are to have integrity. Yet we know that we are a combination of genetic and biological habits and that our brains are capable of changing (and do in fact change across the life span). This calls into question the idea that you can ever have a stable identity. In fact, a stable identity probably results from focusing on unchanging parts of your brain and inhibiting personal growth.

When you are successful, you have to be open to the possibility that you—and your brain—might change. You will always have access to those stable parts of your brain that you feel give you your identity, and you can control what parts you want to remain the same in many instances. As a human being, you have been given the ability to make all sorts of voluntary decisions. As long as you are open to learning from your mistakes and are self-forgiving, success is nothing to fear. In my experience with people, both the successful and the unsuccessful have good intentions and want to be loved and understood. You will not lose this core value as long as you remain critical, self-forgiving, and open in your thinking. Self-forgiveness allows you to recognize mistakes and make the changes that are necessary for you to honor your own value system.

One brain imaging study showed that the basal ganglia activated during learning, whereas no such activation occurred in the brains of people who were not learning. This suggests that learning changes brain functions and alters the way the brain processes information. If you think that you want to achieve more success but are afraid that it will change you, recognizing that change is part of the success process may decrease your anxiety. Also, your brain naturally tends to reverse changes that you do not want.

To recap these ideas, then, fear of success may be due to:

- Fear of the loneliness of success
- Fear of the disorientation of success
- Fear of the responsibility of success
- Fear of the unknown

- Fear of being unable to maintain the success
- Fear of losing our drive
- Fear of becoming prey
- Fear of losing our identity

Although many of us will initially deny consciously having these fears, one of the reasons success may elude us is that we send mixed messages to our brains: "Make me successful, but see how horrible it will be." Again, our brains find themselves in a quandary when we send conflicting messages to them, and this is likely to delay success significantly.

Lack of self-confidence and fear of competition also have a significant correlation with fear of success. The assumption, for whatever reason, that we do not deserve our successes leads to a tremendous fear about being punished for having success. People are very afraid that they will be "found out." This is called the impostor syndrome, and it has been found to occur in very intelligent, high-performing professionals. Since successful people can account for some but not all of their successes, they often question themselves when a sudden meteoric rise or exponential growth occurs. Many of the mechanisms for achieving success are unconscious, but in some high achievers, not knowing exactly what has enabled them to become successful makes them feel as though they have pulled the wool over everyone's eyes. As a result, some high achievers will thwart their own efforts because they are afraid of psychological heights. They would rather not be scrutinized by others because they are petrified that they will be found out. Researchers who have studied this phenomenon describe how destructive it can be to corporations. From a scientific standpoint, understanding that what we think is luck is actually probably unconscious intelligence may help us to accept how we become successful in the first place. This unconscious intelligence can derive from practice; the more we practice it, the more automatic our actions become. Just as it does for an expert athlete, repeatedly practicing actions removes effortfulness, and when actions become automatic, they make way for inspiration.

Success has very different meanings for different people. For example, for some women, staying at home and raising children meets their definition of success, while other women view continued professional development as success. This becomes tricky because it almost always raises the question of whether each of these groups is avoiding an alternative way of life out of a fear of success.

It therefore becomes imperative to examine what you truly define as success, and then to provide this information to your brain so that it can sketch out a road map to help you reach your goals. Denying the fears underlying the fear of success can be very harmful because it will just perpetuate a state of ambivalence and delay your progress. Examining these fears consciously can help you resolve the tensions of success and refine your intention and actions. But to truly understand the connection between the conscious and unconscious in the fear of success, we need to further contemplate the neurobiology. Before we do, let's examine one of the major obstructions to success: the assumption that capacity for success or dominance is an inherent aspect of a person, or that fear of success is genetic and, thus, unavoidable.

What If Success Is Just Not in the Cards for Me?

I can't tell you how often I hear parents say that their second child is entirely different from the first. "It's really quite striking," they will say. "Jimmy is so quiet and peaceful, and Sarah is just such a firecracker." Later on in life, parents will often wonder why it is that one child drops out of school and the other goes to Harvard. People often speak of a sibling as "the smart one" or focus on some other special thing that he or she can do. When this happens, I like to reflect on the following experiment.

Before her death in 1993, Patricia Barchas, PhD, a social science researcher, examined whether dominance was an inherent trait in heterosexual monkeys in the wild. In one experiment, she set up a laboratory situation in which a dominant and a submissive male monkey from the wild were each observed when in the presence of a female monkey. Dominance was measured by how often the male mounted the female.

In this part of the experiment, Barchas found that the dominant male monkey mounted the female monkey many more times than the submissive monkey did, and her researchers were ready to conclude that dominance is inherent even when an animal is removed from the wild. But a while after she removed the dominant monkey from the setting, the submissive monkey began to behave like the dominant monkey. The experimenters were amazed to realize that the dominant monkey had in fact inhibited the behavior of the submissive monkey. This meant that dominant behavior is relative, not inherent.

I have observed this phenomenon over and over again. You can take a struggling adolescent out of a high-achieving home environment, let her choose to pursue something she loves, and then watch her soar. Over and over again, I have seen people squelched by perceived competitors and unable to exert their dominance in the world even though their potential for holding power was so apparent to me. This does not mean that not all of us can be successful. What it means is that focusing on your own inherent ability to be successful will bring you to this goal more quickly than if you allow yourself to be distracted by the success of others.

Judy, a fifty-year-old woman, discovered too late that her mother's fame and fortune had inhibited her own development. She felt guilty about the possibility of exceeding her mother's accomplishments and scared of her own brilliance, and she spent a decade of her life slowly exploring her own path to success. She found a million valid excuses (she was smart!) to explain why she could not express her own brilliance, and she had a very difficult time admitting that she feared being successful. It was only when she was able to see this that she came to understand how she could make changes to her life to help her move toward her goals. For the longest time, she saw herself as existing in a vacuum, outside of the same psychological system as her mother. As a result, she held herself responsible for whatever she could not achieve. She even went so far as to say that her anxiety about achievement was probably genetic, because she was a chronic worrier. So I told her that recent studies have shown that genes may be responsible for excessive worry in some children, but that we now know that as we get older, genes become less important and the environment and our individual psychological tendencies play key roles in whether or not we continue to worry. Sometimes, it's easier for us to think that we have no control over our destiny. But, as has been seen in people with generalized anxiety disorder (who worry excessively, are easily fatigued, have muscle tension, and do not sleep well), the genetic influence on their anxiety is reduced as they get older, which implies that we do have control over our worrying and that we can take the first step to stop this vicious cycle. For Judy, giving up the "it's genetic" excuse was the first step to increasing her freedom from worry, and she started to see that feeling better was a possibility.

If You Can Imagine Success, You're Halfway There

We live in a time that highlights the importance of doing. When I was taking classes for my certification in executive coaching, one of my teachers said to me, "America is a great nation open to inspiration. But inspiration is not action. And coaching is the intermediary that helps inspiration become action." Inspiring thoughts that we are exposed to on a daily basis make us feel good about ourselves; they help us believe that things are possible, and they give us relief from our fears that we are doing nothing with our lives. They take our attention off our fears and place it on the possibility of achieving greatness. What we have to ask ourselves is how we can act on this possibility and desire for success.

Brain imaging researchers have discovered some interesting facts about action. They have found that the brain goes through several steps before it makes an actual movement occur. We touched on this in the previous chapter, but let's go into a little more detail here.

As we learned in the last chapter, imagined action and actual movement share the same neural substrates—that is, they activate the same parts of the brain. Imagination activates these parts of the motor (action) cortex and related areas at a subthreshold level. It starts the action process. Furthermore, motor areas of the brain have been shown to activate when we speak or write action-related words. Thus, thinking, writing, or speaking about our desire for success can start the action process. For this reason, expressing your desires can be very helpful in beginning the action process.

During my preadolescent years, my brother and I would often watch tennis matches and football games on television and then feel compelled to go outside and play. Watching these games stimulated the primary motor cortex, the supplementary motor cortex, and the parietal lobes and basal ganglia—all parts of the brain that are activated in actual movement. Watching sports was like starting a car, and playing the games was like pressing the gas pedal. We often found that we played much better just after watching a game, not simply because our brains were activated by watching the games, but also because we were imitating the moves we had just seen performed. Simulation or imitation of movement also stimulates these same brain areas and probably increases the level of brain activation even further than imagining making the movement does. (When I learned how to swim, my swim coach often told me to watch other people and then swim without thinking too hard about it.) Simulation, however, also activates other brain regions such as the posterior insula and the ACC more strongly than just observing the actions. Antonio Damasio, MD, PhD, a neurologist at the University of Southern California in Los Angeles and a writer, has proposed that the insula maps our gut instincts and emotional experiences and makes feelings more conscious. In preparation for action, it sets up a representation of the body within the mind. Thus, simulation takes imagination one step further toward independent action.

So, when we desire an action, we first have to imagine it. There are two components to this: Speaking, writing, or observing is part of the inspiration to act, and actually imagining yourself in the act of doing what you desire brings this inspiration closer to action. Taking this desire and imagination to the simulation phase then engages even more brain regions that are critical for independent action to occur.

Despite this push forward that imagination gives us, actual movement is necessary for the desired change to begin happening. In fact, recent research has shown that to make changes in our lives, we have to move from our current situation to a new one. Imagining the change you desire and the actions that are necessary to achieve it are crucial steps that can start this process, but you are still inhibited from making the actual change to a new form of behavior because of the strong human desire to hold on to the familiar. For change to occur, we have to reject the old way of being and accept the new way of being. That is, we have to develop cognitive dissonance. This is not always simple.

As an example, consider the dramatic case of a woman I was called upon to see when I was a resident at Massachusetts General Hospital. Dolores was a thirty-seven-year-old woman who had extensive injuries to her face (facial fractures and black eyes) after her husband hit her during a domestic argument. I expected to have a simple conversation with her in which I would refer her to a colleague for outpatient work, inform her about telephone services and shelters providing help to battered women, and advise her about how best to transition out of the relationship. Upon arrival, I expected to be greeted by a tearful victim acknowledging that she was in a horrible relationship and eager to hear my helpful suggestions. Instead, she stopped me as I entered her room: "Now just wait a minute there. I don't know why they called you, and I don't need you. And I'll speak to you if it gets me the f*** out of here, but let me tell you this: My husband is a wonderful man who has a temper problem. I will never report him or press charges. And I don't want some kid fresh out of medical school thinking he can tell me about love, because this person you see is a victim of love and not abuse."

I stood at the door, shocked. All at once, I realized that the woman I was talking to had prioritized avoiding shame about her relationship over her own safety. Insulting her fantasy of what her relationship was like was worse to her than the physical injuries she had suffered. I saw how her desire to avoid shame had authorized this abuse because it prevented any cognitive dissonance that might have inspired her to change. If she had had cognitive dissonance, she would have been uncomfortable about her life, but she could not afford to have it because the possibility of having any different life was more threatening to her. So she sought to be okay with what had happened. And so I took a step back therapeutically as well, understanding that she could not register fear because shame had trumped her fear and taken over her amygdala.

My challenge was to help her register her fear and pain and then replace this with hope—which would take time. The action centers of her brain were not guiding her out of this miserable situation. And any inspiring thoughts that I could share would not even get close to her motor cortex. Change was going to be a challenge.

For change to occur, Dolores had to develop what scientists call an action-oriented mind-set. No amount of inspiration or consideration of the possibility of leaving would actually promote this change. An action-oriented mind-set is one in which all the brakes of staying in the present state are removed and all the possibilities of future action are imagined with an intention to execute. A recent experiment has shown that when a change is about to occur, the left prefrontal cortex is stimulated. Action orientation is critical to bringing about this state. In effect, you have to be in the "on your mark, get ready, get set" position before you can start the sprint. You have to ignore the internal babble and focus your attention on doing.

Fear of success increases the internal babbling. The specific fears outlined above can instigate an internal dialogue that is all about expressing the fears. This blocks and interferes with imagining success and eventually executing the steps to ensure success. When inspirational speakers say, "You are what you believe" or "Imagine and you will achieve," what they are highlighting is the biological fact that our imaginations are strongly connected to our actions. If you imagine all the reasons that you fear success, this information will inhibit you in making success-related actions. But if you imagine all the reasons why success is preferable to your current situation, you will prime your brain to look for solutions rather than to just comfort you about your current position in life.

When Fear of Success Reflects Fear of the Unknown

From where you stand, you imagine that success is somewhere in the distance, in some unseen land or time in life. Whether you are a single mother looking for the right way of life for yourself and your child or a forty-five-year-old man wondering when you will meet the love of your life, you hang on to the idea that some great reward awaits you at a hypothetical distance from your current position in life. You stand in anticipation of this success. Anticipation activates the amygdala. And this activation disorganizes the frontal lobe that informs your actions as directed by the motor cortex.

Recent research has shown that long-term perspectives or big-picture desires activate the ventromedial prefrontal cortex (vmPFC)—a subdivision of the brain that, as we saw in Chapter 2, lit up when people were being chased by a virtual predator. If you are always viewing the big picture or anticipating a future, this activation of the vmPFC and the amygdala will be continuous and additive. The same experiment that showed that the big picture activates the vmPFC also showed that looking to the moment activates the caudate nucleus—a part of the basal ganglia that is responsible for many functions, including movement. Thus, short-term action will redirect the activation from the big picture and the vmPFC to the small picture and the caudate. That is why we are often told to take baby steps if we are trying to change something. To handle the disorienting effects of too much vmPFC activation, we have to engage the action circuits in the present. Remember that the left PFC—the prefrontal cortex—also activates when you are in an action-oriented mind-set. It appears that action moves the activation to the caudate. Being stuck will move the activation to the periaqueductal gray (PAG), as we saw in the last chapter. The result is unbridled anxiety.

So if you restrict your actions to your thoughts, you strain your brain: You keep the anticipation circuits in overdrive, and there is no consummation of that act. It is akin to sexually stimulating yourself and not reaching orgasm. Action is the orgasm of imagination.

When Your Vision of Success Is Too Vague for Your Brain

We are descendants of wild creatures. We have histories of being pursued by predators—whether it is by lions and tigers or by governments and terrorists. We are endowed with a strong biological persuasion to track these dangers. Yet we pay the price for this reactive vigilance in confusing ways.

One of the critical aspects of fear of success is its paradoxical nature. Success usually connotes a positive outcome, while fear connotes a negative outcome. The ACC is involved in this kind of conflict monitoring. Presented with both of these perspectives—positive and negative—the ACC is likely to fire excessively, thereby activating the amygdala as well. This sets in motion the unconscious fear circuitry we examined at the beginning of the book. Thus, one of the critical variables in the fear-of-success paradigm is the conflict that it presents to the brain and the resulting lack of synchrony in the various brain parts. Usually, the ACC will act in conjunction with other parts of the PFC to start a chain of actions. If the ACC is in a state of chaos, the unclear message it sends to the PFC will likely obstruct a quick, successful outcome. Research has shown that we can dissociate the ACC from other parts of the PFC if we focus on the local demands of a task rather than on the global demands of it. What this means is that taking bite-size chunks out of a challenge will allow us to digest it more successfully and deal with less conflict than we would if we had to contend with all of the information contained within a global perspective. This flexibility is key to getting work done. Although a global perspective sets the scene, maintaining a big-picture perspective of success all the time will delay the accomplishment of immediate actions that are necessary. This is why confining yourself to short-term objectives can be less disruptive. It destabilizes the ACC less and allows the PFC to initiate a course of action.

Furthermore, research has shown that the frontoparietal cortex charts the courses that will result in your achieving your immediate and final goals. Earlier in the book, we saw that this region is critical for attention. When success remains a vague, long-term construct, it likely disrupts the functioning of the attentional circuits at this level, as well. Thus, it is important to immediately plan how to reach your goal after envisioning it.

One of the more intriguing findings in brain research that supports not just early planning but also early action is a study that showed that thinking maximizes its value at some point and that actual change (movement toward success) really can occur only when we perform a small action that advances us toward our goals. Very often, people will sketch out a very detailed plan for success at an obsessional level and then find that they cannot remain committed to this plan because the challenge that they build is too large for their brains to handle. Also, brain activation signifying change in the frontal lobe shows us that actual change is much more likely to occur with small actions than with extensive thought. The message here: Start the process. This is much more likely to keep you committed to a goal than endlessly thinking about it is.

Also, action takes some of the stress out of keeping information online all the time. When the brain is given the task of achieving a success, it will keep some information online, in open file folders, for quick access. However, if we overload the brain with what's online, the system will crash. Just like a computer, having too many files open in your brain also slows down the processing speed of the brain. The dorsolateral prefrontal cortex (DLPFC), which stores online material, needs to be relieved of some of this load by action, which closes some of the files. The DLPFC also communicates with the ACC and the rest of the brain, and if it is overloaded, it will create chaos and the brain will fear any plan that is in the making. In light of this, it is easy to see how important it is to decrease brain loading by closing files after we complete actions.

Lucy was a client who wanted to make more money to put into her children's college fund. She was "stuck" in her two jobs, and because of the bad economy, she was unable to leave either job. She wanted to be successful, but being successful meant making a major change in her life that she didn't have the time to put in motion, nor could she afford to take time off from her current jobs or the possibility that she might earn less money in a new endeavor in the short term. So, she remained stuck in this contemplation for two years before I began seeing her.

When she came into therapy, she ostensibly wanted help with this problem, and she was very ashamed about not being able to solve it (though she felt her hands were irrevocably tied). Any suggestion I made was met with insistence that I did not understand how absolutely impossible it was for her to do anything about her life. She felt misunderstood, and, in the initial phases of her course of therapy, I spent much of my time listening to her voice her desire to "change," which was actually a need to have her frustrations heard. Had I said at the outset that this was just a difficult situation she would have to live with, she would have been satisfied, because she had already told her brain that she had no intention of changing.

We started experimenting with different mind-sets: What if she believed that she could change? What if she were able to tell her brain that she needed a way out, rather than asking it to seek and provide evidence that her situation was impossible to change? She struggled with this, because every time she asked her brain for a plan, it would come up with the idea that something had to change. She could not tolerate this. And right here, we see how, although she desired success, she was not willing to give up what was causing her distress. The message that finally struck home with her was my telling her that her situation was very much like holding on to an abusive relationship because she "needed the money." I also told her that to fulfill her desire for success, it meant that she had to be uncomfortable, because our brains will hold on to the familiar even at the expense of our success. I told her that she was a perfectly intelligent and capable woman who was not helping out her brain. Instead, she was leaving herself a slave to circumstances. To be free, a slave has to leave his or her master, no matter how familiar the situation is. For Lucy, leaving created anxiety, but this was a signal that she was giving her brain and the world a chance to respond to her needs.

It was not until she connected with her unconscious fears that she was able to come up with a bridging solution that changed her life. All along, she had thought that she was afraid of failing, but when she gave this some thought, she realized that if she was successful, she would have to deal with her guilt about making more money than her husband did, and somehow this would compromise the vulnerability that she relied upon for her identity. When she came to terms with this, however, it gave her the idea to start a home business that he ran mostly, because he had the time. She had the initiative to start this, and he could run it. In this way, they were able to increase their income together, and she did not even have to deal with her fears of losing her identity as a wife. She would never have been open to this had she not faced her fear of success. Facing this made her face her potential for success as well, and her brain was all too willing to sketch out a plan for this.

Spirituality and Anticipation in Fear of Success:

The Role of Duality through the Neural Lens

Controlling the vmPFC activation can also be done in other ways. Although a certain amount of imagination and talking are necessary in order to communicate a plan to the motor cortex, relentless imagination without action creates relentless anticipation. Relentless anticipation results because of a duality between the here and now and the future. However, seeing ourselves as already successful as opposed to trying to be successful will eliminate a lot of the anticipation. How can you anticipate if the future and the present are one? One question you can ask yourself is what separates the future and the present. What separates anything? The answer to this is nothing. Separation is merely a way of understanding the world. It is a way of digesting it. By removing separation, we remove anticipation. The present and future flow into each other. Your desires are already connected to their outcome the moment they are born. Success is in your very nature because you have been given the biological link between imagination and action. The moment you imagine something, you start to manifest it. If you see your future evolving toward success and you activate your caudate so that you move now rather than later, the desire is already being sculpted.

Scriptures such as *The Yoga Sutras of Patanjali* provide a context for this biology. They contend that success and attainment of desires are already established. In order for us to perceive this, we have to remove the obstacles. Thus, rather than applying effort toward finding our successes, we need to apply effort toward removing obstacles such as fear. That is how we can know that we are already successful and use this to our advantage. If you are looking for success, then you are ignoring what is already present and creating the tension of anticipation, vmPFC activation, and amygdala activation. If you are looking to remove the obstacles, then you focus on actions that prevent spillover from the vmPFC to the PAG or on actions that will prevent overactivation of the vmPFC and begin instead to activate the caudate. There are many prescriptions in spiritual texts that utilize this biology. "Karma yoga," "serve your society," "trust in God": All of these paths prescribe action and faith to defuse fear.

Faith is the dissolution of duality and anticipation. It creates the conditions for optimal frontal function and focus. My opinion is that, whether your faith connects you to Jesus, Allah, Shiva, agnosticism, or atheism, all of these approaches will help create the necessary conditions to limit anticipation. Whenever you can live your life instilled with your beliefs, your brain (and your frontal lobe in particular) will cease to initiate a civil war that creates perpetual unrest. Success is intricately related to believing and can be achieved through the neurobiology of belief.

Fear of Success:
How Believing Helps to Eliminate This Fear

According to Sam Harris, PhD, who has studied the brain correlates of belief, both belief and disbelief can inform emotion and action and are different from uncertainty. As we pointed out above, uncertainty can arise from anticipation. Harris has shown that uncertainty increases ACC activation (since the ACC monitors conflict, it remains on all the time) and decreases caudate activation (thereby lessening the possibility of action). Increased ACC activation can also cause increased amygdala activation, as we have pointed out several times. These regions are distinctly different from those that belief and disbelief activate (in fact, belief activates the vmPFC, thereby setting up an integration of facts and feelings that might precede an action). Thus, commitment to a belief, regardless of what it is, can help eliminate fear of success by stopping overactive conflict monitoring by the ACC and, therefore, overactive amygdala activation.

Using Science to Dispel the Fear of Success: The MAP-CHANGE Approach

Fear of success also is not an intuitive fear that we face in our daily lives. If we are afraid of crowds, terrorists, spiders, or dogs, we are usually aware of it. Most of us believe, however, that we are in cahoots with our brains to promote our success. Yet, as we have seen in this chapter, this is not the brain's default position. The brain's default is to accumulate doubts and data on the probability of success over a lifetime and then subject us to these doubts—unless we ask the right questions and approach the issue of fear with depth and understanding. The brain is designed to overprotect rather than to expose you to the dangers of change. We can change our brains with effort, but the nature of this effort is tricky. Ramana Maharshi, a Hindu sage born in 1879, was noted for his radical disbelief that the journey toward the self is a means of achieving whatever we want in life. He believed that the self is already present, so there is no journey to be made; there are only obstacles to be removed. This approach works well within the biological perspective because we are prone to incorporating the influences of obstacles both conscious and unconscious in our quest for the truth.

Below are some interventions based on the MAP-CHANGE approach and the science discussed above.

Meditation

As described in earlier chapters, meditation can help us focus on the positive and decrease distraction. Mindfulness meditation has been shown to decrease depression and anxiety, both of which may occur with fear of success. Meditation has been shown to decrease brain pain—the registration of pain in the brain. As a result, when we want to decrease fear of success, meditation can take the edge off this fear. Studies of brain changes during meditation show that certain vital activations and deactivations occur when the brain switches into the meditative state, and certain changes persist as well. Sustained meditation has been shown to increase activation in the head of the caudate, which has been shown to be involved in learning, memory, and feedback processing. Thus, the meditational state may allow for new learning. In the case of fear of success, this would involve rising above these fears. Transcendental meditation has been shown to increase the coherence between the right and left hemispheres of the brain, and this likely decreases the worry associated with fear of success. Thus, although there are no specific studies on the effect of meditation on the fear of success, overall, meditation does appear to have stress-reducing and mind-sharpening effects.

Attention

Recommendations based on the ACC-amygdala relationship: The role of attention and emotion

The ACC-amygdala relationship highlights the importance of the connection between attention and emotion. What this teaches us is that we grow what we attend to. If we fear success, we will not grow success, but rather fear. We know that this will occur because the word *fear* has a stronger impact on the amygdala than the word *success*. To impact the amygdala, you will have to flesh out what you consider to be the meaning of success and create multiple associations so that your brain can understand what you want. Simply telling your brain that you want to be "successful" does not provide it with enough information. Instead, you need to tell your brain more precisely what you want. When your brain responds with something that you don't want to do, don't just throw away your goal. Work with your brain to come up with a strategy for success. Listening to our brains sounds obvious, but few people do it. For every response by your brain, seriously consider the sagacity of its advice. The brain has an amazing grasp of what is possible and what is not possible for you. By allowing your brain to give you this information, you allow it to shine the light of the ACC on the pathway to success.

But what exactly does this mean? If you would like a promotion at work, you might want to admit that you want a promotion—even if you are scared of wanting it. Or even if you cannot see how you could possibly get it. When Edmund Hillary climbed Mount Everest, he could not see all of the mountain. His intention, perspective, and training took him there. Similarly, if you want to climb the corporate ladder, you don't have to see all the possibilities at once. I always like to remind people that before prosthetic legs, nobody could imagine how a person who had had a leg amputated could actually run. Now that they exist, we take it for granted that it is possible. When you engage your ACC to lead you toward success, realize that your brain may at first be wired to focus on the problems related to success. You might have to rewire it. Rewiring takes time. And it takes new learning.

Here is an exercise you can try to help you focus on your goals and navigate toward success.

Draw a road map of your success and then fill in the route and turns that you may have to take in order to get to where you want to go. For example, say you are a senior sales manager and would like to become the vice president of human resources, but the president of human resources will not hire you because he says that your experience is in sales.

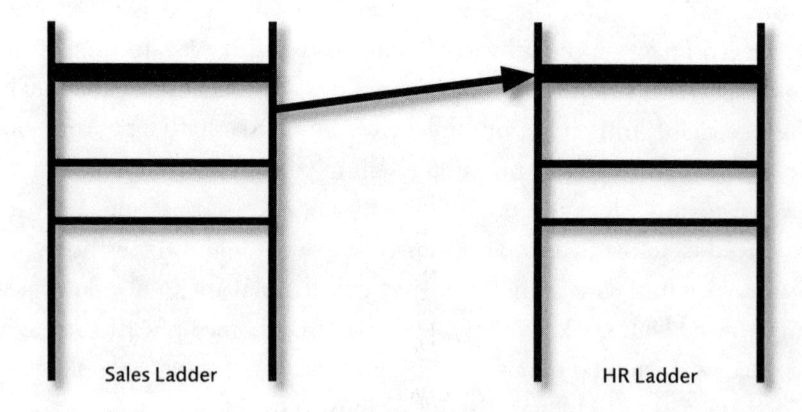

The arrow shows where you are in relation to where you would like to be. This visual image captures the lateral move you would like to make and gets your ACC engaged in imagining your future rather than just thinking about it.

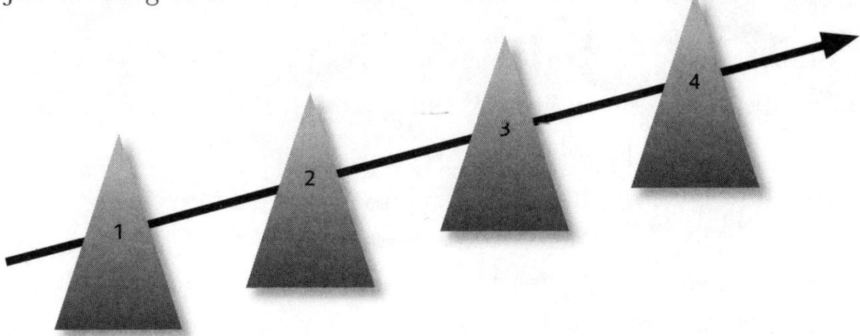

1=No HR experience
2=No good relationship with president of HR
3=Competition with other qualified people
4=Convincing others that you are the best person for the job

Here, each of the triangles represents a mountain you have to climb to get to your goal. Again, you are changing the message relayed to the amygdala by showing it (using the ACC) that what you want is not impossible, but perhaps will require some effort on your part. We call this reframing, something the ACC is good at.

Now, if the amygdala received information only from triangle number 4, it would likely activate like crazy. But when it sees that there is a logical progression of events that is actually addressable, and once the ACC fixes its attention on these things, your brain will start to problem solve because it now knows what to solve.

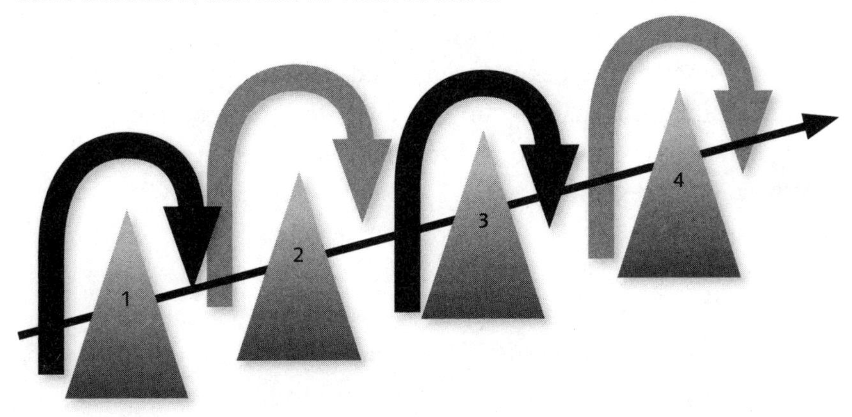

Here, we see that it is possible to jump over each step with an action plan that includes the following:

1. Get some part-time human resources experience.
2. Enlist the help of the president of human resources in enacting a plan that benefits both of you.
3. Take on a challenge within the company that proves your expertise in handling human resources issues.
4. Network and combine evidence of your success with good relationships with others.

These maps can be drawn in a number of ways, but what they do is capture the attention of the ACC and then progressively decrease the obstruction offered by the amygdala so you can focus on your success. Here, what we do is to contextualize the obstacles. Rather than being impossible mountains, obstacles become part of the road leading toward your goals. This is a different way to think of them. People often isolate their obstacles and focus on them. When they do this, they automatically remove the vision of success.

But what can you do if the obstacle seems insurmountable or if you feel that you cannot, for example, take time away from your current duties to get HR experience? This leads us to the second set of recommendations.

Recommendations based on the vmPFC-caudate relationship: The role of perspective

Focusing on the obstacles rather than the success is a perspective issue. Here, the caudate becomes overly involved, showing you only the short-term perspective. It is like standing at the foot of a tall triangle and trying to push it over with your nose when what is required is to fly over it. When you find yourself pushing up against an impossibility, remind yourself to switch perspectives to the long-term goal. I have one important rule that I always tell people: There is no obstacle without a goal. If you find yourself stuck, consider it a message that you want to be elsewhere and that your goal is somewhere else. Switch your activation to the vmPFC so that your long-term perspective can guide you.

For example, in the situation above, you may end up like this:

When you are in this situation, don't let the big, imposing goal increase your fear of success. Take a step backward or look at your road map to change your perspective and reengage the vmPFC.

Remember, however, that reengaging the vmPFC can only be done for so long. You have to switch the activity back to the caudate so that the vmPFC does not become overactivated and spill over into the PAG to cause acute anxiety. So, once you see the road map, you can chart your short-term course, engaging the caudate in making your actual movements rather than remaining stuck. Stuckness comes when the activation stays in the caudate or vmPFC for too long. You have to train your brain to be flexible, and a part of the PFC called the orbitofrontal cortex is essential for what we call cognitive flexibility. You can train this part of your brain by doing exercises to keep it flexible. Remember that your brain is like a thinking muscle. If you do not stretch it regularly, it will weaken and become stiff. Moving beyond obstacles requires you to keep your brain flexible so it can come up with innovative solutions to your problems. A flexible brain has to be stretched regularly, and one of the most effective ways to enhance your flexibility is through using your imagination.

Remember that your imagination can make possible what seems impossible because you give your brain permission to sketch out a plan for reaching your goal by admitting that you are only imagining it. This allows the brain to cooperate with your environment to get what you want.

Here are some exercises that can help you stretch your brain.

1. Imagine how much money you would like to be making. Then ask yourself how much you would need to make to live off the interest alone if you invested the money conservatively. If, for example, you first said that you wanted to be making $1 million a year, this would mean that you would be making about $83,000 a month. If this money represented the 4 percent interest per year on your savings, then you would actually have to make $25 million and invest it to draw $1 million in interest per year. Involve yourself in these sorts of calculations until your brain is comfortable working with money. Start with lower figures if you want more money, because this may help you feel less afraid.
2. Play the "What if?" game. Write down a goal. Then ask yourself what would happen if you actually got to this goal. How would your life be different? At first, write a paragraph about how your life would be different. Then, write out the same paragraph, but write each sentence on a different line. Then, draw what this would look like, as best you can. Then, sing the paragraph to yourself, setting it to any tune you want. (You are forcing your emotions and insula to become involved by doing this seemingly silly exercise; furthermore, you are taking the inertia that accompanies "the usual" out of the equation.) Do this at least twice a week for six months. You will be surprised by how differently you will perceive your success when you do this.
3. Write down a long-term goal. Then write down the first step in achieving it. Then write down ten things that need to be done *before* the first step. After this, do those ten things until you reach an obstacle. When you

reach an obstacle, write down ten more things that need to be done before tackling this obstacle. Here, you are constantly switching perspective and moving between the vmPFC and the caudate.

Psychological Tools

Recommendations based on the social dominance experiment: Overcoming competitive forces

Barchas's social dominance experiment in monkeys showed us that what you think of as your innate experience in fact may not be "innate" at all. Do you remember how the submissive monkey behaved submissively until the dominant monkey was removed? Well, is it possible that you are not succeeding because there is no space for you to succeed? Here are some exercises to perform.

Draw a circle of people in your nuclear family. Segment the circle into sections for the people who have been the most successful. We will call these success pies.

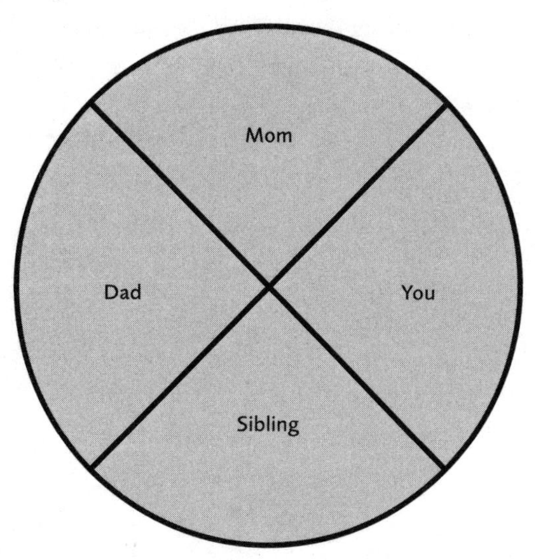

Now, draw the same circle for people involved in your work life. If you work independently, draw the circle to show the relative success of the five most influential people in your field.

In each of these diagrams, see if you occupy less success space than anyone else. Is there enough success pie for you? If there is not enough, realize that this may be why your success has not increased over time in the way that you want it to. You may feel that the success space has already been claimed by someone else. As a result, you may have informed your brain that there is no space for you to expand into.

What can you do about this? For most of us, blocking out, excluding, or firing the dominant people in the world is not feasible or even acceptable, yet we live with this limiting construct and, as a result, we limit our own success. You need to reprogram your brain to think differently about success, and this is what I suggest:

1. Tell yourself that success is not a quantity, but a quality. As a result, there is no "success real estate" that you have to purchase. Owning a quality is an internal process. You do not have to infringe upon the rights or success of others. Tell yourself that you can be as successful as you want, because consciousness is unlimited, and, as such, the potential for success is an individual responsibility that will not take up space that is occupied by others.
2. Reclaim your right to success. Rather than fighting those whom you have identified as more successful than you, set out on a path to define the parameters of your own success. Identify what you think will be your major strengths and weaknesses. Then formulate a plan on how to overcome those barriers. Barriers are a way of delineating the path to your goal. They exist in your head. If you want success, your brain will devise a way to move beyond these barriers.
3. Draw up a list of ways in which you can work cooperatively with the successful people you identified. For example, someone I worked with was unable to sculpt out a path to her success because she felt that her brother was the successful one in the family. She felt unconscious guilt about taking over his

success real estate until she decided that when she made the money that success would allow her to make, she would give some of it to her parents and some of it to him. This helped her let go of her guilt and freed her up to be successful.

4. Although a geographic cure is not the first plan of action that I would suggest, I have seen situations where it has worked wonders. For example, no matter how impressive her mental strength was, Martha, a bright young medical student who struggled but succeeded in getting through medical school, felt that she would never be able to exceed the accomplishments of her two brothers and her sister, all of whom had sailed through their respective careers with honors.

    Earlier in Martha's life, she had excelled at her schoolwork with straight A's, and this was the pattern until she started to flail a bit late in high school. No matter how hard she worked, she just could not consistently get good grades, and all of a sudden her siblings started to flourish. She had submitted to her guilt and they had won the unconscious territorial battle for success.

    Well, when Martha graduated from medical school, she had done well, but not as well as she was capable of doing. As a result, she had to really pitch her worth to good residency programs. Although she could have easily been accepted into a program in her home state, she decided to accept a position in a state very far away. This put a physical distance between her and the family she loved very much, but it also gave her the mental freedom to succeed without feeling like she was stealing the limelight. She excelled then and thereafter, and she was back on track exploiting the very talents that she had always had, but that she had suppressed because of her fear and guilt.

    In light of this story, ask yourself if a geographic

cure is in the cards for you. Is there enough space for you to grow at your workplace? In your home? In your family? Before you decide to leave, perhaps talking to people about this will result in the creation of the space that you want.

The converse of this story is also important to recognize. Adam was a star student who always did his readings and was always up to the mark with new ideas. Adam's classmates liked him, but over time, because success breeds success, Adam's awards and success led to more recognition for him and less for everyone else. On one occasion, his classmates asked the teacher to ask Adam to say less during class. The problem here was not that Adam was taking up all the airtime, but that he was better prepared and therefore better able to respond. His teacher had a chat with him about this, and Adam started to be more silent in class, but in the process, he gave up his success space voluntarily. It was not until Adam realized that this was setting him back considerably that he was able to do anything about it. Until then, he had guiltily given over his domain to the others, who made contributions of lesser quality. Everybody lost out. When Adam sought out extra instruction on a one-to-one basis, he was able to explore his intellect more completely and started to succeed at his goals again. I see this situation come up over and over again in clinical and coaching contexts.

Very talented and capable people are made to be silent ostensibly in the service of being team players. But being a team player still requires you to play your best. It is not only about focusing on your responsibilities with the team, but also about the team making space for your special qualities.

The dominance factor in human biology is an

automatic arrangement, but by using your frontal lobe, you can rearrange this obstructionist idea to give yourself room to fully express yourself.

Recommendations based on the unconscious nature of fear of success: Dealing with hidden motivations in your own brain

The first chapter described many of the principles that relate to the unconscious nature of the fear of success. Periodically revisit the exercises here and apply them to your fear of success. Remember that you are not likely to recognize your fear of success if it is unconscious. One exercise that pertains specifically to this has you rate the strength of the components of your fear of success and then devise an action plan to reduce them one at a time. The key to remember here is that repetition is the only way to convincingly gain access to unconscious obstructions. Your thoughts may be conscious, but your actions may take their instructions from opposite ideas in the unconscious. So, perform the exercise below at least once a week to slowly gain access to your unconscious.

I am afraid that . . .		Rating: From 1 to 10, with 1 being "not at all" and 10 being "definitely a strong influence"									
		1	2	3	4	5	6	7	8	9	10
1	Success will make me lonely										
2	Success will make me unaware of what is going on behind my back										
3	Success will give me too much responsibility										
4	Success will put me in unknown and unfamiliar territory										
5	Success will make people expect more of me										
6	Success will leave me with nothing else to strive for										
7	Success will result in a loss of privacy, and people will observe me too closely										
8	Success will change me too much										

Each week, read the part of this chapter that relates to one of these fears and tell yourself one reward that overcoming this fear will win you.

Recommendations based on left prefrontal cortex activation to action orientation: Moving from "on your mark" to "get set"

For you to become successful, you don't have to do much. You are already successful. The problem is that you are standing in your own way. Negative thoughts disrupt the way your brain sketches out success plans, and the types of thoughts you have determine how successful you are. Passive thoughts of success such as "I want to be successful" will not activate the action centers of your brain to create the successful action or behavior that you want (meaning that the left PFC will remain dormant). They may make you feel positive, but your brain will not interpret them as instructions to do what is needed for you to be successful. Three important principles of success planning are:

1. Be specific
2. Believe: Have no doubt
3. Be action oriented

When the left PFC activates, it is a sign that your brain is ready for action. I like to tell people that they have to marry their goals: For better or for worse, they are stuck to their goals for the rest of their lives. This does not mean that there will be no problems. In fact, like in any marriage, problems often do arise. However, with a combination of a spiritual and an action-oriented mind-set, you will position yourself to achieve great things. Here is one exercise to get you on your way to faster success.

1. Write down one important goal in your life.
2. Write down three steps that you will have to take to get there.
3. For each step, rate your plans from one to ten on each of the following characteristics:

- How specific is your goal?
- How strongly do you believe that it is achievable?
- How action oriented is this step?

If you give each step a ten, you are well on your way to reaching your goal. If any rate less than a ten, spend some time refining what you have written so that your plan rates better on these variables.

Here is an example:
"I am a woman who wants to get married to a man."

Steps:
1. Go out more often.
2. Look more attractive.
3. Be more interesting.

Rating
5 on specificity: Where will you go? Whom will you go with? When will you go out? How will you overcome your shyness?
2 on belief: The nonspecificity of your plan indicates that you do not believe very strongly that the plan will get you to your goal.
3 on action orientation: Your plan should have only impactful verbs. For example, "go out" is impactful, but "be more" is low on impact.

How can you refine your plan? Engage your left PFC and develop action items.

I need to go out more often: I need to go out at least three times a week, once during the week and twice on weekends. I should ask out people I am interested in. For example, Joe, Jim, and Dennis are all interesting to me. I will ask them out this week. If I am too afraid to do this and want to meet other people, perhaps I will get two tickets to something and ask someone if he would like to come. Or I will join a book club this month.

Or I will visit a local community center to see if there are interesting things offered that would help me meet other people. Or I will visit my rabbi and ask how I can get connected to the local Jewish community.

I need to look more attractive: I do not need to look like a model to meet someone I can love. There are all kinds of couples in the universe: overweight women with thin men, young men with older women, Jewish women with men of other ethnicities, shy women with outgoing men. Perhaps I will Google "shy women" and research how shy women find dates and how men deal with shy women. In this way, I will increase my belief that shy women do get married. Or perhaps I will visit a local department store and get some makeup tips. Or perhaps I will buy some nice-looking clothes on Saturday. If I can't afford very expensive clothes, I will go to a discount store. I will get a massage and a facial. I will order a good acne treatment online or visit my doctor. I will join a gym on Saturday.

I need to be more interesting: Why should I be anything other than what I am? Why do I think I am not interesting? Why am I not open to expressing myself? I will read the local newspaper every day so I feel more confident when conversing. I will go on a trip by myself to learn more about another culture. I will meet with a psychologist or psychiatrist to understand myself better.

For each of these changes above, notice how much more action oriented they are. If the left PFC is to be engaged, you must up the ante to the point that the actions are more and more clearly spelled out in order to get to your goal.

Conclusion

Fear of success is an unconscious fear that we can readily address by developing a biological approach to digging into our unconscious and repeatedly asking ourselves if this barrier is obstructing our reaching our goals. If we remain committed to a depth of truth in our lives using biology as a guide, we can undo the layers related to this fear and begin to construct a less fear-based life—especially one that is without the fear of success.

[4]

If It's Hard to Change, It's Not Unchangeable

Overcoming Fear Conditioning in the Human Brain

When there is freedom from mechanical conditioning, there is simplicity. The classical man is just a bundle of routine, ideas, and tradition. If you follow the classical pattern, you are understanding the routine, the tradition, the shadow—you are not understanding yourself.

—**Bruce Lee**

Conditioning, as actor and martial artist Bruce Lee pointed out, is the habit or tradition of feeling, thinking, and acting. It is automatic, powerful, and inevitable, unless we do something about it. When an event occurs, brain circuits that formed as a result of past experiences automatically join us in the moment. Because our early life experiences shape how we see and respond to things, we become a "bundle of routine, ideas, and tradition." We are robbed of the purity of the moment and new experiences. And as Lee pointed out, we are robbed of our selves. But how and why does this occur, and what can we do about it?

Everything we see in life is viewed through the filter of our past experiences. There are elements of every new situation we encounter that resemble elements of our past. In brain terms, when we are confronted with a new situation, the similarities between the new and the past situations stimulate stored memories to join you in the moment. These memories color the way you see things consciously and unconsciously. No new perception is ever truly new unless we train our brains to be richly present without these past filters. And without new perception, we can't change our response.

Since conditioning is a reminder of past experiences thrust onto present events, it's not just our perceptions that are automatically colored: These colored perceptions then color our responses. Our responses are also habitual. As a result, our lives become a series of repetitions, and we cease to grow in new and important ways. We become stuck in the patterns of the past, and we lose the art of being human and being alive. The impressionist painter Claude Monet used to tell his students that every time they painted a flower, they should paint it as if they were seeing it for the first time. In effect, he was asking them to be alive to the moment rather than slaves to the past. But why would the brain be constructed to thrust the past upon every molecule of the present? How does this serve us? How, we may ask, did fear come to marry habit in such an uncompromising way?

Habit often is recognized as a representation of tradition; it provides us with an illusory sense of control as we march toward death. The habits we construct allow us to view the world as static and unchanging. Habits soothe us. No wonder, then, that we develop even habits of fear that define us. The problem with this is that although death is inevitable, being unchanging does not prevent death, nor does it provide any sense of actual growth during this life.

Conditioning occurs when nerve cells within the brain transmit electrical signals in habitual ways. In effect, the brain chooses the path of least resistance, akin to a trench dug to facilitate the flow of water. Shaped by genes, past behavior, and environmental influences, conditioned pathways represent the most efficient means of addressing a problem. It is this motivation to save on energy costs that feeds conditioned brain circuits with an intention of their own, as a self-reinforcing system.

There is a price to pay for this energy conservation, however, and that is stagnation. Fear conditioning can paralyze us. Biologically, conditioning allows us to respond more quickly to a new situation, but this response is only truly useful to us if the new situation is identical to past situations. In most cases, it is not. On the one hand, it is helpful to "remember" things that can cause or protect us from danger. But on the other hand, our brains are built to protect us even at the risk of robbing us of new experiences. We may then be safer from certain dangers, but also averse to learning and new outcomes. Every relationship is not prone to failure just because your first one failed. Every job will not be boring just because most of the previous ones have been. You are not locked into your middle-class roots just because you were born into those circumstances. And pain is not inevitable just because it has been your experience so far. Some things are possible. Conditioning assumes that they are not.

When fear conditioning was first discovered, the idea was fairly alarming. Fear conditioning implied that our brains were automatically set to be afraid, and that if we developed fear responses during our development, then we would be prone to having these responses for the rest of our lives. A substantial number of studies in animals and then in humans showed that our brains worked much like what Bruce Lee was warning us to avoid—prone to mechanical conditioning and habit, with no way of getting around it. Psychologists concluded that if a child was exposed to significant trauma or fear, fear would take root in his or her brain and arise automatically every time something elicited memory of the trauma.

If, for example, a woman grew up with an alcoholic father who abused her, then every time her boyfriend drank a few beers, she might develop the automatic expectation that she would be abused. Or if a man experienced a terrible first marriage, he might automatically expect that every woman he met would be terrible. The human brain appeared to remember "first" experiences and then recall these experiences every time a trigger was encountered. The implications of this idea were far-reaching. If it was, in fact, true that our brains produced learned, automatic reactions in response to fear, then it would seem that we would always be victims of our pasts and that the future would be nothing but a series of repeated behaviors we could never overcome.

Now, more than a century later, this remains the way that most of us live. We experience ourselves as passive recipients, the products of our experiences thus far. If we have come to fear certain things, then we assume we always will. Whether it is failure, success, love, or change, we give in to these fears because our past experience tells us that nothing can change.

If we are to live our lives with greater awareness—with an eye for progress and a drive to transform ourselves and our societies—we must overcome the obstructions of our seemingly unchangeable habits. How can an understanding of human brain biology help us overcome the wily fears that marry habit with caution and stagnation?

Contrary to what we have been conditioned to expect, what may seem unchangeable is actually very changeable indeed, and the human brain, fortunately, is able to execute these changes. My wish is that you will challenge yourself to change one conditioned behavior in your life after reading this chapter.

Myths of Unchangeability:
From Genes to Conditioning

A long time ago, somebody based the myth that we are hardwired on a reasonable but essentially false argument that once the brain develops, like the electrical system in a house, its circuits are fixed and unchangeable. Added to this inaccuracy was the idea that our entire lives are predetermined by our genes; the idea was that we bring what we are born with into the world and live at the mercy of the gifts and curses of our DNA. These concepts of hardwiring and genetic determinism are two of the culprits that have perpetuated hopelessness and immovability at times of suffering. Add to this the fact that we tend to look down on change (the expression "I can't believe how much you've changed" is rarely a compliment) and you have a recipe for stagnation. But what if I told you that the case for hardwiring has been overstated and that we are instead "softwired"? What if I told you that genes are about as fixed in their influences on us as they are on the shade of a leaf in the fall?

As we've discussed, neuroplasticity allows our brains to change physically over time, and increasingly, studies are showing that genes play a smaller role in directing our lives than was once believed. Generalized anxiety disorder (GAD) is a good example of this. People who suffer from GAD experience excessive worry that leads to muscle tension, fatigue, restlessness, and difficulty sleeping. Recent studies have shown that when GAD occurs in childhood, genes play a central role in the manifestation of these symptoms. But as people age, genes play less and less of a role and social influences become more central in the expression of these symptoms.

We now know that the brain—an organ that is prone to genetic influences—can change with the influence of drugs, talking, touch, and smell. Certain things may be more unchangeable than others, but in my experience, no fear is so deeply entrenched that addressing it is futile. Even when old, habitual pathways seem unalterable, new ways of thinking can set up new pathways that dominate the old ones.

If this is the case, then why is it so difficult to make changes and stick with them? Why on earth would the human brain enter into such a dubious transaction with itself that it accepts boredom, life paralysis, and stagnation in exchange for the habitual responses of fear conditioning? How do our basic needs seek to justify the deleterious effects of fear conditioning? How can we start to address these needs in different ways?

Priorities That Challenge Change

Below are some of the reasons that I have discerned during my clinical practice for why habit and conditioning serve important individual and social functions. If we can understand why our brains become so inflexible with conditioning, we can begin to have some power to change our conditioned responses.

Reason 1—"Love is not love / Which alters when it alteration finds" (William Shakespeare): The human drive for love is a powerful mechanism underpinning the survival of the species. Without this love, men and women would not come together to have children, and same-sex couples would not want to raise children either. Raising children requires people to stay together for a long period of time. For a relationship to last, change cannot be too rampant and the habit of being together has to be solidified. This is one possible motivation for choosing stagnation over excitement—the need to be stagnant enough to form and maintain relationships. Evolutionary psychologists believe that the function of romantic love is to create the motivation to stay together for long enough to propagate the species.

In fact, brain imaging studies show that when we scan the brains of people who are in love, it is the motivational centers that are lit up (as opposed to the purely emotional centers), providing evidence for this theory of love as an evolutionary drive. As unromantic as it sounds, this is a strong basis for maintaining habits for long enough to encourage survival of the species.

While at some level this might seem to make a mockery of romance, it also substantiates prevalent patterns of human existence. It provides an explanation for several common consequences that arise when the drive to have children is not present. For example, it is possible that couples divorce after having children because love dies away when the motivational aspect (to propagate the species) is no longer present. It also explains the changed emphasis of relationships from friendship to romance in adulthood—many people lose their friends after college, during their most fertile years.

Tied into this love-based motivation to propagate the species is the fear that if we don't contribute to growing the population, we will not be valuable. A woman's fear that her biological clock is ticking may not be a response only to her own values, but also to a deeper sense of responsibility to contribute to society. Love, partnering, copulation, and child rearing are powerful proponents of habit and shape our brains in powerful ways.

Reason 2—The desire for permanence: At the core of any human quest is the yearning to surmount the transience of this life. With mortality looming over our heads, this vast and frightening unknown is enough to make most of us duct-tape ourselves to the nearest fixed situation in an attempt to avoid the grip of death. Whether it is marriage, tenure, long service to a company, loyal friendships, or a routine morning walk, we establish rituals and habits to prevent ourselves from facing mortality. We cultivate these conditioned habits in order to create the comfortable illusion of repeatability and constancy. This illusion creates the impression that we are not moving toward death, that our lives are fixed in time.

To deal with fears of mortality, we develop habits that distract and comfort us. We create a feeling of control where there is fundamentally really none. I am not opposed to feeling in control. Sometimes it is necessary. But is it possible to create behaviors that both help us feel in control and also accentuate happiness and a sense of purpose in life?

This same light can illuminate our propensity for substance addiction: The satisfaction derived from repeated behavior distracts us from existential questions and comforts us. Addictions provide an opportunity to attach ourselves to a mind-altering behavior to avoid thinking about the agony inherent in the human condition.

Death is perhaps the greatest uncertainty we will ever face. It is no wonder, then, that our brains refuse to act when we are engaged with this uncertainty. As we've learned, uncertainty reduces basal ganglia activation and probably keeps more information online, creating information overload and confusion. Fear of mortality may similarly cause information overload and the confusion that results from it, prompting us to hold tightly to the habits that define us.

Reason 3—Repetition compulsion: Sigmund Freud coined this term to describe the propensity of adults to repeat traumatic experiences. Freud viewed this tendency as unconscious. He first observed it in a child who threw his favorite toy from his crib, became upset, and then, after his mother returned the toy, threw it out again. Freud initially understood this to be an unconscious, primitive drive to be destructive that he called the death instinct. Another interpretation of this behavior suggested by Freud is that it is a desire to gain mastery over the sensation of loss. That is, the child was practicing getting better and better at dealing with the loss of his toy. Freud believed that on an unconscious level, the child used this behavior as a way to come to terms with the presence and absence of his mother. When Freud observed the same child a year later, however, he saw the same act as one of anger in response to the absence of the child's mother. Whatever the psychological narrative is, repeating behavior over and over again is surprising, but common.

Biologically speaking, repeating a behavior is a well-recognized form of learning. Repetition enhances long-term memory. The effect of this consolidated information is seen in parts of the brain responsible for long-term memory (such as the hippocampus). When long-term memory is enhanced, a concept or action can be mastered. However, when this learning becomes a compulsion or impedes change, it can be destructive. Sometimes people will continue to seek to develop mastery over a concept long after they actually have achieved mastery. One common example of this is people who repeatedly engage in long-term romantic relationships for two to five years and then break up to prove to themselves that they can survive alone. These serial monogamists could have realized this the first time. The conditioned fear that they cannot survive alone requires that they prove it to themselves over and over again.

This propensity for repetition is commonly seen in the behavior of people who suffer from obsessive-compulsive disorder (OCD). One study found that people with OCD become fixated on and sometimes respond more quickly (have faster reaction times in button-press tests) to familiar words. That is, long-known words seem to have special meaning for them, implying that they may get stuck in the past and are therefore more prone to continuing conditioned behaviors. This specific problem may correspond with deficits in the frontostriatal system, which is critical in forming memories. Essentially, people with OCD hang on to old ideas longer and respond to old ideas more quickly. Since we know that anxiety underlies OCD, we can deduce that anxiety and fear both engage habits (old ideas) more readily than change. The old or conditioned pathways are less anxiety provoking.

One brain imaging study examined repetition compulsion—the

behavior exhibited by those with OCD—through the lens of overlearning. Overlearning is the process by which one learns something to the point that reproducing it becomes highly automatic. This study found that inhibiting overlearning (or repetition compulsion) requires an intact frontoparietal network, which is a part of the brain responsible for attention. That is, by specifically directing attention at not repeating past behaviors, we can inhibit the conditioned response. Paradoxically, this redirection of attention will probably have to be repeated and integrated with other important faculties, such as emotion, for the new behavior to stick. An intact frontoparietal network that stimulates change instead of habit retention requires specific exercises to make use of its intactness. Having the ability to attend to something with maximum focus and the ability to change the attention's focus to a new, more relevant focus are just two of the factors that signify that a person has the intact frontoparietal network that is required to rid him- or herself of the habit of repetition compulsion.

Reason 4—The delusion of omnipotence: Psychological explorations have led clinicians to understand that a sense of omnipotence—the belief that one has the power to do anything—is intricately tied to masochism, or the desire to hurt oneself. That is, for some reason, in sustaining the idea that we are all-powerful (and not facing our vulnerabilities), we engage in destructive behaviors that we cannot change. Psychoanalysts have conceptualized this as a clinging to pain in the face of mortality that competes with a sense of omnipotence. This habit of clinging to pain may be conditioned and may explain why it is that we sometimes "inadvertently" hurt ourselves over and over again.

Another connection that substantiates the link between masochism and repeated or habitual behavior is Freud's conclusion that masochism is related to the death instinct, and therefore is also connected to repetition compulsion. When we repeatedly do something that is harmful to our lives, whether it is engaging in destructive relationships or smoking cigarettes, we are, in part, controlling our self-harm rather than giving in to the unpredictability of death.

Repetitive intentional self-injury has been connected to damage to the insula and lenticular nucleus, the latter being a part of the basal ganglia. Once again, we see how the basal ganglia, critically involved in both OCD and self-injury, are caught up in repetitive behavior, preventing the institution of a different action plan that avoids repetitive harmful behavior.

The insula is responsible for mapping internal states so the conscious mind can understand them. When it is damaged, repetition occurs in part because we lack any translation of instinctual knowledge; instead, this knowledge stays in the unconscious. As a result, we cannot stop these behaviors because we are not even translating them for the conscious brain to understand. The repetition of self-destruction therefore has a license to repeat itself because it is not being policed by the conscious brain.

When the basal ganglia are damaged, one of the consequences is that the ability to filter information is diminished. As a result, we overload our brains with too much new information that cannot be learned. With this condition, as with insula damage, the conscious brain does not translate repeated self-injury, but this time it is because the conscious brain is overloaded.

The above, then, provides some insight into the psychological and neurobiological bases for the brain choosing to remain stuck. But why do our brain cells seem to automatically gravitate toward conditioned behavior?

When Neurons Fall in Love

The human brain is made up of neurons. We are born with loose neuronal connections, and as we grow, neighboring neurons and even neurons from far away explore ways to come together and create neural connections. As they do, it becomes progressively more difficult to separate them, and at a certain point, they become "married." Change is easier when they are more loosely connected. That is why childhood is such an important time in brain development and habit formation. When fear becomes a conditioned response, the cells that make up this circuit of fear have become closely connected, or married. But just like other forms of marriage, this bond can be broken.

As discussed, the experience of fear is converted into electrical energy in the brain. This electricity is delivered to the first cell in a series of cellular interactions. If it is delivered over and over again to that cell, the electricity will modify the second cell in the chain, making the connection between these two cells stronger. This connection grows stronger through a process called LTP (long-term potentiation), which eventually enables the two neurons to be stimulated simultaneously. Once the connection is this strong, the neurons are able to communicate even better. This relationship becomes consolidated over time, and the memory of it is stored in the brain.

When another fearful experience takes place, the electrical energy experienced as fear stimulates those neurons that have already formed a long-lasting connection and been stored as "fear memories." All of the cells connected in that chain then fire simultaneously, stimulating a memory and all of the fear associated with that memory. As a result, fear memories are very powerful. Due to the preexisting close connections of these neurons, they dominate new neurons that might want to channel the information through a different route.

Overcoming or changing this habitual response requires challenging these strongly formed connections by repeatedly stimulating a different neuronal set and establishing LTP in new neuronal neighbors. This is how the power of positive thinking that we examined in Chapter 2 works at a neuronal level. Repeatedly exposing yourself to positive ideas will start to stimulate new connections in the brain. This attracts more positivity because it creates LTP in a new, positive circuit of neurons. This often affects the entire brain and can also change the way you perceive new experiences. For example, I once spoke with a very successful salesperson who told me that even though he'd experienced many more rejections than sales over the years, he never remembered his rejections. As a result, he always felt motivated to sell. This gave him a love for his work (recall that love activates the brain's motivational system), and he became exceptionally good at his job.

Pessimistic people often seem to feel that optimistic people must be deluded and can't possibly be in touch with the suffering that exists in the world. This is partly because pessimistic people have a difficult time overcoming the LTP of negative events. When you are trying to change your attitude, it is important not to deny that negative things exist, because your brain will always tell you that you are deluded. Instead, realize that what you are trying to do is to activate LTP in neurons that see life positively until they are able to take over. Often, it is helpful to switch to neutrality before proceeding to positivity.

Stimulating a new neural circuit to overwrite your brain's fear programming requires a tremendous amount of energy and new learning. In order to change our automatic fears, we have to create strong connections and new LTP so we can generate new automatic responses.

Phases of Fear Conditioning

Neutral events occur daily in our lives without our notice. Birds fly, cars are driven down the road, the sun rises and sets, and we go on without flinching. We are, in effect, habituated to these neutral events and do not generally ascribe any meaning to them. However, if on three different days that are not good ones for us we notice that we see red cars (as well as noticing that on great days, we do not see red cars), we may come to associate red cars with problem-filled days. This association is a form of learning we call acquisition. That is, we acquire an association between a neutral stimulus (red cars) and bad days. If we see a red car on another day, we may become anxious even *before* problems occur because we anticipate that we are not in control of what is about to take place. Our fear becomes conditioned through the learned association. At a certain point, though, after we've experienced enough days in which we see red cars but experience no bad events, we start to feel less anxious—we extinguish the conditioned fear response. This phase is called extinction.

The relevance of these phases is that just as conditioned fear can be acquired, it can also be extinguished. Thus, unlearning a response is possible under the right circumstances. Although our brains can develop automatic responses to some things, they can also unlearn these responses and develop new responses. This is the reason that we can be optimistic about changing the ways in which our brains work. LTP applies to new learning, as well.

The applicability of this concept is widespread. In any situation in which our attempts have resulted in failure, we have to give up this conditioned fear of failure to try again. Giving up this fear requires extinguishing it, as well as convincing our brains that another attempt is worth it.

The Amygdala as Artist

The human brain is like a canvas on which life paints its experiences in different colors, forms, and degrees of permanence. Where fear is concerned, the amygdala wafts its brush through much of the brain so its bristles thickly pick up the paint of fear. But when the amygdala picks up the color of fear, it also picks up other colors in the spectrum of fear, alerting itself and the brain in general to the neighbors of fear in addition to fear itself.

We are born with an amygdala that quickly responds to fear, but fear is not only borne of our genes and our hardwired brains. It is also learned, and the amygdala is where learned fear resides and from whence it travels. The sayings "Once bitten, twice shy" and "A burned child dreads fire" both refer to the large impact that negative experiences can have on the brain. If you encountered a lion while on safari, your fear of being eaten alive would be logical and sensible. But if you experienced acute anxiety and fear every time you saw a lion on television after that experience, it would pose a problem in your life.

As we know, the amygdala sometimes overcompensates and generalizes. Its fine-tuning ability is limited, and it requires input from the cortex (the thinking brain) in order to change. Once the amygdala makes associations, its paint is resistant to the turpentine of new learning unless the new learning is done in a very particular way and repeated. Other parts of the brain, such as the orbitofrontal cortex, involved in learning to make associations between the fearful and neutral components of an event (bad days and red cars) can more easily relearn information than the amygdala can. The amygdala will continue to alert you even if only the neutral context (a red car) is present. It only knows the neutral context in association with the feared outcome. It cannot appraise the neutral context alone. It cannot be "in the moment," since its job is to be on high alert and to respond to memories of fear.

If fear were blue and neutrality were white, the amygdala, after encountering blue and white together, would always see white alone as tinged with blue. Is it possible for the amygdala to ever see white as only white again?

Scientists were first able to understand the phenomenon of conditioning by introducing a negative event (such as an electric shock) shortly after a neutral event (such as showing a blue circle). Whenever a white circle was shown, however, no shock was delivered. Participants in the study slowly came to understand that seeing a blue circle meant that a shock was to follow it, so every time they saw a blue circle, they would sweat more and their skin conductance would increase. In the acquisition phase, people came to learn this association automatically to the degree that it was totally unconscious. Subsequent research has shown that the amygdala is in fact instrumental in learning to fear something and in making these associations. Some experiments have shown that the hippocampus (classically considered to be involved in forming long-term memories) is also part of this initial learning process, suggesting that the amygdala feeds the hippocampus these learned associations so it can cement the memory and keep it alive and ready to be recalled when necessary.

Remember from our earlier discussion that these processes are also occurring at a cellular level. LTP is part of this phenomenon of acquiring fear memory. We are blissfully unaware of how many of our memories are formed in this way. In any given millisecond, the brain takes in chunks of information, and this information is often packaged as is, forming memories that sometimes last a lifetime. Because much of this occurs outside of conscious awareness, can you imagine how prone to distorted perceptions we are at any given moment in time?

We are convinced that we are right because we have a feeling of conviction, but conviction is nothing other than cemented learning.

The feeling that we are right is not something that we can ordinarily overcome, even when we are wrong. Multiple sources of inaccurate information can increase amygdala activation, thereby convincing you that the fear you are experiencing must, in fact, be real.

When a patient named Kate first came to see me, I observed that she was quite sensitive and very easily hurt. Years before, she had broken up with a boyfriend and become very distraught. She had cried a lot and was upset, but her behavior had been in no way abnormal. When her friends saw how distressed she was, however, they thought she needed professional help and took her to the psychiatric emergency room, and she was then committed to a psychiatric hospital. This experience had traumatized her.

Since that time, she felt that every relationship she began was doomed unless the man she was dating had some experience with the psychiatric system. She felt labeled by that experience and believed that she was "crazy." She believed, therefore, that a "normal" man would never stay with her. This erroneous belief was self-fulfilling. Every time she met a man (a neutral stimulus), her amygdala would recall the learned association between "man" and "I am crazy" (a negative stimulus). Even when the men she dated liked her, to her, every moment in the relationship was about proving the truth of this learned association. Her anxiety would lead the man to become anxious as well.

So, within a short period of time, she would test the strength of the relationship with her sadness or anger, but without a desire to continue the relationship. Superficially, she thought that she wanted the relationship, but on a deeper level, the learned association was something like "If I cry, it will freak out this guy and he will leave." This was the conviction that her brain held on to. Our work consisted of slowly working through this belief. What was striking was that even when she became aware of this association consciously, she was still unable to stop her amygdala from going through the automated process.

Now, Kate and I are probing this learning in a complex manner. To really get at it, we have to evoke and access the emotions that formed this "false memory." The emotions are real, but once we access them, they have to be recontextualized. In Kate's course of therapy, the first six months consisted of her crying most of the time and my reassuring her that those emotions were not evidence that she needed to be committed to a hospital. Although her behavior was definitely concerning, it was also the only way to start to rewire the amygdala to reject the associations that it had formed.

Often, people identify the feared association and then mistake it for a thought. The idea that "emotions are bad," for example, is part thought and part emotion. So rewiring, in this instance, involves rewiring the thought and the emotional circuitry.

This rewiring is necessary because after the amygdala acquires the learned association, it becomes conditioned. Brain imaging studies have shown that the process of conditioning (not just acquisition) involves the amygdala as well. In fact, extinction also involves the amygdala centrally. As a result, much of the rewiring needs to occur in the amygdala. But because the amygdala communicates extensively with other brain regions, the rewiring must occur in more than just the amygdala. The ventromedial prefrontal cortex, for example, is primarily involved in extinction and the retention of extinction. As we learn more about these connections, we are better able to help people free themselves from their conditioned behaviors.

Remember that extinction occurs when the negative stimulus is no longer automatically paired with the neutral stimulus—when Kate no longer thinks that her sadness will drive men away from her. It is important to understand that this new learning is not immediate, and that even after it is learned initially, the old learning can come back. You have to keep reinforcing the new learning for it to take root, but this change is always challenged by old habits that are entrenched in the brain. The subgenual ACC (a part of the ACC activated in extinguishing fear) is extensively connected with brain regions that process threat and reward, so a continuous brain equation remodeling is occurring as new learning occurs.

The good news about all of this is that the more regions there are that connect with the amygdala, the more access we have to it, and the greater the likelihood is that we can take advantage of plasticity (change the neuronal connections) to diminish fear.

Are You a Victim of Automaticity?

If automaticity were inherent, unchangeable, and eternally fixed, there would be no hope of ever overcoming our conditioning. But our brains, at their current state of evolution, have been blessed with numerous possibilities for alteration.

In order to understand the role of attention in learned fear, scientists examined whether attending to unrelated but difficult thinking tasks changed the way the amygdala responded to conditioned fear. They found that attending to more difficult mental tasks decreased amygdala activation, whereas activation was greater when the tasks were easier. What this means is that the amygdala depends heavily on attention to learn automatic responses to stimuli. In essence, if you are busy attending to something else, the amygdala will not condition as easily. This is clearly important, because it suggests that focused concentration removes fear and automatic fear responses. Simply put, if you focused on getting to work on time and not on the cars that were driving by, you would lose the association "red car = bad day."

In your own life, if you find yourself feeling threatened in a situation because of a previous life experience, recognize that there is a biological means for decreasing this fear by concentrating on the matter at hand. For example, say that you once had a bad experience with a male boss and in your new job, your boss is male. In your first meeting, making an effort to focus your attention on the agenda will help you feel less anxious, because you will be diverting brain resources away from your amygdala. This thinking technique is best applied at first in low-anxiety situations, and after practice it can be used in higher-anxiety situations.

In fact, researchers have found that if you are highly anxious, it is less likely that you can interrupt the amygdala's fear response by attending to something else. People who were less anxious were able to engage these attentional systems. Once you have a lower level of anxiety, you will be able to attend to and decrease your automatic fear associations. This is why the time to decrease your anxiety is now. The longer you wait, the longer you will be exposing yourself to automatic fear responses.

Further research into how fear is learned and then made automatic found that not all types of exposure lead to equal automatic amygdala activation. Researchers have studied two other types of conditioning called delay conditioning and trace conditioning. In both situations, subjects are exposed to one neutral event and then, shortly after, one event that is associated with a negative outcome. In delay conditioning, there is little time between both exposures (to the neutral event and the negative outcome). That is, there is some overlap in the brain's processing of both events. Although the brain starts to process the negative event after the neutral event, it is still processing the neutral event when the negative event is happening. Stick with me here, because this has tremendous application in your life.

In trace conditioning, there is enough time between the neutral and negative events that the brain has completed processing the neutral event. There is no leftover activation when the negative event arises. Research has shown that attention can modify skin conductance in trace, but not delay conditioning. That is, when we attend to something with great intensity, we can modify our previously acquired conditioned fear if there was a long enough period of time between the neutral event and the negative association.

So, here is where we get to an important idea in negative life experiences and fear. That anxiety is worse in delay conditioning suggests a biological reason to avoid relationships on the rebound. Essentially, when you are on the rebound, you have not given your amygdala enough time to deactivate from your previous relationship. As a result of this, the new situation could be affected by past amygdala activation and you could confuse the two, creating more confusion for yourself. There is no clear idea about how long you should have to wait, but at the very least, you can approach a new relationship with the realization that leftover activation may intrude upon your current situation.

I saw this in another context when Irene, a capable and intelligent fifty-year-old woman, kept getting fired from jobs within six to twelve months of starting a new position. Many of her co-workers and bosses happened to be Jewish, and she believed that they would fire her eventually because they were prejudiced against people of Irish descent.

Obviously, each of them liked her well enough to hire her, but because of her biases, she was unable to attend to her work and her performance suffered. It was only when she examined the premise of her assumptions and explored her need to be a victim that she was able to let go of these fears enough to hold a job for the next two years. I am not sure if she has let go of this fear entirely, but she appears to be much better adjusted than she had been when she was on autopilot.

Keeping some temporal distance between negative events or working out the negativity at least in part before you move on helps, but neither provides complete protection from repeating a previous error. The hippocampus cements into the long-term memory the associations formed by the amygdala during both delay and trace conditioning, though we are less vulnerable to it during trace than during delay conditioning.

The Role of Anticipation

Anxiety is not just an acute condition. In many instances, it is also anticipatory. That is, some of the worst forms of anxiety occur when we are anticipating a dreaded outcome. Sometimes the anticipation is even worse than experiencing the outcome. Often, we carry our anticipatory fear into a situation.

We often compartmentalize life because it makes things easier to deal with. In reality, however, life is continuous. If the past, present, and future were all one big moment (which they are), then we would have no future and, therefore, nothing to anticipate. Having a future makes the moment one big drumroll. If we lose the drumroll effect, we can exist in greater peace and not fret about an "unknown" future. Many people complain about the unknown future, but the truth is, for many people, even the present is unknown because when they are in it, they are seeing it through the lens of the past.

We regard time as a fundamental truth, which it is not. Jiddu Krishnamurti, a famous philosopher, wrote extensively about how much of our fear comes from contemplating a future that does not really exist outside of the confines of the clock. Simply put, clock time, as it were, is an undeniable reality. We all have to get up at a certain time (most of us, anyway!); we have to show up at places, eat, cook, and sleep at certain times as well. But this time did not exist until we invented a way to measure the rising and setting of the sun. The sun does not set in stages. It is a continuous action. But time, as it was invented, segmented the rising- and setting-sun movements into seconds, minutes, and hours. Similarly, there is no real boundary between the past, present, and future; these words exist only in reference to themselves. Krishnamurti's argument, then, is that there is no "naturally occurring" past, present, and future, but instead one big "now" that is this life. Sure, we can say that what happened yesterday was the past, but what if we did not have the words *past* and *yesterday*? It would mean that all of yesterday and today would be one continuous experience. Fragmenting time also creates a future. It is in the context of this future that people experience anticipatory anxiety. Is it possible to have anticipation without a future? If there is no future, then anticipation and its associated anxiety are not possible.

Part of what creates this anticipation is the larger context into which the possible fear is introduced. Below, we will take a close look at the science of context.

The Importance of Your Surroundings

We understand that repeated brain stimuli of the same variety (optimism, fear, pessimism) cause LTP in chains of neurons that activate in distinctive patterns, resulting in their corresponding outcomes. To break the "chain of fear," we have to break this pattern of LTP and fear conditioning. At any given time, however, there are a number of factors that set up our brains to be conditioned by fear. Apart from the frightening stimulus itself, the context surrounding it (for example, the roads on which the red cars were seen) also "reminds" the brain to activate conditioned circuits. We call the latter contextual conditioning.

Recent experiments in humans have proven that contextual conditioning does, in fact, exist. That is, when a fear-inducing event is first experienced, not only is the fear remembered, but the context of the fear is also remembered in a circuit that includes the hippocampus and amygdala. This context is then tightly associated with the fear itself. The nerve cells that remember fear are so intricately connected to those that remember the context that if you stimulate only the context circuits, the fear circuits automatically start firing.

When a person unlearns this fear, then, the context surrounding it also is important. Even if you unlearn the same fear in an unrelated context, the fear may arise again when the original context is presented. Thus, when we unlearn our fears, we must be careful not to forget to also treat the context. For example, if you once lost all of your money during the springtime, every spring might become a mournful and frightening time if you associate loss of money with tulips in your front yard and rising temperatures. To get over this fear, you would need to rethink this association, meaning that you would need to consciously decouple losing money not only from spring, but also from tulips and warm weather. These kinds of associations are held more deeply in the brain, so when we try to understand our fears, details are important.

What Happens If You Have Too Little Fear Conditioning?

People who have too little fear conditioning receive insufficient warning signals when danger is present. In the best of circumstances, these people become harmless thrill seekers and risk takers, but in the worst of circumstances, they end up hurting themselves and others. In fact, poor fear conditioning, in conjunction with a lack of conscience and poor decision-making skills, is associated with damage to the prefrontal cortex that is typically found in sociopaths.

For example, Andrew was a patient whom I had seen in therapy. He was a sharp, good-looking, HIV-positive, gay executive who was single and very frustrated with his romantic relationships. One relationship in particular left him feeling isolated, alone, and unable to get what he wanted. On a particular day, Andrew revealed to me that he had been frequenting bathhouses and having sex with strangers. Perhaps dangerous, but I wasn't yet concerned. Then Andrew went on to explain that these strangers were teenage boys and that he hadn't used condoms. He said that he was angry that he had to suffer with HIV infection alone, so he had lured in these young boys with his good looks and attempted to infect them. I immediately felt myself thrown into a dilemma over whether this man was homicidal. He firmly denied wanting to do this again and told me that he was talking about it because he felt guilty, but during the next session, he admitted to having repeated this behavior. I sought consultation and terminated the relationship, in part because it was a gray area in terms of reporting it (I am obligated to warn potential victims of homicide, but because Andrew traveled and I had no idea which bathhouses he frequented and he would not tell me, I had nobody specific to warn) and in part because I was not comfortable with participating in the dialogue because I felt immensely angry and afraid for both Andrew and his victims. I knew that I could not help Andrew anymore, but I also realized that although he was initially guilty and afraid, he was now on a rampage because he had lost all sense of control over his own life. His fear conditioning circuits were no longer functional. Apart from probably having prefrontal deficits, his amygdala was underfiring and his hippocampus was not remembering the context or actual fears that he initially felt in relation to his behavior. Here we see a classic but disturbing case of when a little more fear conditioning would be helpful.

The same thinking applies to other kinds of psychopaths, such as rapists or serial murderers. Why do they perform these acts? Are they not affected by what they do? A conditioning experiment in Germany has shown that whereas people normally acquire fear and then develop associations that remind them of these fears, psychopaths do not even acquire these fears or associations. Their brains appear to be underactive. Their emotions and thinking also appear to be disconnected, with no activation occurring in the limbic–prefrontal cortex during acquisition of a conditioned response. The limbic–prefrontal cortex connection is a vital link between thinking and feeling. When this circuit is not activated, people have no conscious access to thinking about what they feel. Even if psychopaths can feel (and I believe that they mostly do), they are cut off from their own and other people's feelings.

Furthermore, psychopaths have also been shown to have atypical structural abnormalities of the hippocampus—the part of the brain responsible for long-term memories. Thus, their ability to retrieve memories of their behavior is compromised, and, as a result, fear conditioning may also be compromised.

Conditioning and Addiction

Why is so much of human behavior addictive? Whether it is drugs, alcohol, sex, food, or sports, we find ourselves drawn to certain habitual paths that keep us engaged regardless of whether they serve our greater needs. For example, an alcoholic may know that she is progressively destroying her life, but still feel unable to stop her behavior. A gambling addict may be in dire financial straits, but continue to roll the dice. What is at the root of these kinds of addictive behaviors?

While the answer is complex, one of the central concepts related to addiction is conditioning. Typically, people acquire a fear through learned association. For example, if you were attacked when you were downtown, you might avoid downtown for fear of being attacked. After several more trips downtown, however, you might learn that, in and of itself, being downtown does not lead to being attacked, and your fear response will decrease every time you go downtown. That is, we eventually habituate to our fear. Once we do this, we can extinguish the fear until something else provokes it.

In addiction, this habituation and extinction does not occur. Instead, what takes place is intermittent reinforcement, a condition in which the addiction sometimes leads to enjoyable results (like feeling great while drunk) and sometimes leads to unpleasant results (like hangovers). The problem arises when the unpleasant results are not predictable. Most people stop drinking excessively because the subsequent hangovers and energy drain become frequent and predictable. But what happens when they are not? And what happens when the positive effects or rewards are also unpredictable? It sets up the brain to want more, because it starts to search for "one more" positive result.

Research has shown that as unpredictability increases, the amygdala and short-term memory and attentional structures in the brain fire for longer. They do not habituate to or extinguish the fear because they are unable to know whether the feared result is gone. This hyperstimulates the brain and keeps you in a state of high expectation. In fact, the amount of activation in these brain regions decreases when expectation is higher. In a predictable situation, this is consistent, so eventually, the brain response decreases. In an unpredictable situation, the brain response does not diminish, because the state of expectation is lower in an attempt to control anxiety.

One sees this pattern often in relationships in which one partner is emotionally guarded but sometimes generous. The other partner often sticks around, waiting for the occasional reward. This waiting is, in part, accounted for by the amygdala and other anxiety-related structures being activated by the intermittent and unpredictable reward. The other partner may even interpret this as a sign that the relationship is working, since that partner is always anxious and activated and the anxiety makes him or her feel alive. It is the exact opposite of this that makes people in long-term relationships want to leave relationships that are trusting and predictable. There is less amygdala activation, and although this feels more restful, it also activates the anxiety centers less and makes them feel less alive. For some people, the rest provided by trust is enough to keep them attached, whereas others consider it a disconnection from their anxiety centers that makes them feel less alive.

Taking Up the Challenge of Deconditioning: The MAP-CHANGE Approach

The management of conditioning is multifactorial and challenging. In part, this is because it is indeed very difficult to tolerate the repetition that is necessary to change habits, and the length of time that it takes to depart from established ways of behaving may be frustrating. Nevertheless, the pages that follow offer several approaches to changing fixed habits and reducing the automatic fears that are associated with conditioning. Repetition is key to new learning and new LTP; however, repetition needs to occur with emotional commitment, mindfulness, and lack of strain.

Meditation

While changing our brain circuitry is a viable and sometimes necessary option, meditation affords us the chance to go more deeply and explore the fears that are troubling us. Also, a meditative state of consciousness decreases the anxiety that accompanies change. Meditation allows you to connect with your deepest sense of self, and it allows the process of change to involve as little strain as possible. Working from this place of minimal strain can be helpful in instituting the changes that we want.

A study was done on a woman who had the habit of biting her nails. She had done so for years because she was conditioned to do this. She had immense difficulty stopping this habit no matter how hard she tried. Over twenty-eight days, she monitored the events that preceded her nail-biting and determined that when she was anxious, she bit her nails. She then used deep muscle relaxation and transcendental meditation to successfully stop her habit. This example illustrates the importance of discerning what the precipitating causes of a behavior are.

Over a period of a month, monitor yourself and jot down a few notes about what leads to an undesirable behavior. For example, a man I was seeing noted that anger and boredom with his wife led to a desire to cheat on her. Instead of going out to look for sex, he learned to discuss this with her, and he became much less anxious and did not feel the need to cheat on her. Meditation offers the relaxation that is necessary to let go of a previously ingrained habit and follow a new, desired path in life.

Studies done on Zen meditators and yogis have found that they are relatively unresponsive to negative stimuli. Conditioning is thought to arise in the mind. A more profound effect of meditation is to transcend the mind to allow the practitioner to operate from the more undefined, real self where there is no anxiety.

One review of the effect of meditation on therapy suggested that meditative exercises offer three therapeutic gains: insight into repetitive, self-defeating patterns of behavior; desensitization of painful thoughts; and conditioning of the central nervous system. In effect, meditation "loosens" the associations between different things, thereby decreasing the propensity for feelings to be evoked by mere association. It increases the sharpness of the brain, allowing it to respond appropriately.

Attention

As outlined above, paying attention to what feelings precede a conditioned behavior may help you to stop the behavior the next time those feelings arise. Thus, attention can be very helpful in decreasing conditioned behavior. In addition, paying attention to the expectation also matters. Conditioning may be reduced (extinguished) when we learn not to associate things with a negative outcome. Thus, rather than expecting the worst, we can consciously tell ourselves to expect better, and then practice this.

Attention becomes deeper and more meaningful when we allow it to rise in all of its purity. When anxiety forces the full thrust of your attention on a subject, it is difficult to remove the fear conditioning. Attention brings you into the moment. When it does this, it reduces the fear of anticipation because there is no sense of the future.

If we want to register less fear, we can divert our attention to something much more captivating. You can make a list of what this might be for you. If you are afraid of flying, you might think about deplaning. If you are afraid of a new job, you may think about the relaxing view you will have from your office window. Distraction is helpful if what we are distracted by is interesting enough, because it will activate the amygdala instead of the fear.

Psychological Tools

Remind yourself when something seems impossible that it may not be. Ask yourself whether you are using the excuses of "genes" or "habit" to avoid pursuing your dreams. It is simply not true that if you have the genes for something, there is a 100 percent probability that it will happen. This is almost never the case. And all that *hardwiring* implies is that something is ingrained, not that it is unchangeable.

Changing relationship assumptions

Changing our basic beliefs about love and relationships is challenging. For the most part, we are prone to seeking security. Hence, we justify habits and encourage our own and others' brain cells to never change. Yet, this same, unchanging pattern compromises freedom. And without freedom, love is compromised. You can address this more deep-seated need for constancy (and thereby start the battle against conditioning) by changing some basic assumptions about relationships. Here are a few things you can do or reflect on.

1. Do not judge your partner for being inconsistent. Consistency is an imagined quality and not really the way the brain functions.
2. Rather than being threatened by your own or your partner's desire for freedom, engage this desire. Talk about its costs and benefits, and discuss how you can maintain your long-term goal of being together while tolerating jealousy, fear, and insecurity. When you examine the need to be free, you will eventually find out that it has nothing to do with wanting to be separate. Rather, it is the nature of who we are.
3. Allow one night for the discussion of "illicit" thoughts with your partner, or if this seems too threatening at first, with a close friend. This will remove the tension. Seek to understand your desires. Your own stillness will allow this.
4. Remove the dynamic of one of you loving the other more. Instead, seek to be realistic in allowing both of you to be equally vulnerable.

These new ways of dealing with a relationship will not happen automatically. Nobody wants to fully embrace the total freedom of his or her partner. But talking about this will help to alleviate some of the concerns. For every couple, the tolerance for each of these new ways of thinking will differ. Be open to them, but form your own parameters. Just make sure that something about them allows for the possibility of change within the relationship without removing love.

Accepting mortality

Recognize that most of your fear of mortality is unconscious. Check in with yourself on a regular basis—and more frequently than you have been—to evaluate whether you are actually changing in the direction you want to. Ask yourself, "What in my life am I tolerating that I would like to change?" Write down three things. I guarantee that there are at least three things that you are tolerating right now. A suboptimal job, a narcissistic lover, and a boring social life are just some of the things that people tolerate. Then write out a commitment that you will not tolerate this anymore. Reflect deeply on how you have been tolerating this.

Acceptance of mortality does not imply stagnation and resignation. If anything, it is a tool that will help you live life more fully. You cannot get the love you want by controlling anything or anyone. Let go of this and concentrate on developing yourself. A coach I once worked with told me about an important exercise he had performed. He was told to imagine what would be on his tombstone. The most frightening epitaph he could imagine was: "Here lies Peter. He had lots of potential." *Potential* means nothing if it is not tied to an action plan. Make up your mind today to manifest your potential through action. Ask yourself what you would like to have engraved on your tombstone.

Reconditioning the brain

Many people wrote poetry or kept a diary as youngsters. If you still have them, read them over and notice that it seems as though very little has changed since your childhood. For example, Jack, a good-looking, intelligent, fun guy, always felt that he needed to do something to keep the women he dated from getting angry with him. In the morning, when they would get up and go to the bathroom, he would wait, wondering if they were going to come back to bed or if they were starting their day. Or, he would go on with his own day, but in the back of his mind, he would wonder when the relationship was going to be threatened by his inaction in some aspect of the relationship. No matter how different the relationship looked at the beginning, it always ended up with Jack in this contemplative state of "What more can I do? Will she be loving today?"

This kind of living is living without faith. It is living in doubt regardless of how many positive thoughts you have. While Jack argued that he had many conscious positive thoughts, he had not been willing to let go of his doubts because they protected him from the losses that he had experienced previously and might experience again. All they actually did was prolong the time to the eventual loss.

Start your day with a newfound trust in what you desire. Practice losing the kind of tension that Jack had, and see if you can do this for longer and longer periods each day. You will see that much of the repetition that occurs with compulsion is not about repeating a behavior, but rather about repeating a fundamental habit of doubting.

We know from scientific research that automatic fears can be reversed if we can teach our brains that they are not associated with the negative outcomes that we expect.

Rex was a patient of mine who had a tremendous fear of flying. Every time he had a reason to fly, he would avoid it by driving instead—even if it was all the way across the country. Since he was an entrepreneur and needed to travel a lot, this made his job exhausting, and he was severely limited in terms of where he could actually go. Rex's last experience with flying was soon after 9/11, when he flew to Chicago from Boston and experienced immense turbulence on the plane.

When we worked on a behavioral plan, I realized that I could not promise him that the next flight he would take would be smooth. But it seemed reasonable to assume that the next ten flights would mostly be okay. So he started out on short trips at first. It was not easy, particularly because his second trip was turbulent, but we revisited the goal, and by the tenth time, even though there was turbulence, Rex had come to grips with the fact that turbulence did not signal that immediate death was probable. This exercise that had him take ten trips created new LTP that then allowed his brain to activate the new pathway instead of traveling along the old pathway that had been formed soon after 9/11.

Conclusion

When something feels unchangeable, do not blame your genes or hardwiring. Conditioning can be resistant, but it is amenable to change. Once you understand how your brain becomes conditioned, you can start to reverse that conditioning. It is not fixed.

[5]

Unlocking a Caged Heart

Melting Ironclad Fear into Secure Attachment

Touch the world, and the world will touch you.

—Swami Sai Premananda

Man is born free, and everywhere he is in chains.

—Jean-Jacques Rousseau

How can you touch the world if the hand with which you touch it is tethered to a caged heart? Why is it that our hearts, once free to produce gurgles and groans, yearn over time to restrict their openness? How can we become unafraid of repeating the painful event that has motivated us to protect our hearts in the first place? How are people who are securely attached different from those who are not?

Finding the key to a caged heart can be daunting, but it has never been more necessary. Consider the following facts: Single households are on the rise. In 2006, one-person households accounted for 28.9 percent of all households in Western Europe, 26.7 percent in North America, and 25.7 percent in Australasia. Between the mid-1970s and the beginning of the '90s, the percentage of adult women who were single grew dramatically in the United States from 17 to 30 percent, and the percentage of single mothers grew from 12 to 17 percent. Between 50 and 67 percent of first marriages end in divorce. About 20 percent of couples in second or third marriages remain happily married, which means that 80 percent of repeat marriages end in divorce. More than one million children watch their parents divorce each year, and half of the babies born this year will suffer through the divorce of their parents before the children turn eighteen. These and other statistics reveal the direction in which we are headed—deeper into the cage and much the worse for it.

Consider the fact that when solitary confinement was studied in prisoners, the effects of isolation were discovered to be profound. Being alone has a dramatic impact on both the psyche (increasing the incidence of depression, anxiety, hallucinations, claustrophobia, and an impaired ability to think and concentrate) and on the body (impairing vision, hearing, and the immune system). Being around other people provides your brain with feedback that stimulates your development. If you subscribe to the use-it-or-lose-it principle, imagine what you are losing when you have no input from other people. Simply put, when you have no input from others, your brain has no material to stimulate its growth. Isolation shrinks vital parts of the human brain and, by inference, human existence, too.

Apart from this, divorce has other disadvantages. Research suggests that children of divorced parents experience a multitude of problems: They begin drinking at an earlier age than their peers; suffer from depression, withdrawal, poor social competency, health problems, and diminished academic performance; and display a variety of conduct-related difficulties. Divorced adults experience a higher incidence of sleep problems; an increased risk of psychopathology; increased rates of automobile accidents; and increased incidences of physical illness, suicide, violence, homicide, significant immunosuppression, and mortality from diseases. Many times divorces are necessary, but they are not without physical and psychological repercussions.

It is no wonder, then, that I have never met a person who, deep down, does not want to find someone to spend his or her life with. Life's vicissitudes and the peculiarities of being human can sometimes deter us from being connected, but cynicism usually arises as a defense against the primary desire to be with someone. The function of this drive is integral not just to individual development, but to the development of society as well.

Evolutionary theorists believe that successful human attachment builds societies and provides a context for not just individual but also social growth. Psychologically speaking, one of the prototypes of people who reject social growth is the sociopath. Studies suggest that sociopaths develop as a result of abuse or poor bonding experiences in childhood that disrupt the brain's "normal" responses to attachment and instead create deep distrust, fear, and isolation. As a result, the inner life of sociopaths is disconnected from society's needs, and rather than deal with the difficulties related to this tension, they develop brains that do not emphasize social priorities. At a very fundamental level, a two-person relationship with sociopaths is compromised because they cannot trust themselves or others.

While we might possess some sociopathic traits, most of us are not sociopaths. But this extreme example illustrates how our psychology shifts when human attachment is compromised. Trust is one of the essential ingredients in human attachment. It is vulnerable to a variety of factors, but one of the key challenges to trust is fear. Fear controls the extent to which the gates of our emotions and thoughts are open to others. If you think for a moment why it is that you are attached to a job that you hate, you will see that it is the familiarity that you choose over the fear associated with starting a new but more fulfilling job. If you wonder why it is that you are attached to someone who makes your life miserable, it is for the same reason. Or if you ask yourself why it is that you are unattached, sooner or later, you will recognize your fear rearing its ugly head. If it doesn't, it is likely that the idea of challenging this fear is so frightening to your unconscious that you would rather avoid this battle than even envision it.

This connection between fear and attachment has been studied extensively by psychologists and brain scientists. While the brain system for attachment is a unique and distinct one, there is no doubt that this system is intricately interwoven with the network for fear. After all, attachment is really about losing the fear of intimacy or the fear of disappointment. And it is often about finding ways to detach from a fearful past in order to create a present and future that are more rewarding.

In this chapter we will explore the basis of the anxiety that arises in relationships and what fear has to do with it. We will first take a look at three basic attachment styles (secure, anxious, and avoidant) and then see how these styles relate to fear. We will explore the consequences of this fear and then examine some biological underpinnings of the attachment process. From neurochemical and neurological research on trust to the brain changes induced by mother-child relationships, we will come to see the ways in which fear affects how we function in relationships and what we will and will not tolerate.

"Why am I so lonely?"
The Psychological Basis of Attachment Styles

Loneliness is not a product of being without people. It is an internal state of disconnection from the self that leads to disconnection from others. People can be lonely whether they are alone or surrounded by other people. I remember going to a very lavish party in the Hamptons, on New York's Long Island. I was one among a thousand people like me who were there to network and shake hands. Within a half hour, I felt a strong impulse to leave. When I thought about my reaction later, I realized that there was no opportunity to communicate any depth of knowledge or feeling in the brief conversations that were taking place. I felt disconnected from myself, and I was lonely beyond belief. When I retired to a hotel that evening with a friend, we breathed heavy sighs of relief mixed with disappointment as we flopped onto our beds. This party that we had so looked forward to—this opportunity to meet and connect with people—left us feeling exhausted, empty, and alone. Our room-service burgers were the highlight of the evening.

Every person I encountered that evening seemed highly anxious and desperate to form relationships with the right people. I was immersed in a cauldron of anxiety and my own brain mirrored it and freaked out—adding to my own initial anxiety. Forming meaningful attachments in a sea of anxiety and fear is like trying to see your reflection in a waterfall. It's just not going to happen.

Attachment behaviors have been extensively studied by psychologists and brain scientists. Although every individual and situation is unique, researchers have found that there are three basic forms of attachment behavior: secure, anxious, and avoidant attachment.

Both anxious and avoidant styles are insecure forms of attachment. Over the course of your life, you probably have wondered why it is that different people have different kinds of relationships. Why are some people attached and others not? Why do some people marry at such an early age while others never marry at all? Why do some people get along so well with others while some always seem to alienate those around them?

In any one of us, a variety of forces is at work determining how we attach to other individuals and to society at large. Based on the attachment influences we encountered during childhood, adolescence, and early adulthood, we form habits for how we relate to people—we approach, avoid, or remain paralyzed in our relationships, and based on these styles, deep unconscious pathways may form. We develop these styles as a result of genetics, conditioning, and our past experiences, and they become fixed once the brain starts to form connections. But before we delve into the different brain responses, let's take a look at each of these styles of attachment in a little more detail. Bear in mind that it is rare for any person to have only one style of attachment. Typically, we all possess each style to different degrees, but understanding this will help us set the stage for understanding how fear interacts with attachment, how our brains respond to this interaction, and what we can do about it.

Secure Attachment

Secure attachment refers to the ability to form and sustain relationships for extended periods of time. Paradoxically, secure attachment involves letting go of conscious attachment behavior and allowing the relationship to develop while believing in it. This autonomy, independence, or self-confidence stimulates a secure basis for the attachment. Here, even when there are fears, they are appropriately harnessed and are not a dominant force in the formation and sustenance of relationships. With secure attachment, a fight with a boyfriend or girlfriend does not result in weeks of distance and fear that the relationship is going to end. If your partner decides to spend a weekend with friends, you don't fear losing him or her.

In secure attachment, you are not constantly preoccupied with the worry that someone will leave you. You rely on yourself as being "enough" to keep the other person interested. And this is not just a thought or a moment's conviction, but an ingrained way of relating to others. Secure attachment is the result of a deep understanding of how difficult it is to be in a relationship with someone, and it involves an active awareness of the trade-offs between being in a relationship and being alone. Trust, understanding, forgiveness, and commitment are central to this process.

One of the core sources of personal pain is the expectation of consistent behavior from ourselves and others. Underlying this assumption is the idea that our brains do not change—that, somehow, we are at our best if our brains stop making new connections and our personal development stops. The truth is that this is never the case, so why expect it? If we believe in the golden rule, which tells us to treat others as we'd like to be treated, it follows logically that if we change, we fear that others may change too. Thus our secure attachment, which is based on a compatibility that may not exist in the future, will be harmed. Yet secure attachment is impossible if this is our expectation. The simple truth of any human relationship is that sometimes you can rely on people and sometimes you can't. Even people you love can let you down.

In a child, secure attachment means that the experience of connection becomes internalized and the child can go off on his or her own without feeling threatened by a sense of loss. In fact, attachment styles often become consolidated between the ages of three and five years. If a child loses a parent at an early age, or if a parent is absent for a long time, secure attachment is compromised.

Secure attachment allows for a "life unlocked" and is something we all strive to achieve. It should not be mistaken for overt or subtle forms of mutual clinging, in which both people make a conscious or unconscious pact not to be free and to provide solace to the other person because they are themselves afraid. This is often a normal part of early commitments, but it rarely promotes growth as a long-term style. When people are securely attached, not only is attaching easier, but loss can be easier too. In fact, ambivalent attachments that are broken often result in prolonged grieving.

Secure attachment comes from realizing that attachment will create all kinds of conflict, and that considerable resolve is needed to create long-lasting relationships. It is usually characterized by the ability to put negative things behind you and focus on the positive aspects of relationships. Secure attachment involves being accustomed to dealing with the anger of others (for others are just as afraid as you are) and exploring intimacy and the emotional landscape of relationships without judgment. Lasting attachments are rarely smooth or without problems. But secure attachment occurs when one expects this. If both people know this, then new learning occurs: "Just because he is angry does not mean that he is going to leave," or "Just because I can't stand her now does not mean that I will not be able to stand her forever."

Anxious Attachment

An anxious attachment is a form of relationship that most people can relate to. When people have attachment anxiety, they are plagued by a fear of rejection and abandonment. Every relationship interaction is accompanied by an inner fear that they will be rejected or abandoned. Even if they have a positive layer of thought and no conscious realization of these expectations, past experiences have shaped their brains to form pathways that trigger feelings of past rejection and abandonment. The inner workings of this kind of thinking are deep and often unrecognized, and they relate intricately to the inner workings of fear.

Many fights between couples are a result of anxious attachment. Have you ever noticed how you might fight with a loved one when he is about to leave on a trip, or when she seems preoccupied with her own work and less interested in you? Have you ever noticed how people start to fight more as they get older? In each of these situations, there is fear or anxiety that the other person is leaving, and it destabilizes the anxious person. It is similar to the reaction to someone dying: Every time a spouse or loved one leaves, it is like a small death. If there is no stability in one's own sense of self, then that departure causes our self-impressions to crumble, and we panic. Fear shakes the foundation of our ability to connect and form meaningful and sustained relationships, in part because fear shakes up the integrated image we have of ourselves.

In our adult lives, anxious attachment manifests itself in a number of ways: during the "first fight" or the first time a loved one goes away, when an attractive co-worker starts to work with a loved one, or when a former spouse or partner reappears. In each situation, our secure attachments are threatened, and we may switch from "secure" to "anxious" mode.

One of the tricky things about anxious attachment is that it is rarely entirely conscious. People will often concoct the most bizarre reasons for separating if anxious attachment is the basis of a relationship. When anxious attachment is conscious, people are always on edge, wondering when the projected loss will occur. Once again, the very thing that is feared becomes a reality when it is the focus of a relationship. "I don't want to divorce just like my parents did" is a mantra that often ends with divorce because an anxious attachment dictates the nature of the relationship.

In my work, I have not seen any forms of relationships that are entirely bad. But red flags that warn about anxious attachment occur to me when certain situations arise. For example, a wide age difference between the two people in a relationship can indicate anxiety and questions. Is the older person anxious about getting older and dying, and trying to overcome this by connecting with a much younger partner? Is the younger person anxious about losing his or her parents, and trying to establish a relationship with a similar age differential in order to hold on to an aging parent? This does not mean that age differentials should not exist in relationships. It just means that understanding this anxiety may help to transform the relationship from a projection of the past into what it actually is. Rather than internally viewing the other person as a parent, for example, one can come to know him or her as a lover. When you relate to someone as if he is someone from your past, forgetting that he is a whole new person, it is called transference.

Another situation in which this might come up is when one or both partners in a marriage are having an affair. Are they anxious about losing control if they offer a full commitment? Are they anxious that the other person might leave, so they leave first? Does this anxiety spill over into other parts of their lives? Are they unable to fully commit to a job or lose themselves in their work because they are afraid of losing control? Have they not come to terms with the fact that they are not and will never be fully in control? Here again, we can refrain from judging situations if we understand the basis for the behavior. Our ideas about what is right and what is wrong are based largely on what we think will hurt us. If we fear losing someone, clearly we will want to get rid of that anxiety. For some people, the answer is to leave the person they are afraid of losing before they are left behind. For other people, the answer is to understand how they may be causing the loss and do something before the loss occurs, or to understand how their anxiety will continue to create this kind of situation even in subsequent relationships unless they address it.

Anxious attachments are very unstable. Usually, they result in one person acting out and testing the other person in the relationship. When adolescents are unable to find the permission to detach from their parents, for example, they will often find it difficult to date just one person. Anxious attachments can be converted into secure attachments, but this may occur at the expense of giving up a level of uncertainty that is often critical to sustaining curiosity and new discovery. So the trick here is to give up the fear of uncertainty enough that the attachment can be secure, but not to give up a sense of entitlement to be curious and learn more about life. If you are certain that you will always grow and try to live for the best outcome, any exploration becomes deeper.

Anxiety in attachment usually arises when one person starts to feel disconnected from the other—one partner feels more aloof, or starts to earn more money, or adopts a different lifestyle or new friends. Changes such as these can be very disconcerting, even when they seem silly, because regardless of how attached we are, we all know how transient relationships can be. Most of us have felt that we would never lose someone, only to suddenly have the rug pulled out from under us and face a devastating loss. All we need is one of these experiences to always be on edge about the possibility of another. This constant tension can be very destructive unless both partners are equally insecure and willing to be controlled. Even then, resentment may grow.

Anxious attachment is easy to address when it is conscious and accessible. But when a person is outwardly calm but anxiety inwardly dictates that person's decision making, it often takes a long time before facing the anxiety he or she has spent a lifetime trying to avoid is possible.

Avoidant Attachment

With the avoidant attachment response, a person may avoid attachment entirely because the anxiety that attachment brings is too threatening. Rather than avoiding the anxiety that comes from anxious attachment, the person avoids the attachment altogether. I think of avoidant attachment as nonattachment rather than detachment. Nonattachment is a defense against attachment. Detachment is a consequence of secure attachment.

People with attachment avoidance often find that they distance themselves from others and shun dependency. They are afraid that if they get too close, their actual need for attachment will be revealed. We can see how this mentality is deeply ingrained in people today by just reflecting on popular relationship advice. "Play it cool" and "don't act desperate" are the mantras that are chanted to the uninitiated. This, however, is just the start of it. When someone is rejected frequently or is anxious in relationships, then he or she will gradually come to regard relationships as unrewarding and avoid them. After all, if I told you that you should eat something that would make you sick, you wouldn't go near it. Similarly, attachment-avoidant individuals avoid the unpleasant feelings that relationships inspire in them.

The result, often, is that other forms of anxiety and sickness eventually start to creep in: fear of loneliness, fear of dying alone, and fear of life having no meaning. The avoidant attachment response often develops in people who have experienced an intense disappointment, such as losing a lover or best friend. In these situations, the person may isolate him- or herself and live a solitary life, or may opt to have "company" as a substitute for attachment. The difference between *company* and *attachment* is that in company, people are with each other, but unattached. The ongoing relationship is perpetuated by the fear of being alone, but a person does not take the risk of attaching.

Essentially, avoidant attachment is a way of avoiding loss. Because death is the fate that finally meets us all, avoidant attachment anticipates this eventual outcome. After all, why attach when we're all going to lose one another eventually?

Avoidant styles of attachment result from having so much fear that it is not even worth forming the attachment. Permanent long-distance relationships, relationships conducted solely online or via the phone, and relationships between "friends" who are romantically and sexually attracted to one another but who never consummate those feelings are all examples of avoidant relationships.

Living a solitary life is also a way of gaining maximum control, as all you have to do is focus on yourself. So what's wrong with this? We will discuss the problems in more detail a bit later. As society has become increasingly work oriented and many more people are open about being unattached or alone, we have sought to rationalize why being alone is okay. Deep down, there is always a discomfort about being alone, and there is always a need to make sense of this condition. The rationalization comes from being dedicated to avoiding attachment.

I have seen this occur in my practice when people experience recurrent disappointments in relationships. They will often choose to spend a prolonged time on their own because they feel defeated by disappointments. Avoidant people will avoid eye contact; they will avoid being attached at all costs. They often enjoy the chase, and even the togetherness, but the idea of a long-term relationship makes them feel trapped. I have also observed this behavior in people who have been divorced.

They will go to great lengths to avoid getting married again because they want to avoid the negative emotions they have come to associate with marriage.

Avoidant attachment, like anxious attachment, is a source and a result of profound loneliness, and both of these insecure forms of attachment have profound physical and psychological consequences. But how does fear relate to insecure attachment, and what are its consequences?

Oxytocin:
The Hormone-Fear-Trust Connection

Beneath the fears of abandonment and rejection is a fundamental inability to trust that things will go well. Fear and trust have an intimate relationship, and recent studies on brain biology have shed more light on it. The link here is that in order to attach securely, we need to have a minimal amount of fear, and in order to fear less, we need to trust more. But is this just a pie-in-the-sky idea, or does it have a basis in our fundamental biology? Recent studies have identified oxytocin as the trust hormone. The more oxytocin that attaches to a person's receptors, the greater a person's ability to trust will be.

Clues to the role oxytocin plays in human relationships were first found in animal studies. Researchers found that oxytocin is essential in nest building and pup retrieval in rats, acceptance of offspring in sheep, and the formation of adult pair bonds in prairie voles. All of these home-building relationships involve significant amounts of secure attachment, so researchers turned their attention to humans to see if this same correlation occurred. Also, given the role of oxytocin in social recognition and aggression in animals, it was a natural next step to examine the role of this hormone in humans.

Some initial observations included the already well-known facts that oxytocin stimulates the ejection of milk during lactation and uterine contraction during birth. In addition, both men and women release it during sexual orgasm. Realizing that oxytocin is released whenever a relationship has to be forged brought us one step closer to suspecting that it must have a role in trust as well. But could researchers shed light on the role of oxytocin in human attachment?

In 2005, a study published in the science journal *Nature* showed that administering oxytocin to humans resulted in an increased ability to trust. What they found was that this trust did not reflect a general readiness to bear risks of any type, however, but instead was related to the ability to bear risks in interpersonal situations. This data showed us for the first time that the ability to form human relationships is a hormonally mediated circumstance and that, most likely, if we want to form more-secure attachments, we have to do something that will increase oxytocin production.

Since that initial study, many subsequent studies have confirmed that negative consequences in social attachment are indeed due in part to oxytocin deficits: One study found that women with a history of severe abuse had less oxytocin in their cerebrospinal fluid (which is connected with the fluid in their brains), while another study found that lower oxytocin levels correlate with social withdrawal and isolation in people suffering from schizophrenia. In addition, a low oxytocin level has been suspected to be in part responsible for the social isolation seen in people with autism. Another group of investigators studied whether administration of oxytocin versus a placebo produced a different response to a breach of trust and found that the behavior of people who received oxytocin did not change even after their trust was breached several times, whereas the behavior of people who received a placebo did change. Perhaps this explains why some of us have the wool pulled over our eyes over and over again: too much oxytocin! This "trust" effect seen with oxytocin increases the chances of looking into the eyes of another person, and when we do, it facilitates trust and connection. When two people toast each other with cocktails and look into each other's eyes, they are increasing their own oxytocin levels, and probably the other person's, too.

It is also interesting to note that one has only to have an "intention to trust" to increase oxytocin in another. One experiment looked at a scenario among a group of experimental subjects in which money was transferred into a subject's bank account. This experiment found that when money was transferred as an intention to trust, the recipient's oxytocin level increased, but when money was transferred unintentionally, there was no change. This suggests that higher oxytocin levels are associated with the reciprocation of trust.

We have accumulating evidence that when trust is involved in human attachment, oxytocin increases. But what is its connection with fear, and how can we link the positive effects of oxytocin on human attachment to fear?

In order to explore this link, researchers began to try to understand how the oxytocin level affected brain function. A number of the studies that were performed are intriguing and compelling.

One of the most reliable studies examined whether oxytocin was different from placebo in activating brain regions. This study found that oxytocin significantly decreased amygdala activation. The link was now becoming clearer! Fear increases amygdala activation and disrupts attachment. Oxytocin decreases amygdala activation and facilitates attachment. So fear and oxytocin are at odds with each other: If one increases, the other decreases.

If oxytocin decreases amygdala activation and its level in the body is increased by the intention to trust, then if we want to reduce our fears (and reduce amygdala activation), we have to expose ourselves to more situations in which we can trust and be trusted by others. It is possible, then, that from an evolutionary standpoint, human attachment serves to moderate the protective discharges of an overactive amygdala and that this provides a strong motivation to seek secure attachment.

For some of us, trusting is difficult, especially if our trust has been broken repeatedly. Although we want to trust other people, it becomes difficult if we are betrayed repeatedly. Does repeated betrayal injure our ability to trust, or does our inability to trust cause repeated betrayal? It seems as though this is a vicious circle. How can this cycle be broken?

Research has proven that when someone experiences an automatic negative response to something, oxytocin administration can reverse the response as well as decrease amygdala activation. Thus, oxytocin can stop fear conditioning. How do we increase our own level of oxytocin to stop this conditioning? By surrounding ourselves with people we can trust or people who will trust us, because this will increase our own oxytocin level and decrease fear-related amygdala activation.

When Trust and Fear Duke It Out in the Human Amygdala

These very sophisticated experiments have brought us that much closer to understanding how fear and trust interact and compete with each other in the human amygdala. Fear increases activation. Trust decreases activation. And because secure attachment relies on a relative absence of fear, trust has to win the fight against fear if we are to remain securely attached. To increase trust, oxytocin has to dominate over the fear-related brain changes.

In attachment-secure individuals, the assumption is that oxytocin has sufficiently reduced amygdala activation to allow unconditional trust and to promote attachment. At first, the idea of trusting or being trusted may seem overwhelming to many of us, but that is why developing trust takes time.

For example, if trust is not well developed in a romantic relationship, then sex and the expectations that it brings may not facilitate attachment. By first developing trust, the fear system is quieted, thereby allowing for attachment to develop. If we do not develop trust first, then the meaning of the physical relationship may be less clear, because sex in the presence of an overactive amygdala may only provide temporary relief from fear or anxiety and have nothing to do with attachment. In this situation, secure attachment has not had the chance to form since there has been no development of trust, just a temporary alleviation of fear. People may become addicted to the act of sex without trust because it relieves the burden of fear (remember that oxytocin is released at orgasm). Many imagine that "trust" will develop if the sex is repeated. Instead, for most people, sex itself does not release sufficient oxytocin, and a new stimulation is sought to reduce the fear. This does not occur when trust is present, because trust, when it secures attachment by decreasing fear, increases the odds of staying together.

In fact, one study showed that a man who was previously unable to achieve orgasm was able to climax when he was injected with oxytocin during intercourse—implying that an enhanced level of trust increased the chances of orgasm. When sexual function becomes an issue for a couple, the subject of trust should always be examined.

The complex interplay between trust, fear, and attachment is well illustrated by an example from my clinical practice.

Bridget is a thirty-year-old woman who has been my patient for a long time. When I first saw her, she was in a troubled relationship with a man, was abusing drugs and alcohol, and was chronically suicidal. She had been under considerable pressure to be as successful as her siblings were, and although she was brilliant, she refused to follow in her parents' and siblings' paths. As a result, her family identified her as the mentally ill one. This was the price that she paid for being different in her family. She was very attached to her father and her two brothers, but also resented them for not recognizing her brilliance and for setting parameters on how she should pursue her life. She eventually processed many aspects of this background and came to a point in her life where she was no longer suicidal and did not use drugs or alcohol. However, she constantly frightened men away.

As she got older, she became angry very quickly when she met men who were not interested in a relationship, because she was intent upon getting married. She was also very attached to her father and, without realizing it, carried the guilt of forming an attachment to any other man into all of her relationships. She gave none of her relationships time to settle in. She was obsessed with being attached, and she pursued her other priorities intermittently, without any consistency of purpose or effort. The constant rejection she faced from men increased her desire to "capture" them, but, of course, it only made them less likely to be with her.

We are now working on developing trust as the first step toward forming a relationship, since right now her high level of amygdala activation just creates a similar level of activation in potential partners and leads to disrupted relationships. She is working on developing deeper emotional connections and being more open about where her relationships will go, but also focusing on trust and reducing her fears rather than constantly trying to become attached and failing. For her, the practice of trust is a challenging one, because she has built up a considerable level of fear after being rejected so many times. Although her intent is to trust when she starts a new romance, it rarely lasts, because the man usually feels her fear and wants to leave when his amygdala activation becomes excessive. Her unconscious fears need to be worked out as she learns how to trust.

Bridget's case illustrates the importance of having a minimal level of fear and a maximal level of trust to cement relationships. Oxytocin and trust interact dynamically with fear circuits to facilitate secure attachments. But we deal with different forms of trust on a daily basis. Some of them are conditional and others are unconditional. What is the difference?

I Love You No Matter What

A recent brain imaging study examined the brain activation seen with conditional and unconditional trust. This study found that conditional trust activated the ventral tegmental area (VTA), which is a brain region that evaluates the expectation of a reward. When the VTA activates, people will trust as long as there is a reward at the end of the tunnel.

Unconditional trust, on the other hand, activates the septal area, which has been linked to social attachment behavior. The septal area is a group of important pleasure centers in the human brain that have extensive connections with the amygdala. Thus, too much amygdala activation due to too much fear can disrupt septal activation and unconditional attachment.

The same study mentioned above showed that another brain region, the paracingulate cortex, plays an important role in building trust-based relationships in which increasing familiarity allows two people to understand one another's intentions. When they do so, unconditional trust is built.

The region around the cingulate may be involved in generating the unique responses children have to mothers, suggesting that early on, this region becomes specialized for predicting behavior on the basis of familiarity. This region may then influence aspects of conditionality or unconditionality in trust and, in so doing, affect attachment behavior. Since fear circuits can disrupt this entire process and since the amygdala connects with all of these areas that cause unconditional trust, it may be difficult for some people to develop unconditional trust when they are afraid, and in low-trust individuals, the VTA may never provide the assurance of reward that eventually leads to unconditional trust. In fact, the VTA underactivates to positive feedback in attachment-avoidant individuals, since their underlying anxiety prevents trust and keeps it, at the very best, in a very conditional state. Thus, fear disrupts the ability to develop unconditional trust, which is necessary for societies to function and for relationships to thrive.

To have unconditional trust in a relationship (that is, to have septal activation), some predictability of behavior or a constant expectation of unpredictability is necessary. It is very difficult for most people to last in a relationship where there is no "certainty." Relationships constantly activate the VTA to assess whether unconditional trust can be allowed to activate the septal area of the brain. Keeping things in an uncertain state can increase anxiety considerably.

One of my patients, Margaret, had a close friend, Eileen, who was in the same line of work as she was. Eileen often turned to Margaret for help with constructing her proposals, but would then take over work projects that Margaret had sought to get, feigning ignorance that Margaret had applied for the same jobs. Margaret liked Eileen a lot, but they held different ideas about their relationship. Margaret wanted to be open about this dynamic, while Eileen somehow believed that she could keep it under wraps for a long time. As a result, they grew apart more and more until Margaret decided to talk to Eileen about the competition between them. Eileen denied it at first, but Margaret insisted on pointing out that they were eroding the trust between them as Eileen continued her unpredictable behavior. We now know that unpredictability prevents brain regions from developing trust circuits, but how can we actually come to expect that everything is predictable when this is clearly not the case for most people? What Margaret said was that she did not want to delude herself into believing that she could trust or predict Eileen's behavior, but that she wanted to remove the hidden elements of this from their relationship. Thus, while Margaret's brain did not move on to develop conditional trust, she and Eileen eliminated one layer of unpredictability as the first step in repairing their relationship. Also, it decreased Margaret's own level of distraction and changed her expectation without necessarily changing her trust.

We also know from the studies discussed earlier that unconditional trust is probably related to circuits that have been impacted by ample amounts of oxytocin. The mother-child relationship offers an opportunity for this early in life. This is when some of the trust-based mechanisms that can counter fear start to develop in the human brain.

The Mother-Child Connection

Trust, attachment, and fear are all relational ideas. That is, one person cannot experience any of these without "another" person or thing. Our brains develop their patterns of behavior from our earliest memories. And there is no earlier memory than that of the mother-child connection.

We know that the brain has mirror neurons that allow it to reflect exactly what it picks up from an environment. When a child is around its mother, the child's brain begins to take shape, in part because it picks up cues, reactions, and ideas from the mother.

The brains of mothers who are looking at their own five- to ten-month-old infants react differently than they do when they are looking at unknown children. All mothers who looked at their own children activated similar brain regions, but when they looked at other children, different brain regions were activated. This ownership and familiarity set the stage for the child's sense of belonging very early in life: He or she has an identified caregiver who knows the child. In the extensive network of regions that is activated in mothers, emotional and thinking circuits interact to prompt the actions necessary to care for the infant, and these brain changes in the mothers relate exclusively to their own children. When they observe other children, these regions are not activated. The implications of this are far-reaching. If mothers develop specific reactions to their own infants, then the brains of infants will in turn be influenced by the changes in the mothers' brains. Thus, if mothers respond in caring and consistent ways that are nonanxious, it sets the stage for nonanxious attachment in children. Mothers are not always this fortunate, however, and for a variety of reasons, the brains of mothers may identify their infants, but also communicate emotions and thoughts that trigger anxious attachment patterns in their children.

For example, reward systems are activated in the brains of mothers when their children are happy, but not when they are sad or neutral. So what happens if a child is crying? In these situations, a mother may react with any of a range of emotions, including fear, shame, disgust, empathy, or disinterest. Mothers who soothe their infants may feel rewarded when the infants calm down. If the infant cannot be soothed, however, the mother may respond with fear. This response, in turn, may set up a fear circuit in the infant's brain. This mechanism is helpful when the fear informs the mother that something is wrong (for example, when the baby is colicky), but it is important to realize that responding with alarm may set off alarm bells in the child's brain. Therefore, although the fear is important in and of itself, it is also important to convert this into a useful action (for example, calling the pediatrician) rather than continuing to communicate fear to the child.

The importance of fear in early maternal responses was illustrated in a study that showed that the amygdala and temporal pole may be key sites in mediating a mother's response to her infant. The increase in amygdala activation is seen in mothers only in response to their own children, not to unknown children. Thus, fear is especially relevant when it concerns your own child. It is important for mothers to realize that maternal protectiveness may increase amygdala activation and activate fear circuits. Mothers offer their children protection in the form of fear and worry or trust, and these reactions produce opposite effects in the child's amygdala. Balancing the two is the most realistic scenario, and it is critical if the child is to develop a secure attachment style.

In general, mothers do respond positively to their own infants, and this positivity correlates with orbitofrontal cortex activation. This is probably why people who have children swear by the uniqueness of the emotions that they experience ("I didn't know what love really was until I had a child")—their brains simply activate differently. People who do not have children often feel that parents are on another planet. The basis for this feeling of alienation could be neurological, because childless people cannot deduce what it feels like to be a parent from their own responses to other children (hence the argument that "it's different when they're your own kids"—it really is).

This attachment between mother and child continues throughout adult life. In fact, another brain imaging study of adult women examined the subjects' responses to pictures of their mothers, close female friends, and two age-matched female strangers. The study found that the ventromedial prefrontal cortex and ACC activated uniquely (showing increased activation) when subjects observed photos of their own mothers, suggesting that we process the faces of our mothers uniquely. Thus, there is a mutual uniqueness in the patterns of activation when children and their mothers recognize each other. This may be why we sometimes cannot understand a spouse's or even a sibling's reaction to a parent. What is going on in your own brain is different from what is going on in their brains.

I recently worked with a couple who are in their sixties. They both identified the husband's mother as controlling, unappreciative, and critical. The husband continued to take care of his mother, however, and the wife assisted. When the husband spoke about his mother, although he agreed with his wife, it was obvious to me that his sentiments were different from hers. It was not obvious to her. When his mother died, he grieved this loss and his wife became enraged that he was being hypocritical. Regardless of how many facts she presented to him, he continued to grieve the loss and explained that she was "[my] mother." His wife could not wrap her head around this reaction. She felt betrayed by her husband. She felt that what she saw in her mother-in-law was the same as what her husband saw, and she just could not understand what he was grieving about. He could not explain his sadness, but we know that it arose because his response to his mother was unique. Children and their mothers have a unique understanding between them, and, whether positive or negative, it is set up early in life and continues throughout the rest of it.

As a child's brain grows, it mirrors what is going on in his or her mother's brain as well as in others who surround it. I recently met a couple at a charity benefit. The wife appeared very together and was a strong and ebullient person. She revealed after a few cocktails that she had a fear of thunder. Her husband, who was more reserved and irritable, said that he knew that his wife dealt with this fear, but he worried that their children were being negatively affected by it. During thunderstorms, the children were probably experiencing reduced oxytocin effects on their fear systems and reduced trust. Even though the mother was able to cope, she might have been better served by trying a cognitive intervention. But she was too ashamed of her seemingly irrational fear to seek help. If she had understood that her excessive amygdala activation was probably affecting the attachment circuits in her children, however, she might have decided to get the help she needed to move past her fear—to the benefit of herself and her entire family.

"You're always so sensitive to criticism"

Earlier in this chapter, we saw that attachment may be secure or insecure, and that insecure attachment manifests as anxiety or avoidance. We also saw that many of the influences on attachment occur early in life and that interaction between hormones and the brain may set the stage for brain responses to different situations later in life. The amygdala, a critical part of the fear circuit, is also affected by trust, which significantly reduces its activation. But what do we know about these different attachment styles and their consequences? Why do people become anxious or avoidant? How are their brains different?

In one study, twenty women participated in a functional MRI experiment in which they thought about—and were asked at a later time to stop thinking about—various relationship scenarios. When they thought about negative scenarios (conflict, breakup, the death of the partner), their level of attachment anxiety was positively correlated with activation in emotion-related areas of the brain (for example, the anterior temporal pole, which is implicated in sadness) and inversely correlated with activation in a region associated with emotion regulation (the orbitofrontal cortex). That is, as they became more and more anxious, the part of the brain that regulates emotions activated less and less. If we cannot regulate our emotions, we tend to feel less in control, making anxiety worse.

This suggests that anxious people react more strongly than nonanxious people to thoughts of loss, and that these negative thoughts spiral out of control since the anxiety interferes with normal brain functioning that would usually suppress negative thoughts. Participants who were highly avoidant also could not use conscious cognitive techniques to turn down the activation in two brain regions (the subcallosal cingulate cortex and the lateral prefrontal cortex), unlike less-avoidant participants. These are among the first findings showing that being anxious affects your brain's ability to control your emotions.

Simply put, being anxious or avoidant sets up a cascade of negative thoughts that cannot be turned off, whereas secure attachment helps to turn off negative thoughts when they occur. This knowledge has applicability in a number of situations. One is if you are afraid that your partner might leave the relationship. Rather than focusing on your fears of this loss, try to understand that giving in to anxiety or avoidance will just force you to focus on negative things. Here, you have to do the equivalent of a mental workout—force your brain to turn off those negative currents. Focus on positive ideas, or focus on thinking about the security that you do have in your life or your relationships. For example, you could write down what aspects of your life are secure. Do you have all four limbs? A working heart? The capacity to survive on your own? A college degree? Friends who love you? Family support? Whatever you can come up with will help to balance out the way your brain functions. I call this part of the mental workout the stepping-back approach. It's effectively a time-out to get your positive game (and your brain) back on track.

Getting to your positive game by just forcing yourself to focus on positive things does not automatically turn on positive emotions in your brain. Sometimes, even being told positive things has no real effect. One brain imaging study looked at whether the brains of secure and anxious individuals differ with regard to positive feedback and found that the brains of people who are anxious about attachment do not register smiling faces as positive feedback as much as they do in people who are secure about their attachments. Two brain regions, the ventral tegmental area and the striatum (the reward centers in the brain), do not activate sufficiently in response to positive feedback in anxious individuals who fear attachment. Also, the left amygdala activates more in anxious people when they perceive angry faces associated with negative feedback, and the degree of the amygdala activation correlates with the degree of anxiousness. We can take this to mean that the more anxious you are about attachment, the more your brain will be hypersensitive to negative feedback and less sensitive to positive feedback. This is a very important finding, because it underscores the idea that if you feel anxious about your relationships, you should take a step back before you respond to either positive or negative feedback. The longer a relationship has continued, the more likely it is that you will be able to experience the depth of your own responses, and many people who hop in and out of relationships are victims of their own anxiety.

Another study confirmed these findings by showing that unresolved attachment—a type of attachment usually associated with significant unresolved loss, abuse, or trauma—activates the amygdala, thereby proving that fear is an integral part of unresolved attachment. It is imperative at a personal and social level for us to relieve ourselves of this fear.

Socially, a parallel can be seen in people who are prompted to leave their home countries out of fear. The increased amygdala activation they experience triggers the fight-or-flight reaction, making them flee because attachment has not formed. When people who have the ability to leave instead remain in their countries despite being afraid, it is because their brains are less sensitive to those fears, enabling them to register those fears less intensely. This may be either helpful or hurtful. Being securely attached is only part of the picture. You don't want to be securely attached to a disaster. Thus, although secure attachment may be appropriate in some cases, it is never helpful as a generalized way of being.

The same principle applies to our relationships at work and at home. If we feel afraid of being in a relationship, the resulting anxiety and amygdala activation will make it very difficult to stay in that relationship. This is important to recognize because people often rationalize about why they have to leave rather than confronting their fears and amygdala activation. Remember, *reason* is somewhat irrelevant when fear and anxiety kick in, because your brain will make up reasons to justify those fears. It is imperative to break this vicious cycle and reduce the fear, and to understand your attachment behavior prior to leaving a relationship. Discomfort in a relationship is not a reason to leave. It is a sign that fear circuits have been activated, and at that time, all your brain can instruct you to do is to leave. Any "thinking" you do at this point will only make up reasons to leave in order to reduce your anxiety about attachment. That is why secure relationships that permit growth involve two people who are dedicated at the most fundamental level to always working things out and staying the course. Partial commitments always fail. In my experience, just sitting tight when there is no solution to a problem readily at hand often allows the solution that is needed to form, especially if you are wholeheartedly present.

When fear disrupts attachment, it activates the amygdala, which prevents the development of trust and attachment. It also activates the regions that it connects with, such as the brain stem. One experiment showed that this latter activation may lead to a person being constantly hyperactivated, especially under stressful conditions. Although most people are activated when experiencing stress, in attachment-anxious individuals the response to stress is magnified, making it difficult for them to stay in relationships. This explains why during times of financial crisis, family stress, or advancing age, people consider leaving their spouses or loved ones. The world becomes like a dangerous forest and the desire to run increases.

We tend to remember what we focus on, as well as what makes the biggest impact on us. Not only does anxiety block out positive feelings, it also blocks positive memories. Once a disagreement begins, anxiety mounts more and more, and the brain's decision making is strongly biased toward the negative. In this state, we simply do not have all of the information that is required to make a good decision when we are anxious about attachment, and we should always strive to consciously consider this during our decision-making process. (That's why thinking about leaving a relationship when you are irritated with a partner over financial troubles or some other anxiety-provoking situation is not a good idea.)

Positive emotions communicated by others (whether remembered from the past or experienced in the present) are not registered by the brain when people are anxious. This may explain the confusion that some people feel when their partners or colleagues appear to be unresponsive to positive input. It is not that they want to ignore the good feeling, but that the brain's positive emotion regions simply do not activate in the way that they are expected to. When the amygdala is too activated by anxiety and fear, it may stop any memories from arising from the parahippocampal gyrus, to which it is closely connected. If you look for something through a lens of fear, you will pick up only fear-related things. If you look for something through a lens of hope, you will pick up hopeful things.

I worked with one couple that consisted of a maverick husband who loved his wife intensely and a wife who had a history of being abandoned. No matter how much he professed his love for her, she insisted that he would leave her. She was very invested in this fear, and what she did not see was that she became part of a vicious cycle. They had an unusual relationship: They had both had several affairs and brief sexual encounters with others, but they were dedicated to being together. Whereas she discounted her own affairs as reactions to his inevitable leaving, she paid attention to his admissions as signs that he would leave her. She would drink and use drugs excessively, and when he talked to her about this, she would insult him to the point that he could not even be in her presence, and then she would accuse him of trying to leave her. In her case, her amygdala (the source of her fear) suppressed any positive experiences (they had three children, had been together for twenty years, and had survived numerous affairs and were still in love with each other) and effectively forced her memory centers to recall only negative ideas. When he traveled for business, her anxiety would increase and she would either have affairs or throw a tantrum when he returned. Both people had traits of anxious attachment, and their marriage was an attempt to create security, but again, instead of focusing on the security, once they got married, the anxiety became the emotion that determined how they lived.

"So what?" you may say. How does it help us to know that fear and anxiety disrupt attachment and create anxious attachment styles and that this anxiety then reduces the brain's ability to register and recall positive events? I would say that if you find yourself in a relationship where you are anxious about your partner's behavior, you should first ask yourself whether this anxiety is about your partner only or if it is, as I would suspect, more about both of you. Talk to your partner about how this anxiety in both of you may be causing anxiety in the other, and early on, try to establish a set of clues that will alert you and your partner that the relationship is being set up to confirm the worst fears of both. Recognize that much of this is biologically wired in your brain, and work on trusting rather than on focusing on your anxiety about betrayal.

Overcoming Fear That Underlies Attachment: The MAP-CHANGE Approach

As in the previous chapters, let us now examine the approach that you can use to navigate successful attachments.

Meditation

Meditation may help us reorganize our attachment styles for the following reasons:

1. It helps to decrease the anxiety that results from paying attention to the fears that underlie insecure attachment styles.

2. It helps to redirect your attention toward developing a secure attachment style.
3. It allows for a stronger connection with the transcendental self and decreases the ego-related distress that we have seen can be associated with exaggerating the pain and suffering in our attachments.
4. It may decrease blood flow through old pathways, depriving nourishment to the pathways related to insecure attachment styles.

As discussed, oxytocin reduces fear and promotes secure attachment. A few studies have suggested that meditation enhances the effects of oxytocin, thereby enhancing trust and stimulating secure attachments. In fact, one study showed that when meditation and yoga were combined prior to childbirth, less oxytocin was needed to stimulate labor. These specific effects are in addition to the increased mindfulness and reduced anxiety noted in earlier chapters to result from meditation. Meditation has also been shown to improve attention and sleep, both of which are adversely affected in those with an insecure attachment style.

Attention

Redirecting your attention is a critical variable in learning how to change fear into secure attachment. Essentially, if you ignore the fear and train your brain to automatically attend to positive versions of your attachment-related fears, you will be able to diminish fear. Remember, attention is literally food for thought. What you attend to will grow.

1. Review the table on the opposite page to see if any of the "old frames" of thinking that you currently hold can be changed and then practice reframing them by intensely concentrating on the "new frame" every day. Then write down three old frames every month and practice three new frames to counteract them.

Old Frame	New Frame
I am never going to find the right person to share my life.	My new mental frames will bring the right person to me. I must remember that even though people struggle to break records, when they do, they inspire other people to break those records because what was once considered impossible is now seen as possible. My possibility lens will change my frame to: Other people have found the right person, so I can too.
People disappoint me over and over again.	In my next relationship, I will get past disappointment to arrive at the truth.
I am afraid of being hurt again.	There will be many beautiful things in my next relationship, and I can endure the challenge of being hurt again. I must remember Babe Ruth, who hit the most home runs when he had the most strikeouts.
If I sense that I will get hurt again, I am going to leave the relationship early.	If I sense that I will get hurt again, I will address it with my partner and ask him or her to keep in mind that my first few responses will be transferential (colored by my past) and not necessarily about him or her.
Conflict distances me from my partner.	Conflict is a sign that we have another hill to climb before we get to the other side.
I can't bear the thought of losing someone again.	I must learn to respect and love my sadness as much as I love my happiness. They are both feelings that come from me and mean something. Rather than judging my sadness, I will see it as a sign of the need for further self-development.
I just can't get past this roadblock in the relationship.	My partner might want to hurt me so I can understand the pain of his or her hurt. What if I reflect on this?
Every time I get close to asking someone out on a date, I cop out.	Whenever I ask someone out on a date over the next few months, I will think of the period as being like the first few months of working out, remembering that I will get better and better as I get myself in shape.
I am anxious about attachment.	Everybody has some degree of anxiety about attachment. I will remember that some have more than others, and that it is not always visible.
I hate my partner.	I will feel better when I relieve myself of the burden of hate by focusing on what I need to develop in myself.

2. Rather than focusing on the anxiety-inducing elements of the relationship, focus on the calm aspects of your connection. Consciously practice calling to mind one positive aspect of your relationship every week. Write it down. Then look at it, take it in, and practice remembering it when you can. Do not force the issue. Just allow yourself to remember it when this thought comes up. It will gradually make its way to your unconscious.
3. Dream about new scenarios that may seem out of reach right now. Think of them as internal maps that you will construct to guide your brain. Draw out a map of the relationship of your dreams with your current partner or create a story about how you will meet the person of your dreams. Repeat this exercise until you feel deeply connected with the story you tell yourself. Countless examples show that the first step in obtaining is believing, and that the second step is allowing your brain to do what you cannot consciously think of by using its unconscious powers and your vision for direction.

   Here are some examples.

	Critical Event
January	My partner will learn to focus on and love new things about me because I will focus on these things about myself.
February	My partner will feel a strong desire for me as I become quieter internally with meditation.
March	My partner will want to spend much more time with me as I come to see myself as interesting.
April	My partner will become sexually closer to me and be able to integrate sexuality and love and not see me as a source of satisfaction, but rather as a source of love energy that can be shared.
May	My partner will want us to move in together or buy a place together because the idea of being together will be far more attractive than the idea of continuing to be separate.
June	My partner and I will develop creative interests that will keep us both engaged and interested in an authentic way.

Now, this is a good six-month plan. When I propose this approach to my clients, some people tell me that it sounds delusional and ignores the problems that will arise. Then, when they try out the idea, they actually experience problems, because when you expect problems—when you feed them—they will occur. Do not give up if this exercise seems impossible at first. It will definitely feel out of reach to your conscious brain.

4. Write down three positive things about yourself once every week and reread them every day without forcing yourself to remember them. Take in their positive truth and let it nourish your brain circuits by opening up these new and enhanced ways of thinking. If you often think about your past negatively, write down one positive thing about your past every week and look at it daily. If you do this for three months, you will see how powerful this exercise is.
5. When you next are thinking and feeling negative, ask yourself what lens you are using: hope or fear? Then immediately change to the lens of hope. Practice this habit repeatedly and your life will change.

Reframe your fears as things that you will overcome. This stimulates the ACC, which monitors for fear and, in its role as an attentional center, redirects your attention away from that fear and toward the solutions offered with the techniques above. If you can't just change your focus of attention, then use your fear to help you formulate what you want to change. For example, if you decide that you want to meet more people, rather than saying, "I'm never going to find the person I want," experiment with alternative approaches, such as thinking of three completely different people whom you might like to be with and where you might meet them. You will be surprised by how informative this exercise can be. When I once asked a woman who was looking for a relationship what her ideal man was like, she said, "Someone who I can bring to the family barbecue, who would get along with my kids, who would be loving and kind, and who would cook for me." I then asked her to define a completely different kind of man whom she also would like, and she replied, "A guy who has sophisticated taste in music and who likes going to the ballet, but is not effeminate." When she said this, she suddenly realized that she avoided going to the ballet to meet people because she automatically assumed that all the men there would be too effeminate. The next guy she dated was someone she met at the ballet. And he barbecued, too!

These are some of the attentional exercises that will guide you through difficult situations related to relationships. What other tools can help you create the change that you want in your life?

Psychological Tools

1. Closing yourself off from the world is deleterious as a habit of living. As an occasional respite, it is fine, but as a habit, it challenges the social parts of your brain (and body). Always make an effort to be around people at least once a week. If you have friends, spend time with them. Or look for a club or online community that feels safe to connect with and use it to meet people. Socialize with people at work at least during your lunch breaks or around the watercooler. If you are at home, perhaps you could set up a community of househusbands or housewives to spend time with. The world is bustling with people. Choosing to be alone is harmful to your mind and your body.
2. In order to get a sense of what kind of attachment behavior you exhibit in life, complete the five-minute questionnaire posted at www.web-research-design.net/cgi-bin/crq/crq.pl.
3. If you are a mother, recognize that your own amygdala is going to have heightened activation due to concern about your child. This may influence your feelings about and responses to your spouse or partner, who in turn may find it difficult to tolerate your anxiety. Therefore, make a conscious effort to separate your concern about your child from your

reaction to your spouse or partner. Also, remember that your brain's reaction to your baby is unique, as is your baby's reaction to you. Do not expect that other people (even your spouse) will see things as you see them. Use this information to prevent a fight the next time one is about to begin. When you get to the point of saying, "We just don't see eye to eye," stop and recognize that you are stating the obvious. We rarely do. This is something that you can even laugh about and use to eventually help you recognize the limitations of our existence as humans. We expect consistency and agreement from others when we should be looking for them from ourselves.

4. While concern about a child is protective, this anxiety can get out of control for you and your child. Don't keep your concerns online. Rather, recognize that you may be "addicted" to concern and that it may be affecting your own and your baby's brains in negative ways. Action usually dispels the anxiety of concern. Most concern is anticipatory. Stay in the present and address what you need to and the anxiety will be gone. A teacher of mine once said, "The substance of your future is the present. Invest in the present and the future will grow exponentially. Every time the 'moment' slips away from you, bring yourself back to the present."
5. Remember that change is uncomfortable: You may be inclined to choose what you fear because it is familiar and makes you feel like it is impossible to fall, but you are then also giving up a chance to fly. If you remain afraid and avoid attachment, it may be deleterious to your physical and emotional health.

It is amazing that so many of us share the same fears, yet we all worry that others will judge us for these feelings. Who can blame us for wanting approval? Yet it is this very desire for approval that often leads us to feelings of alienation. At any point in time, we are most likely to be happy if we are free of an inner voice that is "observing" us critically. Our brains make us believe that this inner voice is actually an "outer voice" of judgment. If we can get rid of this inner voice, there will be no outer voice.

So, how do we do this? Here are a few key things to remember.

1. Practice being comfortable with being alone. Go out alone to a bar or restaurant. Go out alone to a movie. When you start to feel self-conscious, ask yourself, "Why should I feel like I belong here less than anyone else?" If you start to imagine that you know what other people are thinking, ask yourself, "Is it them or is it me?" Assume that it is you and hold on to your equal ownership of the world, just as everyone around you does.

   Focus on giving yourself more freedom: Somehow, by the time people become adults, they lose track of their childhood dreams of freedom. Most of us have our own definitions of freedom: Some of us think of it as financial freedom, others as spiritual freedom. Mostly, we need to connect this idea to actions in our lives. When did you last seek to tolerate your aloneness to give yourself the freedom of ideas? Have you been to a movie recently? Taken a walk in the park? Responded to a spontaneous feeling to meet with friends? Spoiled yourself by getting someone to care for the children as a way of taking care of yourself for one day?
2. Make some positive relationship rules and stick by them. One good one is that all fights have to be resolved before you go to sleep or cannot last more than twenty-four hours. This is an effective way to incorporate forgiveness as a part of your style of relating. Remember that forgiveness does not have to be based on reason. It is an act of generosity and is based on a deep understanding of the imperfection of being human. In my experience, this is one of the main ingredients present in successful long-term relationships. Another good rule is not to fight while hungry. Doing so can lead you to say things

that have more to do with hypoglycemia than the relationship.

3. Ask yourself if you are trying too hard in the relationship. Very often, we become martyrs in our relationships, not realizing that our "giving" is just a form of justifying why the relationship will not work. Giving is a complicated action. When we give knowing that it is going to create guilt in someone else, we should stop and ask ourselves what our intentions are. If we intend to express love and generosity and it results in guilt as a consequence, then you can be more comfortable giving. If, however, you are just giving and feeling increasingly disappointed, ask yourself if you are just letting the disappointment build up, then talk about things with your partner before you make the situation too difficult to address.
4. Fear and trust work hand in hand in the human brain. When one is dominant, the other is less present. Most of us have an idea of how we'd like our relationships to be. As a result, we go out of our way to create routines that make us feel safe. While some routines are helpful for the familiarity they create, others are setups for disappointment. Whenever you find yourself irritated about a break in a routine, stop and ask yourself what your underlying assumptions are. Recognize that the biggest problem is that you are unconsciously catastrophizing, probably because the break in routine is activating an anxious attachment style. Realize that you can choose to do something meaningful rather than moping around because your routine has changed.

Conclusion

Forging the key to a caged heart requires melting ironclad fear into more secure attachment behaviors. Psychological and brain research shows us that we have built-in biases about what we attend to and what we remember when we are anxious about attachment or avoid it. Melting your fears requires an in-depth understanding of the types of fear that underlie insecure attachments—such as fear of rejection or fear of abandonment—and then introducing insight into discussions with loved ones and taking ourselves and others less seriously by using forgiveness and reframing to understand our own vulnerabilities.

[6]

Fear and Prejudice

The Biology of Bigotry

We are each burdened with prejudice; against the poor or the rich, the smart or the slow, the gaunt or the obese. It is natural to develop prejudices. It is noble to rise above them.

—**Unknown**

To have prejudices, or to be a bigot, is to be intolerant of other people's race, gender, appearance, opinion, lifestyle, or identity. Such intolerance would not be a problem if we lived in a homogeneous society, but our world is diverse, populated by many different kinds of people. How, then, do we balance our personal preferences—which result from a phenomenon that social scientists suggest is most likely innate—with the fact that we have to live among other people, and that our optimal survival relies on tolerating differences? Is it possible to challenge—or change—what appears to be innate in our thinking in order to create a more harmonious world?

The first step in trying to understand prejudice is to look at the core of intolerance. When prejudice represents a preference, it is less malignant than intolerance and an expression of a value that is held but not necessarily adhered to. In this state, it is possible for us to still live side by side with those who are different from us. Prejudice that reflects intolerance, in contrast, signifies the existence of many deleterious processes. Fear and prejudice are two sides of the same coin, the psychological and the biological. If we shine a flashlight into the dark corners of prejudice, we will meet the darting eyes of fear. This fear is a result of:

- Feeling ignorant and not wanting others to see this.
- Feeling afraid of being attacked for your views.
- Feeling threatened about the potential dissolution of your identity.
- Feeling that a particular essential item in life is in short supply and that others may take your share.
- Feeling afraid to look beyond the value and definition provided by superficial aspects of our identities to the less linear but oftentimes more important elements of being human.

It is my strong contention that discouraging the admission of prejudice has not been helpful to us as individuals or as a society. We still experience war, terrorism, economic downfalls, and massive erosions of the human spirit regardless of how prohibited these feelings are. Of course, I do not believe that prejudices of action should be allowed, either. Rather, I believe that handling the issue of prejudice requires a more nuanced approach that honors the authenticity of our fears while simultaneously providing a context for new learning.

I recently watched a reality TV dating show in which the bachelors—who were unusually close to and dependent upon their mothers—allowed their mothers to help them choose women to date. One of the mothers revealed on camera that she did not want an African American woman, a Jewish woman, or any type of woman other than a good Catholic girl for her son—a wife who would iron and clean and continue to provide the comforts that she had provided as a good Catholic mother. Of course, the other women on the show, shocked by her overt expression of preference, called her a racist.

I wondered if it was fair to call her a racist. Was she simply afraid that her son wouldn't be happy if he chose a lifestyle that didn't reflect her experience of family life? What if someone could sit down with this woman and acknowledge the flaws in her perspective, but also try to understand her fears? Would it be possible to teach her new perspectives? How is her preference for her son's wife to be Catholic different from that of a father wanting his daughter to marry a businessman instead of a blue-collar worker? Certain cases of preference have adverse effects on society that need to be taken into consideration, but forcing people to express different views in private and in public may not help us meet the goal of fairness for all. In this chapter, we will explore the biology and psychology of prejudice and how fear relates to it.

Understanding Racial Prejudice

To most of us, the idea of being prejudiced is abominable. We like to think of ourselves as fair, objective people who make rational decisions based on what we know and what we think. And we believe this with certainty.

There are different levels of overtness of racial prejudice. The term *racial microaggression* refers to subtle but impactful attitudes toward people of minority races. For example, a study that examined racial microaggression directed toward Asian Americans identified many themes. These included assumptions that Asian people are intelligent, that Asian women are exotic, and, in the most extreme cases, that there are no differences at all among Asian Americans of different ethnicities. These gross generalizations ignore the diversity inherent within this population and typecast Asian Americans. For people who generalize, a fear of Asians, as in this example, represents a fear of the unknown. Many people would deny that these prejudices impact how they think or act, and this may be true. But does it impact their innermost thoughts and feelings, which are largely beyond conscious control?

When you think about your own prejudices, do you speak truthfully about your innermost beliefs? Are you aware of them? Is there a difference between what we say and our most deeply held prejudices, and can we detect these differences? Extensive research on this subject has shown that two scales—the Modern Racism Scale and the Implicit Association Test (IAT)—tap into two different levels of prejudice. The Modern Racism Scale measures and scores what you say, while the IAT measures and scores your unconscious beliefs. You can see for yourself how this is done by going to https://implicit.harvard.edu/implicit/demo/selectatest.html, where tests probing your implicit preferences for light or dark skin, race, age, weight, gender, religion, and other categories are posted.

In the late 1990s, researchers were able to show that the IAT is sensitive to picking up differences between conscious and unconscious ideas about race. That is, the IAT is able to show that we have automatic stereotypical associations about skin color, even when we consciously disavow them. A study conducted with white students from the University of Washington showed that both male and female white participants associated more white people with positive ideas than black people with these same positive ideas. This same test was also conducted with groups of Korean American and Japanese American students, and again, each subgroup showed a greater association of positive traits with its own ethnicity. Furthermore, this study also showed that the IAT results were completely different from the participants' explicitly disavowed prejudices. This was pretty powerful information, because it gives us a means of accessing and understanding our innermost prejudices.

Aside from the IAT, there is also another way to look at implicit attitudes about race. By using electromyography (EMG) to measure activity in the smiling and frowning muscles of the face, researchers found that they could separate implicit and explicit attitudes about race. In one study of white college students who identified themselves as having a low level of prejudice, researchers found that EMG activity in the facial muscles increased at the cheek region (indicating smiling activity) when the participants viewed pictures of white people.

Interestingly, studies have also shown that when white people are asked to smile when viewing images of black people, they have a more favorable opinion of black people. This suggests that the act of smiling can actually disrupt the brain's automatic racial assessments. It may also explain, in part, why humor (or comic relief) is often such an effective vehicle for communicating racial and cultural differences (notably in stand-up comedy).

A question that emerged from these studies detecting unconscious racial biases was how early in our lives these biases are learned. In one study, researchers examined the racial preferences of six-year-olds, ten-year-olds, and adults and found that preferences for white people develop in white children as early as six years of age, and that both implicit and explicit measurements of this bias match. By age ten, however, we begin to see some divergence, with greater implicit than explicit racism present until adulthood, when a complete dissociation between the two takes place.

What we think overtly and what we say about prejudice may be the same, but our conscious thoughts and attitudes may not match our unconscious biases. Why would the conscious and unconscious brains carry different kinds of information? Here again, fear raises its ugly head.

Because we fear that we will be ostracized for or made to feel guilty about our innermost biases, our brains protect us by making sure that these controversial thoughts never make it to the conscious level. The problem with this is that, as a result, we never gain access to these thoughts—and if we don't gain access to them, we don't have an opportunity to rewire our brains to match what we explicitly think and feel. There are many people who do not wish to be racist but are. Fear keeps this divide alive and leads to many prejudicial actions. Some studies have shown that the more highly educated a person is, the less racist they are. But I question whether education can truly have an impact on our unconscious beliefs, which are formed early in life.

If we are to truly understand and change our prejudices, we have to deeply explore how bias is held in our brains. Our fear of being found out sometimes causes us to experience conscious and unconscious levels of shame and guilt. I have to admit that when President Barack Obama was elected, I was a bit surprised by the enthusiasm with which our diverse country embraced him. Although I understood that his victory represented new hope for the United States, relief about the end of the

George W. Bush presidency, and a genuine happiness about his policies, I couldn't help wondering how much of this zealous enthusiasm was due to the relief of both conscious and unconscious guilt over not having previously elected a nonwhite president. On that day, a white friend of mine whom I love dearly wrote, "Today is an amazing day. We have broken a field of prejudice that could assist all of humanity to do the same." While this resonated with me, it also helped me understand that many people may have experienced a sense of relief from their internal tension over their unconscious biases and conscious intellectual thoughts.

If this guilt is so burdensome, why would our brains hold on to bias in the first place?

The Toxic Sweetness of Prejudice:
How Racism Serves Us

At a psychological level, for our brains to maintain unconscious biases about race, there must be some intrinsic need for us to hold on to these thoughts. Although there is no clearly defined explanation for this, I believe there are several possible reasons.

First, racist ideas protect us from knowing our true selves. If we focus on the exterior, we never have to focus on the interior. If we think we are different from others, we can define our self-worth according to these external differences rather than recognizing and acknowledging our sameness. Knowing our true selves is intimidating because it involves navigating uncertain terrain for which there are no labels. The old Buddhist lesson that pointing at the moon is different from being on the moon applies here. When we label ourselves, we are really just pointing at ourselves and not living as ourselves. To live as ourselves requires knowing how to live without the external identifiers and labels, and it is threatening to our egos. Racism creates a label, and in that way it prevents us from having to deal with who we truly are.

Another theory is that racist ideas protect us from fears of merging. If we focus on how we are different, this theory says, we do not have to deal with merging with other people. If we recognize our similarities, we then have to deal with channeling a consciousness much more vast than the one we think we own. This is frightening. There is something crushing to the ego about believing that we are all one. We can see this reflected in the arbitrary divisions of land on a world map. Just look at the boundaries we have created to make something our own, despite the inner desire (through mediums like the Internet) to move beyond these boundaries and acknowledge that we are, in fact, connected. All of the technology that we have developed attests to the fact that, first and foremost, we crave human connection. Telephones, fax machines, and e-mail all facilitate connections from remote locations. But our egos trap us into living at the level of the perceived differences because of the feared anonymity of being "merged."

Racist ideas also allow us to bond with other members of the same race: When we distinguish ourselves from others, we can form a group or exclusive club. Without these subsets we are just one big society—and we have to face the fallacy of a world with borders. Racist ideas give us overt reasons to feel as though we are part of a group.

Racist ideas can also feed into a fear of contamination: Externally, we look different, and sometimes we have different habits and ways of upbringing. Rather than dealing with the discomfort caused by otherness, we choose to focus on what we are accustomed to and comfortable with. Indian people like spicy food. White people like steak and potatoes. What would we do without these classifications? The idea of not being separate means that we would have to merge with the biases we hold. The differences of others frighten us and feel threatening.

Differences also allow us to impose a sense of order, to divide people into categories. Race, like any other category, serves our need to organize things in ways we can understand. From South African apartheid to the genocides of Rwanda and the Holocaust, an obsession with categorizing people by race or ethnicity for the purpose of creating a nonthreatening social order underlies some of the darkest moments in history. We believe that we "know" ourselves better when we are all neatly labeled.

Racism can be an expression of man's need to dominate and have power, but at its separatist core, it does not take advantage of the power of all who are available. When we view the world through racial preferences, it allows us to create an overt context for focusing on similarities. Perceived commonalities unify members of a group and create a false sense of power that ignores how much more power could be had if everyone unified as one.

The Irony of Preference

A group of researchers conducted an experiment in which white participants took the IAT and then discussed race relations with a black or white partner. The white participants who scored highest on the IAT (that is, the most racially prejudiced subjects) received the most positive feedback from black participants (but interestingly, not from other white participants). Black participants reported that the more racially biased whites were more engaging. That is, black participants were more interested in racist whites. This finding is highly controversial, but it is possible that identifying with (and therefore preferring) an aggressor may occur as a result of needing to feel accepted by that aggressor. A similar phenomenon can be observed with Stockholm syndrome, in which hostages express positive feelings toward their captors.

It is a standing joke that having a friend of a different race qualifies a person as "not racist" ("I have a friend who is black/Asian/Indian—I can't be racist!"). Although this seems absurd on the surface, a 2004 study actually supports this idea. When people have a friend of a particular ethnicity, they are less likely to show even implicit biases on the IAT. This supports my belief that familiarity reduces fear—and thus prejudice—because our biases come from deeply rooted fears based on surface inferences rather than a deeper understanding of people.

For people of mixed race, the question of cultural identity is often a struggle. Do Americans with one Asian and one non-Asian parent identify with Asian or American culture? How about Americans with one Mexican and one non-Mexican parent? One group of researchers used the IAT to investigate whether mixed-race individuals experienced cultural preferences and found that the majority of study participants identified with both of their genetic cultures. This suggests that cultural homogeneity in explicit responses (which does not exist in implicit testing) may be a defense against being singled out.

We often choose familiarity over the unfamiliar because the unfamiliar is threatening and usually is accompanied by a host of learned responses. Even if the unfamiliar is preferable, we may reject it because it creates too much fear. Think of how relevant this may be to choices that you have made in your own life, when it came to choosing a life partner or a job, for example. It is important to be vigilant about our initial assessments because "automatic" feelings do not necessarily indicate what is best for us—they just acknowledge what we are familiar with.

The amygdala is involved in implicit racism, as are other brain regions. One study that looked at racism's effect in the frontal cortex found that when research subjects implicitly made biased associations with regard to gender or race, the ACC and part of the prefrontal cortex activated more, whereas when they did not have these implicit biases, the dorsolateral prefrontal cortex (DLPFC) was activated. The ACC, as you remember, is an error monitor in the brain and is intimately involved in attention. It fires excessively when the amygdala activates and disturbs attention. The ACC's greater activation with implicit biases is evidence that it is detecting an error in its comparison of intrinsic and explicit attitudes. The DLPFC is involved in short-term memory, and its increased activation against the stereotype suggests that active memories called into short-term memory may decrease our intrinsic biases. Thus, if we can remind ourselves of recent positive memories instead of negative memories, we may be more likely to negate bias. This may apply not just to race, but also to interpersonal situations in which people would benefit from remembering positive rather than negative experiences.

Can We Stop Racism with Effort?

Some studies have shown that, like the smiling effect, if an individual focuses on specific counterstereotypical thoughts when he or she comes into contact with an object of prejudice, automatic stereotyping is reduced. This implies that it may be possible to train yourself to alter long-held beliefs that may have become ingrained in your life and actions. But in order for this "retraining" of the brain to succeed, people must strongly desire it—they have to really want to change their bias.

Research has suggested that nonracist people make more positive automatic associations than negative ones. There may be a fundamental difference in the way some people integrate new information. There are also subtle differences in how we address racism. One study showed that when whites are told of inequities that are framed as "white privilege," they are less responsive about redistributive policies and more threatened than when such issues are framed as "antiblack discrimination." At its most basic, this study illustrates that the privilege concept evokes threat and fear, and that this threat prevents action against intrinsic racism.

Four studies investigated how stereotype threat—the fear that you will reinforce a negative stereotype held about your race or ethnicity—produces racial distancing behavior. Researchers hypothesized that the threat of appearing racist may have the ironic effect of causing whites to distance themselves from black conversation partners. In the first study, white participants distanced themselves more from black partners when they were perceived as the "white racist" stereotype. In the second study, it was demonstrated that whites' interracial distancing behavior was not predicted by explicit or implicit prejudice. That is, the distancing behavior was likely due to feeling insulted by having been stereotyped rather than to having an intrinsic prejudice. In the third study, conceiving of interracial interactions as opportunities to learn led to fewer negative consequences of threat for whites than not recognizing them as such. And in the fourth study, researchers found that when whites have conscious access to their experience of stereotype threat, this awareness may decrease the feeling of threat and distance. This last finding was hopeful because it means that if people understand their reactions to being stereotyped, they have a greater chance of doing something about them. These studies elegantly show that the accusation of being racist does not encourage white people to be less racist, but the insight that they may react to being called racist helps them react less automatically, with more curiosity, and without defensiveness. When Nelson Mandela visited an Afrikaans university in South Africa in 1991, he addressed the crowd in Afrikaans. Afrikaans was regarded by black South Africans as the language of the oppressor. This was a remarkable example of how, when we want to reach out to people across racial or ethnic lines, expressing empathy and understanding is much more useful than denouncing the negative connotations of perceived differences.

One strategy practiced by many whites to regulate any appearance of prejudice during social interaction is to avoid talking about race or even acknowledging racial difference. Four experiments investigated what may lead to and result from this avoidance. The first study found that whites' acknowledgment of race was highly susceptible to normative pressure and most evident among individuals who were concerned about self-presentational aspects of appearing biased. This tendency was often counterproductive, however, because avoiding race during interracial interaction led to negative nonverbal behavior and a decreased capacity to exert inhibitory control over prejudice. Thus, avoidance of race did not make things better, it made them worse. Two studies examining white and black observers' impressions of color-blind behavior in simulated social interactions revealed divergent assessments of the actors' prejudice in situations where race was clearly relevant, but convergent assessments when race was less relevant. That is, black and white study participants had a more favorable attitude about color blindness when the race of the actor was not clear, but when it was, black participants felt less positive and were more skeptical. These studies show that avoiding talking about race may not help the interaction at hand. Although people may fear that pointing out a difference will feel accusatory to the "different" individual, avoiding the issue sends negative signals and makes it difficult to change prejudicial attitudes.

How Can We Reduce the Fear That Underlies Prejudice?

The MAP-CHANGE Approach

The MAP-CHANGE approach to reducing prejudice is less well studied than it is for other fear-related phenomena. The suggestions below may be helpful in understanding yourself and addressing your prejudices on a deep level.

Meditation

On an overt level, a deep contemplation of prejudice will likely reveal egoistic tendencies that we may hold because of our own insecurities. At a general level, we can use meditation to reduce our anxiety about losing our identity if we empathize with people. At a more basic level, the increases in heart rate that have been shown to coexist with the expression of bias may also be managed with meditation.

Perhaps the most exciting data on meditation as it relates to prejudice were found in a study that examined the brain changes that occur with empathy and compassion during meditation. This study showed that people who had practiced meditation for a longer time (experts) were much more compassionate than people who had practiced it less (novices) and that these differences involved increased activation of the amygdala, insula, and ACC. It appeared that the pain of others could be felt more deeply by expert meditators. The ACC probably activated more in response to their attending to the pain of others.

This study illustrates that meditation increases empathy, and that the increased sensitivity to the pain of others causes related changes in the brain. It may also explain why prejudice exists: It is easier to be biased than to experience someone else's pain. To me, this indicates that we have to be sensitive to the guilt and pain experienced by people who are prejudiced if we want this prejudice to change. This argument supports taking diplomatic and nonjudgmental approaches to prejudiced individuals, along with cultivating a sensitivity that society as a whole has to be interested in the well-being of the biased if the well-being of the victims of the biased is to be ensured.

Attention

Most of the studies on effort as an intervention to change racism showed that effort does, in fact, decrease prejudice. Most people give up after their first attempt, but repeated efforts are more likely to be successful.

Psychological Tools

How can we encourage the admission and exploration of prejudice in work and social situations? Here are a few examples of things we can do.

1. In diversity training, employees can learn not just that different cultures have different habits in such things as eating and dressing, but that there are also numerous common goals that different cultures can achieve. Recently at my workplace, a secretary went out to buy lunch and brought back Chinese food. The other secretary, who was of the same race, reprimanded her for eating in the conference room, commenting that she wouldn't mind if her co-worker were eating American food, but that Chinese food made the whole office smell bad. I found this a very difficult situation because I often prefer fragrant to nonfragrant food, and I wondered if she would have had the same reaction to tuna, egg salad, or Caesar salad dressing. Still, there was a part of me that understood how abrasive strong smells can be in an office. Even in myself, I find these profound hypocrisies.

   Research related to diversity training also suggests that intergroup interaction may help people come to understand each other better. This exposure is especially effective when it occurs early in life, so it is important to make sure that your children interact with people of all races to help them eliminate their prejudices and to help them grow into less biased adults.

2. Remember that conscious and unconscious biases do not correlate. Whether the biases are based on race, gender, or sexual orientation, it is important to realize that what we think may not be what we feel. This may occur because when we are prejudiced, we may feel so guilty about or afraid of this that we have to hide our innermost feelings and, thus, keep these feelings in the unconscious. The basic idea here is that it has to be socially acceptable to talk about biases so we can then work to overcome them. Being open in trusting situations may help us to confront our biases and work with them more effectively.
3. Start antiprejudice efforts early. However, I personally am not fond of "anti" anything, and I find that "anti" campaigns are not as successful as "pro" campaigns. So, although I think that the effort to reteach is important, I believe that it is much more important to learn to eliminate prejudice through promoting self-acceptance, less guilt, and appreciation of others. Whether taught by a teacher, parent, or public person in an influential role, it is clear from this research that efforts to prevent prejudice need to start early in life if we hope to transform society.
4. Appearing to represent the mainstream can be nonthreatening and helpful at times. "When in Rome, do as the Romans do" has long been embraced as a sophisticated approach to navigating cultural differences, one that allows you to appreciate and celebrate the value of a different culture.

   I do not believe that this is always necessary, however. For example, I had dinner recently at a popular spot in New York City that serves American food. I asked for hot peppers and jalapeño peppers with my meal, and the friend I was with warned me that I would be culturally stereotyped. I told him that I simply wanted to enjoy my meal, and that I would be surprised if a restaurant of that caliber couldn't accommodate my request.

5. The media are notorious for fueling ideas about many different kinds of prejudice. These messages can be very influential, so it's important to be vigilant about your exposure to them.
6. If you are a victim of any form of prejudice, remember that prejudice arises from fear and familiarity decreases fear. The more open you can be in conversation about yourself and your ideas in a way that does not make people defensive, the more likely it is that people will come to know you. This idea is consistent with research that has shown that self-disclosure creates an atmosphere of empathy and trust and reduces bias and prejudice.

Role models play an important role in destigmatizing certain ideas. When you are positively regarded, you are in a much better position to eliminate prejudice, and this can usually be done by putting other people at ease by doing the job well or representing yourself with ease and nondefensiveness.

When I was chief resident in a training program, the residents complained to me that they were overworked. Rather than complaining to the staff that the residents were overworked, I compiled a list of ways in which residents' lives and performance were being affected by the workload and appealed to the empathy of the senior staff to think with me about ways to prevent this. The seniors were very sympathetic and lost the my-way-or-the-highway attitude after we talked about how people were being affected.

Remember that when we threaten self-esteem, we increase fear, which only increases bias. This relates to another piece of research discussed earlier in the chapter that revealed that the threat of appearing racist may have the ironic effect of causing whites to distance themselves from black conversation partners.

Conclusion

Prejudice and fear are intricately connected. By decreasing our own and others' fears, we can significantly reduce prejudice. Working with rather than against prejudice is often more fruitful. A combination of effort, understanding, openness, and reassurance can decrease fear and bias and help people see eye to eye and support each other. Furthermore, our own prejudices may signal unconscious fear and associated guilt as well. By excluding ourselves from a group, we risk harming ourselves through fear, guilt, and feeling threatened as a result of our own views. This can profoundly affect our ability to be successful.

[7]

How to Develop Emotional Superglue

Fear, Trauma, and Piecing Together the Human Psyche

Sometimes a breakdown can be the beginning of a kind of breakthrough, a way of living in advance through a trauma that prepares you for a future of radical transformation.

—**Cherríe Moraga**

The issue of trauma is central to our identities. Who we are is shaped by the experiences we have. When those experiences are traumatic, they inevitably influence the ways in which we speak, think, and act. What constitutes a traumatic experience differs from person to person. There is little doubt about the traumatic nature of events such as being a victim of a violent crime, abuse, or sexual assault; participating in military combat; and being in a physically traumatic accident. Other life experiences may be quite upsetting, but are less clearly defined as trauma: your first romantic breakup, leaving your parents' home as a young adult, going through a divorce, losing your job. Our experiences of events such as these differ depending on our coping mechanisms and the intensity of the situation. But regardless of the trauma, our outward reaction only hints at what's going on inside the brain.

I have counseled rape victims who are utterly devastated and unable to cope, and others who are shocked, but seemingly not traumatized. There is no one way or right way to react to trauma. While the person who appears to be mildly affected may seem better off initially, who is to say that a breakdown might not have been a more effective way of expressing and dealing with the incident in the long run?

Any person who has experienced any disappointment, sadness, or loss knows how unforgettable such experiences can be. Eventually, we may choose to move on—but do we, really? Can we ever really move on from an event that has become indelibly incorporated into our brains? One that has etched itself into our memory like initials in wet cement? The unforgettability of such traumas is twofold: They may register in your memory and always feel close at hand, coloring the way in which you see the world, or they may seep into your deeper memory (your unconscious memory), but reappear at the slightest provocation.

Take the example of Jeanine, a fifty-year-old divorced woman of considerable charm and beauty. Jeanine had never been able to find a man with whom she could settle down despite having numerous relationships. She had divorced her husband because he was too boring for her, and she had looked upon her single life as an opportunity to "do this over, but do it right this time." Yet, regardless of how much any man loved her, and despite her devotion and dedication, no one ever committed to her. Gradually, she began to feel that she would never be able to attract someone who would want to be with her. Each disappointment was anchored in her memory, and these accumulated memories formed an unconscious paradigm in her mind: "Why am I not worth it?"

Jeanine had been sexually abused repeatedly when she was fifteen by an uncle who had helped to raise her. She was reluctant to use the term *abuse,* however, because she enjoyed his attention and the initial thrills of his touch in the secrecy of his bedroom. When her aunt began to suspect what was going on, her uncle spoke negatively about Jeanine in front of his wife and talked directly with Jeanine less frequently. At the tender age of eighteen, she ran away with a romantic acquaintance to Rio, where she was stopped at the border. When her uncle found out that she had been caught, she had to return home. These early experiences had colored the filter through which she viewed men and life.

Although she was not one to overtly hold any resentment, and she had very admirably overcome these adversities with a good sense of humor, a life full of friends, and a stable job, Jeanine held deep within her memory her initial experiences with men: "Do not get too close, because you will be used," and "If you try to get what you want, you will be stopped." These messages had become a part of her memory, and memories are the filters through which we live life. Jeanine's biggest challenge was that she had never confronted her fears. Deep down, she was afraid that she was a bad person and a sexually promiscuous woman, and she did not want to see this any more clearly.

Every time Jeanine met a man, these memories would seep into her behavior, and eventually these men would pick up on it. They would become confused, and they often left on good terms because there was nothing they could actually complain about. Both she and they were unaware of how these past traumas had set up fears in Jeanine's brain that inevitably caused the men to also become afraid and then to want out of the relationship.

The traumas we experience in life may have consequences we are entirely conscious of, but we should never assume that we have fully grasped the unconscious impact of these events until we have examined them. The impact is sometimes obvious, but most times subtle, and grappling with these traumas requires grappling with the fears that have become stimulated on account of them.

Every bad situation sets up the brain to anticipate any similar bad situation. While this is protective, it is also obstructive when the fear system becomes too automatic and nonspecific. It is not helpful if, for several years after a car accident, a woman develops panic attacks whenever she is in a car. Or when, after being mugged at night, a man is too afraid to walk after dark again. Caution is helpful. Too much caution is destructive and can severely limit your life.

Any trauma, then, causes a disruption of a person's life, not just in terms of what we see, but also at the level of the brain. In this chapter, we will take a closer look at what happens in the brains of traumatized individuals, how this relates to fear, and what we can do about this once we understand the potential impact of trauma in our lives. We will explore how people like Jeanine can come to know the inner workings of their minds and what they can do about them.

The Shattering Effect:
A Look Inside a Child's Brain

When researchers look at the brains of children who have been maltreated, it appears that the major structural problem lies in the corpus callosum—the fiber tract that connects the right and left halves of the brain. This is the brain bridge. It appears that this connecting group of brain fibers is smaller in children who are mistreated or abused. The potential impact is substantial. The consequences of a broken bridge in a child include disconnection between thinking and feeling, loss of the sense of self, excessive worry, feeling as though something is missing (called the gap), and chronic fatigue syndrome.

Disconnection of Thinking and Feeling

Our brains rely on effective communication between both hemispheres. Thinking (a left hemisphere phenomenon) and feeling (a right hemisphere phenomenon) need to act in concert for us to make sensible decisions. If the connection between the brain's hemispheres is damaged, information from each hemisphere cannot cross the midline, and thinking and feeling are not integrated. The result is that people are disconnected from their feelings and they experience a sense of numbness. They feel as though they're fine when they are not. They only realize that they aren't okay when their lives begin to fall apart. Then they wonder, "Why is this happening?"

Even though they are not in touch with their feelings, the emotion or feeling circuits in the brains of people who have been traumatized are still active, they just don't consciously experience these emotions.

One of these feeling circuits is fear. When thinking and feeling are disconnected, fear cannot be reached or understood. Traumatized people cannot make sense of their fear. A child whose brain bridge has been damaged suffers from feelings of fear, but doesn't know why. These children seem restless for no apparent reason and often need to self-soothe because they feel so much internal unrest.

Loss of a Sense of Self

In his book *Descartes' Error,* neurologist Antonio Damasio explains how a sense of self is critically dependent on the integration of thinking and feeling, and that without this integration, our ability to make decisions is compromised. Emotions carry important information that can influence decisions. Without this information, we lack the fuel necessary to move others or ourselves.

Here is one example from my clinical experience. Sally was a Harvard sophomore whose parents had divorced when she was five. Her mother had left her father when he had one too many affairs. Sally blamed her father for her unhappy childhood. Her anger was so extreme that she couldn't deal with it consciously, so she ignored her feelings of rage.

When she began therapy at the age of nineteen, she ignored the fact that she never developed successful relationships despite the reality that she was strikingly beautiful, incredibly smart, and loving. Superficially, she liked herself for being "more like a guy" in that she was incredibly rational, always "not that emotional," and all of the other stereotypical characteristics that one associates with men. She had many guy friends to help her neutralize the immense fear that she had of her rage toward men.

She was completely cut off from her feelings of anger, although she was able to identify it superficially. She did not realize that this immense anger actually frightened her, and that the fear was what kept her disconnected from her emotional life. As a result, she was never open to dating, because when she started to develop feelings for someone, her fears about relationships with men became activated. So she put out a friendly vibe instead of a romantic one, and therefore struggled to attract romance to her life.

Her parents' divorce left her to cope with an incredible amount of anger, and she "chose" to ignore this by disconnecting her thinking and feeling. But did she really choose this? Or was her brain bridge damaged as a result of childhood trauma? In all likelihood, Sally probably did suffer damage to this part of her brain. Even as an intelligent Harvard student, she mocked the notion of connecting with her feelings, and she avoided taking any courses that required creativity.

Excessive Worry

The brain bridge has also been shown to play a role in worry. What is worry? Worry, as most people would describe it, is being unable to stop thinking about negative things. It is the brain's way of coming up with stories to continually occupy our minds. What most worriers do not realize is that these stories are not the actual issue; the underlying cause of these stories is the problem. When a child has been traumatized, the brain bridge is disrupted, and the child starts to develop worry stories to distract him- or herself from focusing on the traumatic experience. Worry is like a stuck record; it is akin to circuits that carry the flow of electricity because the electricity has nowhere else to go. Usually, thinking and feeling come together to make sense of the world, and this decreases worry. When the brain bridge is disrupted, however, the thinking circuits continually fire and are unable to quiet down.

Excessive worry is a sign that emotional information from the right hemisphere is trying to make it over to the left hemisphere, but can't. So the left, thinking hemisphere starts to look for stories to account for this absence. In fact, studies have shown that in order for us to think about threat, threatening information has to go from the right to the left hemisphere. In people who worry excessively, this crossing over via the brain bridge occurs much more slowly. Thus, children who are maltreated may also worry much more and may appear to be overly concerned about things that are beyond their control.

Ricky was a thirty-year-old man who was filled with emotion and an exquisite ability to think in the deepest ways, but he was unable to integrate his thoughts and feelings, which felt like two completely separate mental experiences to him. He had been sexually abused as a child, an event that he had pushed to the recesses of his unconscious thought. He wasn't constantly plagued by memories of it, and he did not feel that the experience affected his choices or relationships in any way.

Yet any time Ricky sought out romantic relationships, he found himself with sociopathic women or prostitutes—women who also were disconnected from their emotions—because it made him feel better about his own disconnection. In the rare instance when he was in a relationship with someone who was emotionally healthy or relatively self-assured, the woman posed an immense threat because she reminded him of the connection between both hemispheres that he had spent his life trying to avoid. Of course, this wasn't an intentional choice: He secretly grappled with the idea that he did not actually "feel" for people, and this compounded his fears of ever getting close to anyone.

When he was with lovers who were extremely emotional, he would have mixed feelings. Although he would sometimes enjoy it, he also found it difficult to cope with. He remembered having been sexually abused as a child by a man he knew, but he could not recall any specific details. Emotions exert a strong influence over memory. Strong emotions create strong memories—up to a point. If the emotion was immense fear or shame, the brain is less likely to want to recall this tornado to disrupt its otherwise peaceful existence.

Ricky had problems remembering the abuse because, in part, his emotions had crossed over very slowly from the right to the left side of his brain as a child, and his thinking and feeling had become increasingly disconnected. He had no idea of how to connect thinking and feeling. He felt as though his brain was going to explode.

Although Ricky knew about this disconnection within himself—he could identify it—knowing this was not enough for him. His self-esteem spoke for itself. He ran from each opportunity for a romantic relationship. For him, emotional, intellectual, and sexual intimacy needed to come from different individuals, because getting them from one person was too threatening.

The brain bridge damage that Ricky likely suffered as a result of childhood trauma left his thoughts and feelings disconnected, and this set him up for his adult relationships. Because he was unable to connect his thoughts and feelings, he felt he had no right to be angry when the women he dated had affairs or mistreated him.

With therapy, he gradually began to stop or limit some of this self-destructive behavior, but the challenge that connecting with his emotions presented was significant.

The Gap

As we've learned, damage to the brain bridge can affect how feelings and memories are integrated and connected. When memories are formed, much of their emotional content is lost in storage. For nontraumatized people, remembering childhood may bring on a whole flood of emotions associated with certain events. But when a person has experienced significant trauma, the emotions attached to it are either held back or stored even more deeply than thoughts. As a result, when a person experiences trauma early in life, he or she may not be able to recall aspects of childhood or emotions associated with certain events; that is, there is a deficit in the memories. Some things are remembered while others are not, to an even greater extent than in the general population. Traumatized people may in fact be storing their brain bridge disruptions as their memories.

Beyond discrete major life events, another form of childhood trauma is more generalized but nevertheless as impactful: emotional neglect. This may lead to a sense of desperation or sadness that is too much for the thinking brain to process. As a result, this sadness becomes stored in the brain as a partial memory. Since memories are an indicator of the past, and since the past contributes to how we define ourselves, disrupted memories lead to a disrupted sense of self.

For most nontraumatized people, the past is only partly remembered, but the brain creates a sense of continuity by filling in the gaps between experiences so there is an internal sense of coherence. This ability of the brain to fill in the dots has been shown in a literal way by drawing two horizontal lines very, very close together. At some point, even when there is a gap, the brain sees them as a single line. This is also what the brain does with our past experiences. It makes them single and continuous so that we feel an inner sense of continuity.

When someone has been traumatized, the gaps between experiences are too large and the brain is unable to create a coherent story about the past. Trauma victims suffer from the immense fear that they are not whole, that pieces of themselves or their lives are missing. They often experience panic attacks or immense anxiety as a result of this. How can they exist in the present when they have no continuous past? Did they fake their way to where they are? These are the kinds of tortured questions that their brains ask in the present because they cannot make sense of the past.

At birth, the brain is pretty much a blank slate, and our experiences contribute colors, pictures, and textures to this slate, creating a lifetime filled with memories. Having a past that you remember creates a sense of internal continuity. It provides a marker of where you have been and where you are going. Since traumatized individuals cannot remember parts of the past, they lose these markers. As a result, when they have reason to recall something that is in the gap, they suddenly feel disoriented, as if the environment is unfamiliar. The feeling is similar to what some people feel when they go to a party that they are anxious about attending, or when they get lost. Imagine being lost in the middle of a forest and losing sight of the path you took to get where you are. Imagine how frantically that might make you search for a way out. These fears are akin to experiencing a gap between memories. This gap itself is anxiety provoking and can lead to a frantic but fruitless search to fill it with memories of what actually happened. As a result, the fears associated with this gap can multiply with the increasing realization that the gap is not going to be filled. What, then, ends up happening?

People either make up stories to fill these gaps or walk around feeling "broken" in some way. Their pasts have riddled their identities with holes, and they feel as though they have been shot multiple times, but never died. To a certain extent, they have to make up stories. I remember first meeting Alison, a woman who said she was sexually abused when she was five years old. She told the story of how her family (which seemed quite "normal" by conventional standards) held ritual abuse ceremonies in the backyard of their home, in a quiet suburb of Washington, DC. She related how her family members chanted magical incantations, progressively taking away her self-esteem. She talked about how she was convinced that on one or two occasions, aliens were invited to attack her sexually, and that she could not bear to remember the details, except that there were scars to prove it.

The more bizarre her stories became, the more frustrated I grew, because I did not believe her, and I could not connect with her because of it. When I challenged her story, she withdrew and became distant, so I pulled back and just listened. I sought consultation from a colleague who had worked extensively with patients like Alison. He advised that as absurd as her stories might sound, I needed to listen to them. So I did. For the next three years, I heard them every week. And one day, in the middle of her third year of therapy, she burst into tears and began to sob uncontrollably midway through a story. When she was able to speak again, she told me that she had suddenly realized how important it was to her that I had listened to her stories, and she also told me that they had all been lies. She was afraid that she now had no license to feel as she did.

I explained to her that they were not lies, but rather interpretations of a real feeling that she'd experienced. They reflected something that had truly gone on in her life at that time. The real story that eventually came out was not that she'd been abused, but that her parents had favored her brother so much that she felt as though she did not exist. Their favoritism was so great that she had wished that she was a boy and wanted to disown her own gender. As a result, her stories of being assaulted by aliens were amended to be about being infiltrated by self-doubt and negativity about her gender, making her hate herself for not being the child she felt her parents wanted.

Suddenly, she had filled in this gap caused by disruption of the brain bridge, and when a critical amount of emotional information was able to cross over to the thinking side, her story made more sense, to me and to her. Since then, she has become incredibly functional and is in a very satisfying romantic relationship.

Even in people without a history of trauma, experiencing a gap can be a significant psychological limitation that can lead to frantically sampling all of their past experience without finding the answer to the question of being human. They might sample different sexual experiences or different drugs, for example, without examining how this sampling behavior prevents a sense of depth. Being human, in my experience, involves coming to terms with these gaps. In traumatized individuals, however, the emotions within these gaps are intensified, and this accentuates the feeling of being broken in some way. Experiencing any one thing in depth is too scary, because it feels like a deep hole.

Chronic Fatigue Syndrome

People who experience childhood trauma are six times more likely to develop chronic fatigue syndrome as adults. In fact, many people, including Mary, Ricky, and Alison—find themselves sleeping for up to twelve hours a day without understanding why they are so tired. It is understandable how fatiguing worry can be when the brain bridge is disrupted, and how this ongoing search for an inner sense of continuity can be exhausting.

Many of the phenomena that I mention here—from a feeling of internal fragmentation to preoccupation with worry—are not just experienced by people who suffered childhood trauma. But in children who have been abused, their effects are exaggerated.

When Trauma Occurs in Adulthood:
Shrinking Memories of a Shrinking Self

We often are told that we should be present in our lives, but how can we be present when there are constant internal distractions? Why do our brains create these distractions? To be present is to look into a pool of calm water and see your reflection unperturbed. To be distracted is to throw multiple rocks into that pool and see yourself in bits and pieces.

When severe trauma occurs, any reminder of the trauma, no matter how distant, is a potent distracter that is equivalent to throwing multiple rocks into that still pool of water. Traumatic reminders create earthquakes in the brain. They destroy any attention directed toward the present, sometimes from outside of an individual's awareness.

How Trauma Colors the Filters of Perception

Have you ever wondered why you make the same mistakes over and over again? Why you keep choosing the same kind of romantic partner and experiencing the same kind of trauma? When we discussed the effects of conditioning, we examined one possibility: Your brain is trained to look for the same thing once the circuitry for your preferences has been established. However, here we will examine another possibility.

Transference happens when our past experiences unconsciously intrude upon a present moment. That is, we "transfer" what happened in the past to the present without realizing it. When we get angry with someone, we may in fact be angry with him or her, but the magnitude of our anger may be related to a similar past experience. For example, Joe, a client I was seeing, became enraged with his wife because he had invested a lot of time and energy in her business, but she was not able to make it viable. She had spent much of her energy trying to make it work, but could not succeed. He became so angry that on one occasion, he grabbed her by the shoulders and shook her. She was petrified, in part because this anger seemed to come completely out of nowhere. Over time, however, Joe came to understand that his anger was in part related to his wife, but mostly to his mother, who, like his wife, had not been home most of the time due to being involved with her own career. Rather than discuss his ambivalence with his mother, he became angry with his wife and transferred this anger onto her. It was only when he began to separate his wife (who was quite doting and caring even though she was so busy with her work) from his mother that he was able to help the relationship develop. It took a long time for him to "detach," or view the situation differently, however, because he was unable to be flexible in his thinking to shift his perspective from the past, because his anger toward his mother was so significant.

Another example is Angela, who repeatedly sought out neglectful relationships after breaking up with her boyfriend of six years. When she described her latest boyfriend to me, he did not seem neglectful at all. In fact, he seemed to really care about her, but she could not see this. "He's just never around enough," she would complain. When we explored her feelings more deeply, we recognized that once they had settled down together, she had started to bombard him with accusations about how she knew he was going to be neglectful, to the point that he started to avoid her to avoid this conversation. She had placed a filter of the past over her current situation and created her past all over again. Once she realized this, she backed off from this perspective, and her boyfriend reengaged in the relationship.

What you think of as "the same old problem" in your relationships may not actually exist. The same old problem may be your lens. Our lenses are filters formed by the past and through which we view all current and future experience. These filters are memories stored in the brain that are stimulated and join attention circuits when something related to them is happening in the present. Trauma can affect this lens, so all you see is past trauma projected onto the present.

To a certain extent, we all do this. But in traumatized people, the filter of the past is more fixed, and the flexibility needed to let go of it is compromised. Research has shown that having this flexibility in thinking can help reduce stress. When it is absent, stress levels are sky-high. It is almost as if the brain is frozen in the past and can't let go despite experiencing soaring stress levels.

Psychological tests in trauma survivors of political violence have shown that the absence of this flexibility prevents recovery. If you are glued to your memories or caught in them like a deer in the headlights, shifting your attention elsewhere feels impossible.

This inability to shift attention elsewhere is also seen in cancer survivors with post-traumatic stress disorder (PTSD), whose inability to shift attention or change behavior learned in the past distinguishes them from cancer survivors without PTSD. That is, if the trauma of having cancer fixes you in the fears associated with it, even if you survive, the fears do not go away. For these fears to dissipate, you have to shift your attention away from them. While this sounds like an easy enough exercise, it is not if you have been traumatized, because trauma fundamentally changes how your brain behaves.

One of the basic brain changes that occurs is that the orbitofrontal cortex shrinks. This brain region is widely known to be involved in flexibility in thinking and behavior. If it is rendered less functional by trauma, flexibility feels impossible to the person. Add to this the other, more deeply embedded structures in the brain—like the basal ganglia—that are also involved in flexibility of thinking, and you can see the added burden that trauma inflicts upon survivors.

Special Effects of Trauma on Attention

In addition to impairing flexibility in thinking, trauma also affects the brain's ability to attend to things. The difference is that when someone has been traumatized, both superficial and deeper attentional systems in the brain are affected.

Brain circuits at the surface as well as deep within the brain are coordinated to allow us to focus our attention on something. For example, if you want to attend to your work and get things done, these different circuits help you to attend to whatever you need to. Or, if you need to learn new information, both of these systems steady your attention. Or, if you're reading this book, both of these systems act in concert to allow you to attend to reading.

The superficial system is related to the short-term memory system in the brain, which is housed in the dorsolateral prefrontal cortex, or DLPFC. This system processes content that has just been learned or observed. If you are given a new telephone number to remember, or if you are given instructions to convey to someone, the DLPFC is responsible for holding on to this information. If, in the midst of this, you suddenly look out the window and see a car accident and you have never been in a car accident, your DLPFC will be disrupted and you will likely forget the telephone number or be distracted by the crash. But what if you had been in a car accident before? Would this make a difference in how your brain responded?

The answer is yes. It turns out that having prior personal exposure to a trauma also causes disruption in the deeper brain areas that coordinate attention. That is, the ventral emotion-processing regions, such as the amygdala and ventrolateral prefrontal cortex, are also disrupted. So what? Well, this means that areas of the brain that are more difficult to reach immediately are also affected, and so the effects of trauma on attention are more deeply rooted. This is one of the reasons that the distraction is so strong when traumatized individuals are exposed to reminders of their trauma. When trauma victims encounter reminders, the distraction travels far and wide in the brain's attentional system.

Victims of trauma already have a fragmented sense of self, as we learned earlier. When they remember more of their trauma, they disrupt these pathways of attention that carry emotional information. Thus, they feel even more fragmented. This creates too much anxiety for them to handle. This is the reason that in therapy, a therapist generally proceeds very cautiously with people who have been traumatized. Even when patients want to "face what happened," they cannot tolerate the intensity of the feelings that have been held back and repressed for all those years, and they often flee from the situation. The consequences of this distraction can be far-reaching, and they can be seen in the story of Liz.

Liz was sexually abused as a child by her aunt. She was able to cope well with most distractions, since they did not distract her at the level of the amygdala. When she fell in love with a woman as an adult, however, her amygdala became activated by the dilemma. To escape the disconnection between thinking and feeling, and to escape the distractions of her trauma that were triggered by her love affair with a woman, Liz would often hide in what she believed to be the "real" nature of the universe. This was a place where chaos was alive and where things flowed without boundaries. As long as life reflected her internal chaos, she felt there was some company for her inner self. She created chaos to mirror her internal distraction rather than trying to decrease the internal distraction.

Although she was in love with a woman and this relationship brought her much in the way of integration, dedication, love, and comfort, Liz could not face this. So she chose to also sleep with men to create more chaos in her life. If Liz developed a peaceful love with this woman, she would have to confront her anger with the aunt who had abused her. This was too difficult for her.

Activating her amygdala with memories of being with a woman was too anxiety provoking for her. In fact, Liz considered herself to be the more dominant partner sexually in the relationship, but when the time came to dominate her lover, she would experience strong feelings of disgust that went far beyond a healthy level of fear or apprehension. Because she could not accept the idea that someone could love her completely, she needed to run away from time to time.

So Liz continued to have sex with men and only limited sexual experiences with the woman she loved. In fact, in their limited sexual experiences, she rarely was an active participant. She unwittingly repeated her childhood behavior of being a passive participant in a relationship, in part because this passivity meant that she was not a lesbian but was being made to be, and in part because she unconsciously blamed herself for the abuse because she had experienced pleasure when her aunt had stimulated her sexually. As a result, Liz would disappear for long periods at a time, and she engaged in unprotected sex with her male partners. Her recklessness was an attempt to re-create the carefree childhood that she never got to have. Shame enhances risky behaviors in adults, and in traumatized individuals, it is constantly evoked by this inner sense of fragmentation and the inability to attend to any one thing for a sustained amount of time.

Most of us fill our lives with distractions that hold our attention so we can deal with the intrusive memories of negative life events. This can obviously be helpful because it calms the brain, but it can also be harmful when trauma is able to exert its power unconsciously. In traumatized individuals, there is a constant need to master this distraction. Because it is occurring in the ventral attentional system, the distraction is deep and difficult to access.

The problems with thinking that accompany PTSD are extensive and fairly defining. Having a constant reminder of background trauma affects thinking in specific ways. These include being slow to prepare for a thought or action, taking time to switch attention, taking time to react, and reacting when there is no reason to react. Life for these individuals is a series of inaccurate or late reactions that feed into how they experience their lives.

Liz was acutely aware of how this affected her judgment, but could not do anything about it. She allowed people who used her to continue to use her, and she felt threatened by people who loved her. In some way, she perpetuated the familiar and rejected the unfamiliar. The unfamiliar was associated with a new fear, whereas the familiar was an old fear. The problem was that these old fears were slowly but surely eroding her being.

Usually, when we are about to react to something for no reason, the brain will pull the brake. For PTSD sufferers, there is no brake. The reaction, once begun, will be performed at full throttle, in part because reminders of the trauma put the brain in overdrive and it will start to process stimuli whether they are relevant or not. This leads to a lot of chaos in the brain's functioning.

Disgust and Mapping Gut Feelings

The insula maps out gut feelings, making them conscious and, therefore, overtly understandable. It is also involved in the registration of disgust. Studies have shown that, compared to women who have not been traumatized, women who are victims of intimate partner violence have increased insula activation when exposed to negative stimuli, indicating a heightened level of disgust and, possibly, a greater translation of gut feelings into conscious thoughts. This heightened level of emotionality and constant translation of gut feelings can also be distracting.

Why Dissociation Cannot Protect against Unconscious Fears

When people are traumatized, they may become dissociated from their feelings or emotions. A person may appear to be spacey, or will simply deny that anything is wrong even though daily functioning is disrupted. Dissociation allows a traumatized person to be distanced from feelings that are too difficult for the brain to process all at once. Although this can be a useful defense mechanism, there comes a time when being dissociated does not serve a person well, because he or she may pursue the same type of dysfunctional relationship over and over again without realizing what happened previously. When researchers examined the brains of traumatized people who were dissociated versus those who were not, they found that dissociated people experienced different brain responses to conscious and unconscious fear. Dissociation is thought to involve prefrontal circuits in the brain that are turned on to prevent connecting with inner fears. As such, it protects against any fears that are presented consciously.

It turns out that dissociation can turn off conscious fears that activate the prefrontal cortex, but it cannot turn off unconscious fears that activate the amygdala, insula, and left thalamus. These parts of the brain continue to fire when dissociation occurs. Even though we can dissociate from our conscious fears, we cannot dissociate from our unconscious fears. The importance of this is underscored in the example below.

Mary was a forty-year-old woman who had been sexually abused by her first husband. She was raped several times before she eventually sought help when the level of violence escalated and resulted in her jaw being broken. The relationship finally ended in a divorce.

Mary eventually began dating again and met a man, Aaron, whom she thought was very attractive, loving, and caring. He was hot-tempered, however, and she said that when they fought, he would grit his teeth, glare at her, shake his fist at her, and occasionally shake her by the shoulders. She accepted this behavior.

The relationship became serious and the two of them decided to move in together. Mary still didn't speak to him about his anger and never really connected with her own fears. She practiced yoga regularly, and used breathing exercises to calm herself down whenever she became afraid of his anger.

After three months of dating, Mary and Aaron got into a huge argument. Aaron went through his usual routine of screaming, gritting his teeth, shaking his fist at her, and grabbing her by the shoulders. But this time, when she did not respond, he punched her in the face, fracturing several of her facial bones. At no time prior to or during the attack did Mary expect the upcoming violence.

When she entered therapy, she spent the first two years performing a very logical deconstruction of her relationships, not once showing any emotional impact. She teared up when she talked about the end of those relationships, and she became sad when she talked about the violence, but she never once showed any loss of control. One day in the middle of the third year, however, she came in infuriated by her boss's abusive behavior. He had been raising his voice in front of other people, banging on his desk in his office, and flinging papers at her. I asked her if this reminded her of other men in her life, and then the penny dropped.

Mary recognized that for all these years, she had been dissociating from her fears because they were too much to handle. Rather than face them, she chose to "get a handle on them"—but this handle only reached her conscious feelings. She never really acknowledged her deepest awareness and fears.

What followed was months of intense emotionality—at times verging on a need for hospitalization—but Mary recognized that she could not hold back any longer. She had long held this emotional knowledge of being abused as a deficiency within herself, and, as a result, she never sought to reach for anything that would cause her to have to express herself deeply. As a result, her relationships had been superficial, her jobs had been mediocre, and her entire life had been one characterized by coping rather than freely expressing who she was. Within months of recognizing this, she left her job, got a very senior position at a new company, met another man, and ended that relationship long before the anticipated violence became an issue. Instead of using dissociation as a defense, she trusted her gut instincts.

This case illustrates how trauma can use dissociation from fear as a way to protect a person from overwhelming feelings, but until people connect with their deepest and unconscious fears, they are not truly protected because they are not accessing knowledge that could be helpful in making future decisions.

Cementing the Memory

When traumatic memories are formed, they are etched into the cement of our brains because high anxiety drives them in. In fact, one study showed that if you give people morphine soon after a traumatic event, the impact of that event over time will be much less. By relaxing the person soon after he or she experiences trauma, you prevent the memories from having as strong a hold on the brain.

People with PTSD have a smaller hippocampus—the part of the brain that is involved in long-term memory. Somehow, their ability to remember is compromised, and trauma shapes the way in which the brain develops memory systems. A smaller hippocampus is one result of this memory shaping. Early on, soon after the trauma, blood flow is increased in memory systems involving the hippocampus and amygdala, signaling that memory changes are taking place, but the long-term effects of trauma are decreased blood flow to the hippocampus. Severe stress increases the circulating blood levels of a hormone called cortisol. It is believed that cortisol is, in part, responsible for the smaller hippocampus suppressing memory.

More recent studies have shown that it is not the entire hippocampus that is smaller in PTSD. In fact, if we divide the hippocampus into front and back parts, it is the back part that is affected. It is this part of the brain that is responsible for storage, processing, and retrieval of memories of space and time.

The smaller hippocampus in traumatized people leads to what is called an exaggerated startle response. That is, people startle at the slightest provocation, even when it is not necessary. This sets up a cycle of stress. In my experience, this startle sometimes leads to a paralysis of function in traumatized people, even when they are not physically reactive. Can you imagine being startled at the slightest provocation over and over again? (Talk about chronic fatigue!)

Working Memory:
The Biology of Denial

Working memory refers to short-term memory. For example, when we remember a telephone number just after being given it, these numbers are held in working memory. As we function in our daily environments, working memory is continually updated as we send new information to our brains. In between, working memory has to be maintained for long enough that relevant tasks can be done or information can be sent to long-term memory. In people who are severely traumatized, there is malfunction in the updating system, and even when the system is supposed to be quiet, it starts to update. This may be why concentration is affected and why engaging in day-to-day tasks is difficult for those who suffer from PTSD.

Ricky, Liz, and Mary didn't appear to truly grasp their anger on a day-to-day basis. While they recognized that they were temperamental, they usually remembered their angry reactions in an understated way, partly because they could not hold on to this information. Perhaps more disturbing to me was their lack of awareness of others taking advantage of them. In part because Ricky, Liz, and Mary were financially successful, the people in their lives constantly used them for money. These trauma survivors seemed to "forget" past incidents and allowed friends and family members to use them time and again. When reminded of previous incidents, they could identify what had happened, but were not emotional about the negative outcome. This kind of denial is common in traumatized individuals.

Often, several traumatic events may converge. In Ricky's case, he had been sexually abused as a child. Also, his mother had been relatively absent. His thoughts and feelings were rarely synchronized because these multiple traumatic events were even more difficult to bear. Intelligent people who are traumatized will fill in the gaps in their lives with almost believable stories. But deep down, they are always unsettled by something not jelling. Faulty working memory and hippocampal damage are partly responsible for these gaps in remembering. One study has shown that the greater the trauma, the greater the loss of memory specificity. People who are traumatized do not have great specific memories. As a result, they have a less coherent sense of the past.

Alexithymia:
How Trauma Impairs the Ability to Feel

Alexithymia is a condition in which people have less ability to experience and/or express emotion. In severely traumatized people, this inability to feel or express emotions becomes more severe. As a result, traumatized people will often seek out highly evocative (and frequently provocative) situations in order to experience emotions that will relieve their feelings of fear and anxiety. Furthermore, corresponding brain regions will activate or deactivate depending on the severity of the alexithymia. Also, people who have experienced severe trauma have a decreased level of emotional awareness.

There are two main divisions of the ACC: the dorsal, thinking part, and the ventral, emotional part. In people without a history of trauma, the activation of the ventral ACC increases as emotional awareness increases. In traumatized individuals, however, the opposite occurs. The more aware they are, the less the ventral ACC activates. Overall, traumatized individuals have a lower level of emotional awareness than nontraumatized individuals. This lack of emotional awareness can significantly impair decision-making processes that require emotion.

Failure of Extinction:
How Trauma Makes It Difficult to Adjust to Fears

As we have discussed, in order to overcome our fears, we have to develop extinction so we learn not to be afraid of neutral stimuli that are associated with a negative outcome. For example, if a woman was sexually abused by a man with dark hair, with extinction she may eventually come to be less reactive to men with dark hair. In life, when trauma has not occurred, we learn to overcome our fears by learning how to extinguish responses to previously feared neutral situations. After a few successes, we can extinguish our fears. But in traumatized individuals, this extinction does not occur as readily.

This is, in part, because their brains are usually on hyperalert when a feared situation is replicated in any way (by war movies for war veterans, by romance for the sexually abused, by cars for victims of motor vehicle accidents). This state of hypervigilance correlates with an increase in amygdala activation. Usually, when we reexperience situations like these, the medial prefrontal cortex and ACC activate to extinguish or remove our fear responses. In people with PTSD, they do not activate. That is, certain brain regions that ordinarily help us identify situations as harmless are turned off.

Can you imagine how fatiguing this must be? No wonder PTSD is associated with chronic fatigue. The brain is constantly in overdrive and has to use a tremendous amount of energy to sustain its daily operations. The emotional operating margins are slim in people with PTSD.

How Long Can the Effects of Trauma Last?

It is clear that the effects of trauma can last for a long time. One study that used MRI to measure blood flow in survivors of the 9/11 terrorist attacks found that, compared to people who were two hundred miles away from the incident, people who were within one and a half miles of the attacks still showed increased amygdala activation three years later when they were shown images of fearful faces. This suggests that the effects of trauma can not only be long lasting, but also that the more directly one is involved in a trauma, the longer its impact lasts.

Thus, the effects of trauma in adulthood are widespread, affecting the brain systems related to short- and long-term memory, attention, emotion, and the various systems that coordinate these functions.

How Can We Reduce the Impact of Trauma on the Brain?

The MAP-CHANGE Approach

Following are some of the ways you can change your fear response if you have been a victim of trauma. It is important to remember that apart from these suggestions, techniques such as psychotherapy and eye movement desensitization and reprocessing, a technique involving the manipulation of eye movement, have been found to be helpful. Also, antidepressant treatments and changes in the environment can reverse the effects of stress on hippocampal nerve growth.

Meditation

Meditation involves an inward journey, one that can be very frightening to a person who has been traumatized. As the journey proceeds, traumatized individuals may come across fragments of their traumatic memories that compound the already huge distraction. In fact, at first, it is very difficult for traumatized individuals to meditate for any length of time. Being still means confronting the inner chaos that for so long has been mirrored in chaotic external activity. But as trauma victims learn to bear their inner journeys, when undertaken without forcing any connection or trying to make meaning, there emerges a new possibility of a sense of self beyond concrete narratives. This sense of self is constructed through the "feeling" of the inward journey. By maintaining attentional focus on a mantra or an object, for example, a trauma victim can continually redirect him- or herself back to a place of calm, away from the narratives that are otherwise disrupting life. In so doing, the narratives are trained by meditation to quiet down, and they become less distracting, allowing for a more peaceful environment in which to address the past trauma and reintegrate a sense of self.

There is growing evidence that meditation can be utilized to effect change in trauma victims. One study in which traumatized adolescents used a combination of meditation, guided imagery, and breathing techniques showed that they scored much lower in PTSD symptoms than those who did not use these techniques. These symptom improvements remained at three months.

One case history that came to the attention of the media was that of Trisha Meili, who revealed her identity as the Central Park Jogger—the victim of a brutal assault and rape in New York City's Central Park in 1989—in a presentation at Spaulding Rehabilitation Hospital in Boston in May 2003. Jon Kabat-Zinn, PhD, a professor at the University of Massachusetts Medical School, presented Meili's case history and revealed that mindfulness and meditation had been important in her rehabilitation process. She reported that her self-discovered practice of mindfulness helped restore her emotional and physical functioning. In their presentation, they emphasized the importance of meditation in rehabilitation from trauma.

There is also other evidence supporting the use of meditation in recovery from trauma. Victims of Hurricane Katrina who completed a four-hour workshop on meditation followed by an eight-week home-study program reported an improved sense of well-being that was significantly correlated with the total number of minutes of daily meditation practice they undertook.

Although we can't be certain why meditation is effective for trauma victims, it is possible that focusing attention on something else decreases the fear and pain caused by the trauma. Meditation may also increase the coordination between the different brain regions that are disrupted as a result of trauma, and people may then be able to reintegrate thoughts and feelings that were previously disconnected.

Attention

As outlined in this chapter, trauma can affect attention in a number of ways.

- It can disrupt superficial attention, increasing distractibility.
- It can disrupt unconscious attention, increasing vulnerability to inner fears and internal distraction.

- It can lead to dissociation in an attempt to create distance from conscious fears, but dissociation has no impact on the unconscious brain.

Ricky, Liz, and Mary all had chaotic lives before their attention was harnessed; however, their attention could be harnessed only when their emotions allowed them to harness it. This occurred as they learned to process difficult emotions, engaging the thinking circuits that were otherwise engaged in pointless worrying.

Since trauma causes a disruption between thinking and feeling, and since this disruption leads to distraction, the key intervention is to reintegrate difficult emotions. Difficult emotions "attack" the traumatized brain, however, causing exaggerated responses—either too much emotionality or complete dissociation.

Thus, generally speaking, there are two ideas to be aware of:

1. It is important to take things one day at a time and not to try to process all of the difficult emotions at once. This may even take years, and working with a psychologist or psychiatrist may be very helpful, especially if you are able to form an alliance with the professional.
2. When you are confronted with a big problem, break it into smaller parts. Recalling the full details of trauma may be too much at first. Start with what you are feeling now—maybe you feel shaken, uncomfortable, or anxious—and then focus on the change you want. Rather than focusing only on the "broken" aspects, focus on what you want to fix.

Distraction can be effective in reducing trauma's consequences, such as flashbacks and anxiety. It is different from dissociation in that you allow your brain time-limited, conscious relief by replacing the traumatic flashbacks with another engaging—but positive—experience. Eating a great meal, spending time with friends, playing a video game, and shopping are all examples of distractions. They work because they take the focus off the trauma and flashbacks and train the brain to focus on other things. Ideally, identifying a growth opportunity and planning for it prior to executing it are very productive ways to use distraction. Although processing the trauma is important, relieving your brain of the constant stress is also important and will allow you to process the trauma more effectively.

Psychological Tools

Starting slowly is critical to undoing the destructive effects of trauma. Effective therapy has to be trauma focused. Similarly, if you are looking to help yourself, your efforts should be trauma focused. First, write down the specific limitations that trauma is creating for you. Then, reexamine this from multiple perspectives. Finally, determine what is most easily changed, and change it. For many people, even approaching this is petrifying. They may fall into the prudence trap and do nothing at all. Caution is a result of the amygdala activating. Being overly cautious occurs when the amygdala activates to the point of burning itself out. Then, the entire brain's functioning is paralyzed. It is important to recognize that often, action cleanses us more than more thinking does. When looking to deal with problems, then, it is critical that you do not keep them academic, but rather actually experiment with them in day-to-day situations. The steps are:

1. Identify the trauma.
2. Talk about the trauma with people you trust.
3. Focus on what you want to change rather than only on what happened; teach your brain to think this way.
4. If you find yourself stuck in your head, *do* something: If you are afraid of cars, ride in a car with a close friend; if you are afraid of the war, watch a movie about war in the privacy of your home, but talk about your fears while you are doing this.

Most of us do not choose to have our thinking and feeling disconnected. It is a defense against the fear that if we connect our thinking and feeling, we will go crazy. The truth is, "craziness" usually results from not expressing feelings. So, if you have the chance to express yourself, do so. The basic idea here is to express yourself progressively over time, and only to people you trust. The exercises that follow help to integrate thinking and feeling. Another way to do this is to each week select a movie that explores a theme relevant to your own trauma. Watch the movie and allow yourself to respond to it in an emotionally honest way. You can do the same with songs, as well. Use keywords to search the Internet for relevant songs, and then listen to them to find one that reflects the feeling you are looking to connect with.

Documenting your life can be a rich and fulfilling experience if you continue to add layers of complexity. For example, you can keep track of the important events in your life over the span of several years and assess how variables correlate from year to year. The table below offers a sample of how you can keep track of your life experiences from year to year. Any number of combinations can be created.

	This Year	Year 2	Year 3	Year 4	Year 5
Income					
Number of lovers					
Number of satisfying relationships					
Number of vacations					
Happiness rating					
Serendipitous moments					
Challenging events					

To augment this table, you can also create wish tables for the next ten years and compare them with the past. This will not only allow you to feel more integrated, but will also connect you with a sense of the future. It is very important that you learn to focus on the things you want and not only on the things you do not want. To help you do this, I suggest that you start a journal called *The Book of Dos* (as opposed to *don'ts*). In this book, write down only things that you would like to accomplish in the coming week.

So you don't repress your memories, also start a journal of past traumas called *Lessons Learned.* While all of these books and tables may sound like a lot of work, they will eventually help your life become much more efficient.

Although the efforts outlined above are important and will help you to focus, too much effort can also cause you to fatigue easily. The trick here is to allocate effort during a part of your day, and then to let your practice show itself as you proceed through your day. If you apply effort all day, it will be like struggling in quicksand. Try to apply yourself to changing your life in a way that is predominantly exploratory and punctuated with effort. Effortful psychological practices should probably not take up more than two hours in a day.

Conclusion

Trauma causes disruption to your inner life. As a result, the past, present, and future become discontinuous and identity becomes fractured. This scatters attention and increases fear. The disconnection is reflected in brain activations where the brain bridge between thinking and feeling is damaged, and the memory and attention centers are, in effect, altered in adulthood. To reestablish our brain bridges and to reprogram our memory centers, we have to confront those fears gradually while at the same time allowing ourselves to build a better future.

References

(1965). "Good and bad choices." *Mod Hosp* 105(4): 95–6 passim.

(1975). "Ethics of selective treatment of spina bifida: Report by a working party." *Lancet* 1(7898): 85–8.

(2006). "Ethical dilemma: Letting patients make bad choices. Listening and sensitivity critical." *AIDS Alert* 21(8): 92–4.

(2006). "The Society for Clinical Trials opposes US legislation to permit marketing of unproven medical therapies for seriously ill patients." *Clin Trials* 3(2): 154–7.

(2007). "Combat loneliness to slow the aging process: Feeling isolated could accelerate aging, affecting inflammation and infection at the cellular level." *Health News* 13(12): 6–7.

(2007). "In with the good, out with the bad: Fat, carbohydrate, and protein are all good for you—as long as you make smart choices." *Harv Heart Lett* 18(3): 4–5.

Abel-Smith, B. (1972). "Health priorities in developing countries: The economist's contribution." *Int J Health Serv* 2(1): 5–12.

Aberson, C. L., C. Shoemaker, et al. (2004). "Implicit bias and contact: The role of interethnic friendships." *J Soc Psychol* 144(3): 335–47.

Adolphs, R., D. Tranel, et al. (1995). "Fear and the human amygdala." *J Neurosci* 15(9): 5879–91.

Afonso-Souza, G., P. Nadanovsky, et al. (2007). "[Test-retest reliability of self-perceived oral health in an adult population in Rio de Janeiro, Brazil]." *Cad Saude Publica* 23(6): 1483–8.

Allen, C. T., S. C. Swan, et al. (2009). "Gender Symmetry, Sexism, and Intimate Partner Violence." *J Interpers Violence* 24: 1816–34.

Allen-Wright, S. (1999). "Expanding health promotion to individuals with spinal cord injuries." *SCI Nurs* 16(3): 85–8.

Amiraian, D. E., and J. Sobal (2009). "Dating and eating: Beliefs about dating foods among university students." *Appetite* 53(2): 226–32.

Andersen, H. S., D. Sestoft, et al. (2000). "A longitudinal study of prisoners on remand: Psychiatric prevalence, incidence and psychopathology in solitary vs. non-solitary confinement." *Acta Psychiatr Scand* 102(1): 19–25.

Anderson, A. K., K. Christoff, et al. (2003). "Neural correlates of the automatic processing of threat facial signals." *J Neurosci* 23(13): 5627–33.

Andre, M., L. Borgquist, et al. (2002). "Asking for 'rules of thumb': A way to discover tacit knowledge in general practice." *Fam Pract* 19(6): 617–22.

Armony, J. L., and R. J. Dolan (2001). "Modulation of auditory neural responses by a visual context in human fear conditioning." *Neuroreport* 12(15): 3407–11.

Armony, J. L., and R. J. Dolan (2002). "Modulation of spatial attention by fear-conditioned stimuli: An event-related fMRI study." *Neuropsychologia* 40(7): 817–26.

Arnold, R. L., and K. Egan (2004). "Breaking the 'bad' news to patients and families: Preparing to have the conversation about end-of-life and hospice care." *Am J Geriatr Cardiol* 13(6): 307–12.

Balsamo, R. R., and M. Pine (1994). "Twelve questions to ask about your outcomes monitoring system—Part II." *Physician Exec* 20(5): 22–5.

Baltussen, R., and L. Niessen (2006). "Priority setting of health interventions: The need for multi-criteria decision analysis." *Cost Eff Resour Alloc* 4: 14.

Baron, A. S., and M. R. Banaji (2006). "The development of implicit attitudes: Evidence of race evaluations from ages 6 and 10 and adulthood." *Psychol Sci* 17(1): 53–8.

Baron Short, E., S. Kose, et al. (2007). "Regional brain activation during meditation shows time and practice effects: An exploratory fMRI study." *Evid Based Complement Alternat Med,* doi:10.1093/ecam/nem163.

Baruch, D. E., R. A. Swain, et al. (2004). "Effects of exercise on Pavlovian fear conditioning." *Behav Neurosci* 118(5): 1123–7.

Bauer, H., J. Pripfl, et al. (2003). "Functional neuroanatomy of learned helplessness." *Neuroimage* 20(2): 927–39.

Baumann, M., and M. Trincard (2002). "[Autonomy attitudes in the treatment compliance of a cohort of subjects with continuous psychotropic drug administration]." *Encephale* 28(5 Pt 1): 389–96.

Baumgartner, T., M. Heinrichs, et al. (2008). "Oxytocin shapes the neural circuitry of trust and trust adaptation in humans." *Neuron* 58(4): 639–50.

Bechara, A., S. Dolan, et al. (2002). "Decision-making and addiction (part II): Myopia for the future or hypersensitivity to reward?" *Neuropsychologia* 40(10): 1690–705.

Bechara, A., D. Tranel, et al. (1996). "Failure to respond autonomically to anticipated future outcomes following damage to prefrontal cortex." *Cereb Cortex* 6(2): 215–25.

Beer, J. S., M. Stallen, et al. (2008). "The Quadruple Process model approach to examining the neural underpinnings of prejudice." *Neuroimage* 43(4): 775–83.

Berg, R. F., M. R. Moldover, et al. (1999). "Frequency-dependent viscosity of xenon near the critical point." *Phys Rev E Stat Phys Plasmas Fluids Relat Interdiscip Topics* 60(4 Pt A): 4079–98.

Berkowitz, R. L., L. Lynch, et al. (1996). "The current status of multifetal pregnancy reduction." *Am J Obstet Gynecol* 174(4): 1265–72.

Berns, G. S., J. Chappelow, et al. (2006). "Neurobiological substrates of dread." *Science* 312(5774): 754–8.

Bin, A., and T. Hoshi (2005). "[A study on the availability of subjective health indices for the aged: Focus on Japanese and Chinese studies]." *Nippon Koshu Eisei Zasshi* 52(10): 841–52.

Birbaumer, N., W. Grodd, et al. (1998). "fMRI reveals amygdala activation to human faces in social phobics." *Neuroreport* 9(6): 1223–6.

Birbaumer, N., R. Veit, et al. (2005). "Deficient fear conditioning in psychopathy: A functional magnetic resonance imaging study." *Arch Gen Psychiatry* 62(7): 799–805.

Bishop, S. J., J. Duncan, et al. (2004). "State anxiety modulation of the amygdala response to unattended threat-related stimuli." *J Neurosci* 24(46): 10364–8.

Bisson, J., and M. Andrew (2007). "Psychological treatment of post-traumatic stress disorder (PTSD)." *Cochrane Database Syst Rev* (3): CD003388.

Blackwell, C. W. (2008). "Registered nurses' attitudes toward the protection of gays and lesbians in the workplace." *J Transcult Nurs* 19(4): 347–53.

Blythe, I. M., C. Kennard, et al. (1987). "Residual vision in patients with retrogeniculate lesions of the visual pathways." *Brain* 110(Pt 4): 887–905.

Bonne, O., M. Vythilingam, et al. (2008). "Reduced posterior hippocampal volume in posttraumatic stress disorder." *J Clin Psychiatry* 69(7): 1087–91.

Bourgeois-Bailetti, A. M., and G. Cerbus (1977). "Color associations to mood stories in first grade boys." *Percept Mot Skills* 45(3 Pt 2): 1051–6.

Bouwman, L. I., H. te Molder, et al. (2009). "I eat healthfully but I am not a freak: Consumers' everyday life perspective on healthful eating." *Appetite* 53(3): 390–8.

Bowen-Simpkins, P. (1988). "Contraception by age group." *Practitioner* 232(1441): 15–20.

Boyatzis, R., A. McKee, et al. (2002). "Reawakening your passion for work." *Harv Bus Rev* 80(4): 86–94, 126.

Bracha, H. S., D. T. Yoshioka, et al. (2005). "Evolution of the human fear-circuitry and acute sociogenic pseudoneurological symptoms:

The Neolithic balanced-polymorphism hypothesis." *J Affect Disord* 88(2): 119–29.

Bremner, J. D., B. Elzinga, et al. (2008). "Structural and functional plasticity of the human brain in posttraumatic stress disorder." *Prog Brain Res* 167: 171–86.

Brennan, F. X., and C. J. Charnetski (2000). "Explanatory style and immunoglobulin A (IgA)." *Integr Physiol Behav Sci* 35(4): 251–5.

Brescoll, V. L., and E. L. Uhlmann (2008). "Can an angry woman get ahead? Status conferral, gender, and expression of emotion in the workplace." *Psychol Sci* 19(3): 268–75.

Brosch, T., D. Sander, et al. (2008). "Beyond fear: Rapid spatial orienting toward positive emotional stimuli." *Psychol Sci* 19(4): 362–70.

Brown, M. A., and L. Stopa (2008). "The looming maladaptive style in social anxiety." *Behav Ther* 39(1): 57–64.

Brown, R. P., and P. L. Gerbarg (2005). "Sudarshan Kriya yogic breathing in the treatment of stress, anxiety, and depression: Part II—Clinical applications and guidelines." *J Altern Complement Med* 11(4): 711–7.

Bryant, R. A., M. Creamer, et al. (2009). "A study of the protective function of acute morphine administration on subsequent posttraumatic stress disorder." *Biol Psychiatry* 65(5): 438–40.

Buchel, C., R. J. Dolan, et al. (1999). "Amygdala-hippocampal involvement in human aversive trace conditioning revealed through event-related functional magnetic resonance imaging." *J Neurosci* 19(24): 10869–76.

Buchheim, A., S. Erk, et al. (2008). "Neural correlates of attachment trauma in borderline personality disorder: A functional magnetic resonance imaging study." *Psychiatry Res* 163(3): 223–35.

Buchheim, A., S. Erk, et al. (2006). "Measuring attachment representation in an fMRI environment: A pilot study." *Psychopathology* 39(3): 144–52.

Buenting, J. A. (1992). "Health life-styles of lesbian and heterosexual women." *Health Care Women Int* 13(2): 165–71.

Bunch, W. H. (1981). "Decision analysis of treatment choices in the osteochondroses." *Clin Orthop Relat Res* (158): 91–8.

Burgess, D., M. van Ryn, et al. (2007). "Reducing racial bias among health care providers: Lessons from social-cognitive psychology." *J Gen Intern Med* 22(6): 882–7.

Cabanac, M., J. Guillaume, et al. (2002). "Pleasure in decision-making situations." *BMC Psychiatry* 2: 7.

Cacioppo, J. T., C. J. Norris, et al. (2009). "In the eye of the beholder: Individual differences in perceived social isolation predict regional brain activation to social stimuli." *J Cogn Neurosci* 21(1): 83–92.

Cahn, B. R., and J. Polich (2009). "Meditation (Vipassana) and the P3a event-related brain potential." *Int J Psychophysiol* 72(1): 51–60.

Calabria, M., M. Cotelli, et al. (2009). "Empathy and emotion recognition in semantic dementia: A case report." *Brain Cogn* 70(3): 247–52.

Carr, D., K. J. Jaffe, et al. (2008). "Perceived interpersonal mistreatment among obese Americans: Do race, class, and gender matter?" *Obesity (Silver Spring)* 16 Suppl 2: S60–8.

Carretie, L., J. A. Hinojosa, et al. (2005). "Cortical response to subjectively unconscious danger." *Neuroimage* 24(3): 615–23.

Carter, C. S., and M. K. Krug (2009). "The functional neuroanatomy of dread: Functional magnetic resonance imaging insights into generalized anxiety disorder and its treatment." *Am J Psychiatry* 166(3): 263–5.

Case, D. A., B. O. Ploog, et al. (1990). "Observing behavior in a computer game." *J Exp Anal Behav* 54(3): 185–99.

Castelli, L., S. Tomelleri, et al. (2008). "Implicit ingroup metafavoritism: Subtle preference for ingroup members displaying ingroup bias." *Pers Soc Psychol Bull* 34(6): 807–18.

Cavenar, J. O., Jr., and D. S. Werman (1981). "Origins of the fear of success." *Am J Psychiatry* 138(1): 95–8.

Cemalcilar, Z., R. Canbeyli, et al. (2003). "Learned helplessness, therapy, and personality traits: An experimental study." *J Soc Psychol* 143(1): 65–81.

Cermak, L. S., and D. Stiassny (1982). "Recall failure following successful generation and recognition of responses by alcoholic Korsakoff patients." *Brain Cogn* 1(2): 165–76.

Chandler, R. A., J. Wakeley, et al. (2009). "Altered risk-aversion and risk-seeking behavior in bipolar disorder." *Biol Psychiatry* 66(9): 840–6.

Chapleau, K. M., D. L. Oswald, et al. (2008). "Male rape myths: The role of gender, violence, and sexism." *J Interpers Violence* 23(5): 600–15.

Chatzisarantis, N. L., and M. S. Hagger (2007). "Mindfulness and the intention-behavior relationship within the theory of planned behavior." *Pers Soc Psychol Bull* 33(5): 663–76.

Chen, E. H., F. S. Shofer, et al. (2008). "Gender disparity in analgesic treatment of emergency department patients with acute abdominal pain." *Acad Emerg Med* 15(5): 414–8.

Cheng, D. T., D. C. Knight, et al. (2003). "Functional MRI of human amygdala activity during Pavlovian fear conditioning: Stimulus processing versus response expression." *Behav Neurosci* 117(1): 3–10.

Chorpita, B. F., and D. H. Barlow (1998). "The development of anxiety: The role of control in the early environment." *Psychol Bull* 124(1): 3–21.

Chuang, S. C. (2007). "Sadder but wiser or happier and smarter? A demonstration of judgment and decision making." *J Psychol* 141(1): 63–76.

Clark, R. A. (2008). "Promotion and retention of women physicians in academia." *J La State Med Soc* 160(5): 289–91.

Cole, S. W., L. C. Hawkley, et al. (2007). "Social regulation of gene expression in human leukocytes." *Genome Biol* 8(9): R189.

Collins, R. L., P. L. Ellickson, et al. (2007). "The role of substance use in young adult divorce." *Addiction* 102(5): 786–94.

Compton, R. J., J. Carp, et al. (2008). "Trouble crossing the bridge: Altered interhemispheric communication of emotional images in anxiety." *Emotion* 8(5): 684–92.

Condry, J. C., and S. L. Dyer (1977). "Behavioral and fantasy measures of fear of success in children." *Child Dev* 48(4): 1417–25.

Conn, J., and A. Robeznieks (2007). "'We can overcome this': Optimism reigns supreme at Crescent City confab." *Mod Healthc* 37(10): 22–3.

Connor, K. M., and W. Zhang (2006). "Recent advances in the understanding and treatment of anxiety disorders. Resilience: Determinants, measurement, and treatment responsiveness." *CNS Spectr* 11(10 Suppl 12): 5–12.

Conway, C. A., B. C. Jones, et al. (2008). "Integrating physical and social cues when forming face preferences: Differences among low and high-anxiety individuals." *Soc Neurosci* 3(1): 89–95.

Cools, R., A. J. Calder, et al. (2005). "Individual differences in threat sensitivity predict serotonergic modulation of amygdala response to fearful faces." *Psychopharmacology (Berl)* 180(4): 670–9.

Criado, F. J. (2001). "How poor writing and bad word choices can turn readers off! A 'mea culpa.'" *J Invasive Cardiol* 13(10): 721.

Critchley, H. D., C. J. Mathias, et al. (2002). "Fear conditioning in humans: The influence of awareness and autonomic arousal on functional neuroanatomy." *Neuron* 33(4): 653–63.

Crombez, G., C. Eccleston, et al. (2007). "Is it better to have controlled and lost than never to have controlled at all? An experimental investigation of control over pain." *Pain* 137(3): 631–9.

Crone, E. A., R. J. Somsen, et al. (2004). "Heart rate and skin conductance analysis of antecendents and consequences of decision making." *Psychophysiology* 41(4): 531–40.

Cuellar, N. G. (2008). "Mindfulness meditation for veterans—Implications for occupational health providers." *AAOHN J* 56(8): 357–63.

Cunningham, W. A., A. Kesek, et al. (2009). "Distinct orbitofrontal regions encode stimulus and choice valuation." *J Cogn Neurosci* 21(10): 1956–66.

D'Argembeau, A., G. Xue, et al. (2008). "Neural correlates of envisioning emotional events in the near and far future." *Neuroimage* 40(1): 398–407.

Dailey, A. B., S. V. Kasl, et al. (2008). "Does gender discrimination impact regular mammography screening? Findings from the race differences in screening mammography study." *J Womens Health (Larchmt)* 17(2): 195–206.

Dalgleish, T., J. Rolfe, et al. (2008). "Reduced autobiographical memory specificity and posttraumatic stress: Exploring the contributions of impaired executive control and affect regulation." *J Abnorm Psychol* 117(1): 236–41.

Das, P., A. H. Kemp, et al. (2005). "Pathways for fear perception: Modulation of amygdala activity by thalamo-cortical systems." *Neuroimage* 26(1): 141–8.

Dasgupta, N., and L. M. Rivera (2006). "From automatic antigay prejudice to behavior: The moderating role of conscious beliefs about gender and behavioral control." *J Pers Soc Psychol* 91(2): 268–80.

Dauchy, S., and N. Bendrihen (2008). "[The announcement of the diagnosis of bronchial carcinoma]." *Rev Pneumol Clin* 64(2): 112–7.

Davis, S. (2001). "Testosterone deficiency in women." *J Reprod Med* 46(3 Suppl): 291–6.

de Gelder, B., J. S. Morris, et al. (2005). "Unconscious fear influences emotional awareness of faces and voices." *Proc Natl Acad Sci U S A* 102(51): 18682–7.

de Gelder, B., G. Pourtois, et al. (2002). "Fear recognition in the voice is modulated by unconsciously recognized facial expressions but not by unconsciously recognized affective pictures." *Proc Natl Acad Sci U S A* 99(6): 4121–6.

de Gelder, B., J. Snyder, et al. (2004). "Fear fosters flight: A mechanism for fear contagion when perceiving emotion expressed by a whole body." *Proc Natl Acad Sci U S A* 101(47): 16701–6.

de Gelder, B., J. Vroomen, et al. (1999). "Non-conscious recognition of affect in the absence of striate cortex." *Neuroreport* 10(18): 3759–63.

de Jong, J. D., A. van den Brink-Muinen, et al. (2008). "The Dutch health insurance reform: Switching between insurers, a comparison between the general population and the chronically ill and disabled." *BMC Health Serv Res* 8: 58.

de Vries, M. F. (2005). "The dangers of feeling like a fake." *Harv Bus Rev* 83(9): 108–16, 159.

Delgado, M. R., R. H. Frank, et al. (2005). "Perceptions of moral character modulate the neural systems of reward during the trust game." *Nat Neurosci* 8(11): 1611–8.

Desclaux, A., and C. Alfieri (2009). "Counseling and choosing between infant-feeding options: Overall limits and local interpretations by health care providers and women living with HIV in resource-poor countries (Burkina Faso, Cambodia, Cameroon)." *Soc Sci Med* 69(6): 821–9.

Desharnais, R., G. Godin, et al. (1990). "Optimism and health-relevant cognitions after a myocardial infarction." *Psychol Rep* 67 (3 Pt 2): 1131–5.

Devos, T. (2006). "Implicit bicultural identity among Mexican American and Asian American college students." *Cultur Divers Ethnic Minor Psychol* 12(3): 381–402.

Dewitte, M., E. H. Koster, et al. (2007). "Attentive processing of threat and adult attachment: A dot-probe study." *Behav Res Ther* 45(6): 1307–17.

Di Paolo, E. A. (2001). "Rhythmic and non-rhythmic attractors in asynchronous random Boolean networks." *Biosystems* 59(3): 185–95.

DiCenzo, J., and P. Fronstin (2008). "Lessons from the evolution of 401(k) retirement plans for increased consumerism in health care: An application of behavioral research." *EBRI Issue Brief* (320): 1, 3–26.

Dickie, E. W., and J. L. Armony (2008). "Amygdala responses to unattended fearful faces: Interaction between sex and trait anxiety." *Psychiatry Res* 162(1): 51–7.

Dimberg, U. (1997). "Facial reactions: Rapidly evoked emotional responses." *J Psychophysiol* 11: 115–23.

DiStefano, A. S. (2008). "Suicidality and self-harm among sexual minorities in Japan." *Qual Health Res* 18(10): 1429–41.

DiYanni, C., and D. Kelemen (2008). "Using a bad tool with good intention: Young children's imitation of adults' questionable choices." *J Exp Child Psychol* 101(4): 241–61.

dosReis, S., A. Butz, et al. (2006). "Attitudes about stimulant medication for attention-deficit/hyperactivity disorder among African American families in an inner city community." *J Behav Health Serv Res* 33(4): 423–30.

Dougherty, C. J. (1993). "Bad faith and victim-blaming: The limits of health promotion." *Health Care Anal* 1(2): 111–9.

Duffy, S. A., F. C. Jackson, et al. (2006). "Racial/ethnic preferences, sex preferences, and perceived discrimination related to end-of-life care." *J Am Geriatr Soc* 54(1): 150–7.

DuHamel, K. N., S. Manne, et al. (2004). "Cognitive processing among mothers of children undergoing bone marrow/stem cell transplantation." *Psychosom Med* 66(1): 92–103.

DuHamel, K. N., C. Rini, et al. (2007). "Optimism and life events as predictors of fear appraisals in mothers of children undergoing hematopoietic stem cell transplantation." *Psychooncology* 16(9): 821–33.

Dvorak-Bertsch, J. D., J. J. Curtin, et al. (2007). "Anxiety moderates the interplay between cognitive and affective processing." *Psychol Sci* 18(8): 699–705.

Elmrini, A., A. Elibrahimi, et al. (2006). "Ipsilateral fractures of tibia and femur or floating knee." *Int Orthop* 30(5): 325–8.

Emanuel, R. (2001). "A-void—An exploration of defences against sensing nothingness." *Int J Psychoanal* 82(Pt 6): 1069–84.

Eng, W., R. G. Heimberg, et al. (2001). "Attachment in individuals with social anxiety disorder: The relationship among adult attachment styles, social anxiety, and depression." *Emotion* 1(4): 365–80.

Esteves, F., C. Parra, et al. (1994). "Nonconscious associative learning: Pavlovian conditioning of skin conductance responses to masked fear-relevant facial stimuli." *Psychophysiology* 31(4): 375–85.

Etkin, A., K. C. Klemenhagen, et al. (2004). "Individual differences in trait anxiety predict the response of the basolateral amygdala to unconsciously processed fearful faces." *Neuron* 44(6): 1043–55.

Exline, J. J., and M. Lobel (1999). "The perils of outperformance: Sensitivity about being the target of a threatening upward comparison." *Psychol Bull* 125(3): 307–37.

Falconer, E., R. Bryant, et al. (2008). "The neural networks of inhibitory control in posttraumatic stress disorder." *J Psychiatry Neurosci* 33(5): 413–22.

Falconer, E. M., K. L. Felmingham, et al. (2008). "Developing an integrated brain, behavior and biological response profile in posttraumatic stress disorder (PTSD)." *J Integr Neurosci* 7(3): 439–56.

Favaro, A., D. Degortes, et al. (2000). "The effects of trauma among kidnap victims in Sardinia, Italy." *Psychol Med* 30(4): 975–80.

Febo, M., M. Numan, et al. (2005). "Functional magnetic resonance imaging shows oxytocin activates brain regions associated with mother-pup bonding during suckling." *J Neurosci* 25(50): 11637–44.

Felmingham, K., A. H. Kemp, et al. (2008). "Dissociative responses to conscious and non-conscious fear impact underlying brain function in post-traumatic stress disorder." *Psychol Med* 38(12): 1771–80.

Feser, D. K., M. Grundl, et al. (2007). "Attractiveness of eyebrow position and shape in females depends on the age of the beholder." *Aesthetic Plast Surg* 31(2): 154–60.

Files, J. A., J. E. Blair, et al. (2008). "Facilitated peer mentorship: A pilot program for academic advancement of female medical faculty." *J Womens Health (Larchmt)* 17(6): 1009–15.

Fisher, E. B., C. A. Brownson, et al. (2007). "Perspectives on self-management from the Diabetes Initiative of the Robert Wood Johnson Foundation." *Diabetes Educ* 33 Suppl 6: 216S-24S.

Fisher, H. E., A. Aron, et al. (2006). "Romantic love: A mammalian brain system for mate choice." *Philos Trans R Soc Lond B Biol Sci* 361(1476): 2173–86.

Fleming, K. K., C. L. Bandy, et al. (2009). "Decisions to shoot in a weapon identification task: The influence of cultural stereotypes and perceived threat on false positive errors." *Soc Neurosci,* doi: 10.1080/17470910903268931.

Floyd, K. (2000). "Affectionate same-sex touch: The influence of homophobia on observers' perceptions." *J Soc Psychol* 140(6): 774–88.

Fonagy, P., G. Gergely, et al. (2007). "The parent-infant dyad and the construction of the subjective self." *J Child Psychol Psychiatry* 48(3–4): 288–328.

Ford, T. E., C. F. Boxer, et al. (2008). "More than 'just a joke': The prejudice-releasing function of sexist humor." *Pers Soc Psychol Bull* 34(2): 159–70.

Fox, N. A., H. A. Henderson, et al. (2005). "Behavioral inhibition: Linking biology and behavior within a developmental framework." *Annu Rev Psychol* 56: 235–62.

Frank, M. J., B. S. Woroch, et al. (2005). "Error-related negativity predicts reinforcement learning and conflict biases." *Neuron* 47(4): 495–501.

Frantz, C. M., A. J. Cuddy, et al. (2004). "A threat in the computer: The race Implicit Association Test as a stereotype threat experience." *Pers Soc Psychol Bull* 30(12): 1611–24.

Freeland-Graves, J., and S. Nitzke (2002). "Position of the American Dietetic Association: Total diet approach to communicating food and nutrition information." *J Am Diet Assoc* 102(1): 100–8.

Frewen, P., R. D. Lane, et al. (2008). "Neural correlates of levels of emotional awareness during trauma script-imagery in posttraumatic stress disorder." *Psychosom Med* 70(1): 27–31.

Frewen, P. A., R. A. Lanius, et al. (2008). "Clinical and neural correlates of alexithymia in posttraumatic stress disorder." *J Abnorm Psychol* 117(1): 171–81.

Fried-Buchalter, S. (1992). "Fear of success, fear of failure, and the imposter phenomenon: A factor analytic approach to convergent and discriminant validity." *J Pers Assess* 58(2): 368–79.

Funk, R. E. (2008). "Men's work: Men's voices and actions against sexism and violence." *J Prev Interv Community* 36(1–2): 155–71.

Furlong, E. E., K. J. Boose, et al. (2008). "Raking it in: The impact of enculturation on chimpanzee tool use." *Anim Cogn* 11(1): 83–97.

Ganzel, B., B. J. Casey, et al. (2007). "The aftermath of 9/11: Effect of intensity and recency of trauma on outcome." *Emotion* 7(2): 227–38.

Garcia, A. V., F. L. Torrecillas, et al. (2005). "Effects of executive impairments on maladaptive explanatory styles in substance abusers: Clinical implications." *Arch Clin Neuropsychol* 20(1): 67–80.

Gatchel, R. J., and J. D. Proctor (1976). "Physiological correlates of learned helplessness in man." *J Abnorm Psychol* 85(1): 27–34.

Gayle, M. E. (1987). "Applying futures' research to nutrition education." *J Am Diet Assoc* 87(9 Suppl): S78–80.

Gaylord, C., D. Orme-Johnson, et al. (1989). "The effects of the transcendental mediation technique and progressive muscle relaxation on EEG coherence, stress reactivity, and mental health in black adults." *Int J Neurosci* 46(1–2): 77–86.

Gernigon, C., P. Fleurance, et al. (2000). "Effects of uncontrollability and failure on the development of learned helplessness in perceptual-motor tasks." *Res Q Exerc Sport* 71(1): 44–54.

Gilbert, S. C. (1993). "Fear of success in anorexic young women." *J Adolesc Health* 14(5): 380–3.

Gilbertson, M. W., S. K. Williston, et al. (2007). "Configural cue performance in identical twins discordant for posttraumatic stress disorder: Theoretical implications for the role of hippocampal function." *Biol Psychiatry* 62(5): 513–20.

Gillath, O., S. A. Bunge, et al. (2005). "Attachment-style differences in the ability to suppress negative thoughts: Exploring the neural correlates." *Neuroimage* 28(4): 835–47.

Giltay, E. J., J. M. Geleijnse, et al. (2007). "Lifestyle and dietary correlates of dispositional optimism in men: The Zutphen Elderly Study." *J Psychosom Res* 63(5): 483–90.

Gobbini, M. I., E. Leibenluft, et al. (2004). "Social and emotional attachment in the neural representation of faces." *Neuroimage* 22(4): 1628–35.

Goff, P. A., J. L. Eberhardt, et al. (2008). "Not yet human: Implicit knowledge, historical dehumanization, and contemporary consequences." *J Pers Soc Psychol* 94(2): 292–306.

Goff, P. A., C. M. Steele, et al. (2008). "The space between us: Stereotype threat and distance in interracial contexts." *J Pers Soc Psychol* 94(1): 91–107.

Goldberg, I. I., M. Harel, et al. (2006). "When the brain loses its self: Prefrontal inactivation during sensorimotor processing." *Neuron* 50(2): 329–39.

Golden, A. M., T. Dalgleish, et al. (2007). "Levels of specificity of autobiographical memories and of biographical memories of the deceased in bereaved individuals with and without complicated grief." *J Abnorm Psychol* 116(4): 786–95.

Gordon, J. S., J. K. Staples, et al. (2008). "Treatment of posttraumatic stress disorder in postwar Kosovar adolescents using mind-body skills groups: A randomized controlled trial." *J Clin Psychiatry* 69(9): 1469–76.

Gottman, J. M. (1998). "Psychology and the study of marital processes." *Annu Rev Psychol* 49: 169–97.

Gottschalk, L. A., J. Fronczek, et al. (1993). "The cerebral neurobiology of hope and hopelessness." *Psychiatry* 56(3): 270–81.

Green, A. R., D. R. Carney, et al. (2007). "Implicit bias among physicians and its prediction of thrombolysis decisions for black and white patients." *J Gen Intern Med* 22(9): 1231–8.

Green, B. C. (2005). "Homosexual signification: A moral construct in social contexts." *J Homosex* 49(2): 119–34.

Greenwald, A. G., D. E. McGhee, et al. (1998). "Measuring individual differences in implicit cognition: The Implicit Association Test." *J Pers Soc Psychol* 74(6): 1464–80.

Greer, J. G., and C. E. Wethered (1984). "Learned helplessness: A piece of the burnout puzzle." *Except Child* 50(6): 524–30.

Gregory, W. L., G. M. Chartier, et al. (1979). "Learned helplessness and learned effectiveness: Effects of explicit response cues on individuals differing in personal control expectancies." *J Pers Soc Psychol* 37(11): 1982–92.

Grundl, M., S. Klein, et al. (2008). "The 'jaguar's eye' as a new beauty trend? Age-related effects in judging the attractiveness of the oblique eye axis." *Aesthetic Plast Surg* 32(6): 915–9.

Guastella, A. J., P. B. Mitchell, et al. (2008). "Oxytocin increases gaze to the eye region of human faces." *Biol Psychiatry* 63(1): 3–5.

Guerrero, M. L., R. C. Morrow, et al. (1999). "Rapid ethnographic assessment of breastfeeding practices in periurban Mexico City." *Bull World Health Organ* 77(4): 323–30.

Gunning-Dixon, F. M., R. C. Gur, et al. (2003). "Age-related differences in brain activation during emotional face processing." *Neurobiol Aging* 24(2): 285–95.

Gupta, A. (2002). "Unconscious amygdalar fear conditioning in a subset of chronic fatigue syndrome patients." *Med Hypotheses* 59(6): 727–35.

Gupta, V. K., D. B. Turban, et al. (2008). "The effect of gender stereotype activation on entrepreneurial intentions." *J Appl Psychol* 93(5): 1053–61.

Gur, R. C., L. Schroeder, et al. (2002). "Brain activation during facial emotion processing." *Neuroimage* 16(3 Pt 1): 651–62.

Hadjikhani, N., and B. de Gelder (2003). "Seeing fearful body expressions activates the fusiform cortex and amygdala." *Curr Biol* 13(24): 2201–5.

Haggard, P. (2005). "Conscious intention and motor cognition." *Trends Cogn Sci* 9(6): 290–5.

Haggard, P., and J. Cole (2007). "Intention, attention and the temporal experience of action." *Conscious Cogn* 16(2): 211–20.

Hakamata, Y., Y. Matsuoka, et al. (2007). "Structure of orbitofrontal cortex and its longitudinal course in cancer-related post-traumatic stress disorder." *Neurosci Res* 59(4): 383–9.

Halper, T. (1980). "The double-edged sword: Paternalism as a policy in the problems of aging." *Milbank Mem Fund Q Health Soc* 58(3): 472–99.

Hamm, A. O., A. I. Weike, et al. (2003). "Affective blindsight: Intact fear conditioning to a visual cue in a cortically blind patient." *Brain* 126(Pt 2): 267–75.

Hammond, J. S., R. L. Keeney, et al. (1998). "The hidden traps in decision making." *Harv Bus Rev* 76(5): 47–8, 50, 52 passim.

Hankey, A. (2006). "Studies of advanced stages of meditation in the Tibetan Buddhist and Vedic traditions. I: A comparison of general changes." *Evid Based Complement Alternat Med* 3(4): 513–21.

Hanssen, I. (2004). "From human ability to ethical principle: An intercultural perspective on autonomy." *Med Health Care Philos* 7(3): 269–79.

Harding, T., N. North, et al. (2008). "Sexualizing men's touch: Male nurses and the use of intimate touch in clinical practice." *Res Theory Nurs Pract* 22(2): 88–102.

Hardy, C. J., and J. M. Silva, 3rd (1986). "The relationship between selected psychological traits and fear of success in senior elite level wrestlers." *Can J Appl Sport Sci* 11(4): 205–10.

Hariri, A. R., S. Y. Bookheimer, et al. (2000). "Modulating emotional responses: Effects of a neocortical network on the limbic system." *Neuroreport* 11(1): 43–8.

Hariri, A. R., E. M. Drabant, et al. (2005). "A susceptibility gene for affective disorders and the response of the human amygdala." *Arch Gen Psychiatry* 62(2): 146–52.

Hariri, A. R., V. S. Mattay, et al. (2003). "Neocortical modulation of the amygdala response to fearful stimuli." *Biol Psychiatry* 53(6): 494–501.

Harmer, C. J., C. E. Mackay, et al. (2006). "Antidepressant drug treatment modifies the neural processing of nonconscious threat cues." *Biol Psychiatry* 59(9): 816–20.

Harnischmacher, R., and J. Muther (1987). "[The Stockholm syndrome: On the psychological reaction of hostages and hostage-takers]." *Arch Kriminol* 180(1–2): 1–12.

Harrell, E. H., J. R. Haynes, et al. (1978). "Reversal of learned helplessness by peripheral arousal." *Psychol Rep* 43(3 Pt 2): 1211–7.

Harris, S., S. A. Sheth, et al. (2008). "Functional neuroimaging of belief, disbelief, and uncertainty." *Ann Neurol* 63(2): 141–7.

Hatfield, E., J. T. Cacioppo, et al. (1994). *Emotional Contagion.* (Cambridge, England: Cambridge University Press).

Hawkley, L. C., and J. T. Cacioppo (2003). "Loneliness and pathways to disease." *Brain Behav Immun* 17 Suppl 1: S98–105.

Hawkley, L. C., C. M. Masi, et al. (2006). "Loneliness is a unique predictor of age-related differences in systolic blood pressure." *Psychol Aging* 21(1): 152–64.

Hedges, D. W., G. W. Thatcher, et al. (2007). "Brain integrity and cerebral atrophy in Vietnam combat veterans with and without posttraumatic stress disorder." *Neurocase* 13(5): 402–10.

Heim, C., U. M. Nater, et al. (2009). "Childhood trauma and risk for chronic fatigue syndrome: Association with neuroendocrine dysfunction." *Arch Gen Psychiatry* 66(1): 72–80.

Heim, C., L. J. Young, et al. (2009). "Lower CSF oxytocin concentrations in women with a history of childhood abuse." *Mol Psychiatry* 14: 954–8.

Hendler, T., P. Rotshtein, et al. (2001). "Emotion-perception interplay in the visual cortex: 'The eyes follow the heart.'" *Cell Mol Neurobiol* 21(6): 733–52.

Higgins, R. W. (1986). "[Can the quality of life be quantified?]." *Bull Cancer* 73(6): 704–8.

Hilton, S., K. Hunt, et al. (2008). "Have men been overlooked? A comparison of young men and women's experiences of chemotherapy-induced alopecia." *Psychooncology* 17(6): 577–83.

Hinson, J. M., P. Whitney, et al. (2006). "Affective biasing of choices in gambling task decision making." *Cogn Affect Behav Neurosci* 6(3): 190–200.

Hirsh, A. T., S. Z. George, et al. (2008). "Fear of pain, pain catastrophizing, and acute pain perception: Relative prediction and timing of assessment." *J Pain* 9(9): 806–12.

Hollway, W., and T. Jefferson (2005). "Panic and perjury: A psychosocial exploration of agency." *Br J Soc Psychol* 44(Pt 2): 147–63.

Holmes, E. A., E. L. James, et al. (2009). "Can playing the computer game 'Tetris' reduce the build-up of flashbacks for trauma? A proposal from cognitive science." *PLoS ONE* 4(1): e4153.

Horgen, K. B., and K. D. Brownell (2002). "Comparison of price change and health message interventions in promoting healthy food choices." *Health Psychol* 21(5): 505–12.

Horstmann, G. (2003). "What do facial expressions convey: Feeling states, behavioral intentions, or action requests?" *Emotion* 3(2): 150–66.

Hsee, C. K., and R. Hastie (2006). "Decision and experience: Why don't we choose what makes us happy?" *Trends Cogn Sci* 10(1): 31–7.

Hsee, C. K., and J. Zhang (2004). "Distinction bias: Misprediction and mischoice due to joint evaluation." *J Pers Soc Psychol* 86(5): 680–95.

Hunt, M. E. (1993). "Abortion in a just society." *Conscience* 14(1–2): 33–6.

Iborra, A. (2007). "Dealing with homosexuality in a homophobic culture: A self-organization approach." *Integr Psychol Behav Sci* 41(3–4): 285–95; discussion 326–34.

Ilg, R., K. Vogeley, et al. (2007). "Neural processes underlying intuitive coherence judgments as revealed by fMRI on a semantic judgment task." *Neuroimage* 38(1): 228–38.

Inzaghi, M. G., A. De Tanti, et al. (2005). "The effects of traumatic brain injury on patients and their families: A follow-up study." *Eura Medicophys* 41(4): 265–73.

Ishak, W. W., D. S. Berman, et al. (2008). "Male anorgasmia treated with oxytocin." *J Sex Med* 5(4): 1022–4.

Ishiyama, F. I., P. A. Munson, et al. (1990). "Birth order and fear of success among midadolescents." *Psychol Rep* 66(1): 17–8.

Ito, T. A., K. W. Chiao, et al. (2006). "The influence of facial feedback on race bias." *Psychol Sci* 17(3): 256–61.

Iverson, P. (2003). "Evaluating the function of phonetic perceptual phenomena within speech recognition: An examination of the perception of /d/–/t/ by adult cochlear implant users." *J Acoust Soc Am* 113(2): 1056–64.

Jackowski, A. P., C. M. de Araujo, et al. (2009). "Neurostructural imaging findings in children with post-traumatic stress disorder: Brief review." *Psychiatry Clin Neurosci* 63(1): 1–8.

Jevning, R., A. F. Wilson, et al. (1985). "Modulation of red cell metabolism by states of decreased activation: Comparison between states." *Physiol Behav* 35(5): 679–82.

Johnson, M. J., N. C. Jackson, et al. (2005). "Gay and lesbian perceptions of discrimination in retirement care facilities." *J Homosex* 49(2): 83–102.

Johnstone, T., L. H. Somerville, et al. (2005). "Stability of amygdala BOLD response to fearful faces over multiple scan sessions." *Neuroimage* 25(4): 1112–23.

Jones, T. E. (2006). "Five questions dentists should ask about their money. Question 4: How do the communities (family, practice, profession, culture, neighborhood, etc.) in which I live affect my financial decisions?" *J Okla Dent Assoc* 96(3): 24.

Jordan, P. W. (1998). "Human factors for pleasure in product use." *Appl Ergon* 29(1): 25–33.

Kaiser, C. R., and J. S. Pratt-Hyatt (2009). "Distributing prejudice unequally: Do Whites direct their prejudice toward strongly identified minorities?" *J Pers Soc Psychol* 96(2): 432–45.

Kanagaratnam, P., and A. E. Asbjornsen (2007). "Executive deficits in chronic PTSD related to political violence." *J Anxiety Disord* 21(4): 510–25.

Kapfhammer, H. P. (2008). "[Therapeutic possibilities after traumatic experiences]." *Psychiatr Danub* 20(4): 532–45.

Kassel, J. D., M. Wardle, et al. (2007). "Adult attachment security and college student substance use." *Addict Behav* 32(6): 1164–76.

Katkin, E. S., S. Wiens, et al. (2001). "Nonconscious fear conditioning, visceral perception, and the development of gut feelings." *Psychol Sci* 12(5): 366–70.

Kawakami, K., E. Dunn, et al. (2009). "Mispredicting affective and behavioral responses to racism." *Science* 323(5911): 276–8.

Kehoe, J. (1994). *Money Success and You.* (Vancouver, British Columbia: Zoetic).

Keri, S., I. Kiss, et al. (2008). "Sharing secrets: Oxytocin and trust in schizophrenia." *Soc Neurosci* 4(4): 287–93.

Kibadi, K., I. Aujoulat, et al. (2007). "[Study of names and folklore associated with *Mycobacterium ulcerans* infection in various endemic countries in Africa]." *Med Trop (Mars)* 67(3): 241–8.

Killgore, W. D., and D. A. Yurgelun-Todd (2005). "Social anxiety predicts amygdala activation in adolescents viewing fearful faces." *Neuroreport* 16(15): 1671–5.

Kim, A. W., M. J. Liptay, et al. (2008). "Contemporary review on the inequities in the management of lung cancer among the African-American population." *J Natl Med Assoc* 100(6): 683–8.

Kimura, M., J. Katayama, et al. (2008). "Event-related brain potential evidence for implicit change detection: A replication of Fernandez-Duque et al. (2003)." *Neurosci Lett* 448(3): 236–9.

Kimura, Y., A. Yoshino, et al. (2004). "Interhemispheric difference in emotional response without awareness." *Physiol Behav* 82(4): 727–31.

Kinoshita, S., and M. Peek-O'Leary (2005). "Does the compatibility effect in the race Implicit Association Test reflect familiarity or affect?" *Psychon Bull Rev* 12(3): 442–52.

Kirsch, P., C. Esslinger, et al. (2005). "Oxytocin modulates neural circuitry for social cognition and fear in humans." *J Neurosci* 25(49): 11489–93.

Kissane, D. W., S. Wein, et al. (2004). "The Demoralization Scale: A report of its development and preliminary validation." *J Palliat Care* 20(4): 269–76.

Klein, D. C., and M. E. Seligman (1976). "Reversal of performance deficits and perceptual deficits in learned helplessness and depression." *J Abnorm Psychol* 85(1): 11–26.

Knight, D. C., H. T. Nguyen, et al. (2005). "The role of the human amygdala in the production of conditioned fear responses." *Neuroimage* 26(4): 1193–200.

Knight, D. C., C. N. Smith, et al. (1999). "Functional MRI of human Pavlovian fear conditioning: Patterns of activation as a function of learning." *Neuroreport* 10(17): 3665–70.

Knutson, K. M., L. Mah, et al. (2007). "Neural correlates of automatic beliefs about gender and race." *Hum Brain Mapp* 28(10): 915–30.

Konstantopoulos, S., and A. Constant (2008). "The gender gap reloaded: Are school characteristics linked to labor market performance?" *Soc Sci Res* 37(2): 374–85.

Kosfeld, M., M. Heinrichs, et al. (2005). "Oxytocin increases trust in humans." *Nature* 435(7042): 673–6.

Kozar, R. A., K. D. Anderson, et al. (2004). "Preclinical students: Who are surgeons?" *J Surg Res* 119(2): 113–6.

Kroon, V., and L. Boyd (2001). "Menopause: Choices for women." *Aust Nurs J* 8(7): Suppl 1–4.

Krueger, F., K. McCabe, et al. (2007). "Neural correlates of trust." *Proc Natl Acad Sci U S A* 104(50): 20084–9.

Kuno, M., H. Yazawa, et al. (2003). "[Learned helplessness, generalized self-efficacy, and immune function]." *Shinrigaku Kenkyu* 73(6): 472–9.

LaBar, K. S., M. J. Crupain, et al. (2003). "Dynamic perception of facial affect and identity in the human brain." *Cereb Cortex* 13(10): 1023–33.

LaBar, K. S., J. C. Gatenby, et al. (1998). "Human amygdala activation during conditioned fear acquisition and extinction: A mixed-trial fMRI study." *Neuron* 20(5): 937–45.

LaBar, K. S., and E. A. Phelps (2005). "Reinstatement of conditioned fear in humans is context dependent and impaired in amnesia." *Behav Neurosci* 119(3): 677–86.

Laird, J. D. (1984). "The real role of facial response in the experience of emotion: A reply to Tourangeau and Ellsworth, and others." *J Pers Soc Psychol* 47: 909–17.

Lau, H. C., R. D. Rogers, et al. (2007). "Manipulating the experienced onset of intention after action execution." *J Cogn Neurosci* 19(1): 81–90.

Lawrence, E. J., P. Shaw, et al. (2006). "The role of 'shared representations' in social perception and empathy: An fMRI study." *Neuroimage* 29(4): 1173–84.

LeDoux, J. (1996). "Emotional networks and motor control: A fearful view." *Prog Brain Res* 107: 437–46.

LeDoux, J. (1998). "Fear and the brain: Where have we been, and where are we going?" *Biol Psychiatry* 44(12): 1229–38.

LeDoux, J. E. (1993). "Emotional memory: In search of systems and synapses." *Ann N Y Acad Sci* 702: 149–57.

Legault, L., I. Green-Demers, et al. (2007). "On the self-regulation of implicit and explicit prejudice: A self-determination theory perspective." *Pers Soc Psychol Bull* 33(5): 732–49.

Leibenluft, E., M. I. Gobbini, et al. (2004). "Mothers' neural activation in response to pictures of their children and other children." *Biol Psychiatry* 56(4): 225–32.

Lemche, E., V. P. Giampietro, et al. (2006). "Human attachment security is mediated by the amygdala: Evidence from combined fMRI and psychophysiological measures." *Hum Brain Mapp* 27(8): 623–35.

Lemm, K. M. (2006). "Positive associations among interpersonal contact, motivation, and implicit and explicit attitudes toward gay men." *J Homosex* 51(2): 79–99.

Lenke, R. R., and J. M. Nemes (1985). "Wrongful birth, wrongful life: The doctor between a rock and a hard place." *Obstet Gynecol* 66(5): 719–22.

Lester, D. (2001). "An inventory to measure helplessness, hopelessness, and haplessness." *Psychol Rep* 89(3): 495–8.

Liddell, B. J., K. J. Brown, et al. (2005). "A direct brainstem-amygdala-cortical 'alarm' system for subliminal signals of fear." *Neuroimage* 24(1): 235–43.

Lieberman, M. D., A. Hariri, et al. (2005). "An fMRI investigation of race-related amygdala activity in African-American and Caucasian-American individuals." *Nat Neurosci* 8(6): 720–2.

Limb, C. J., and A. R. Braun (2008). "Neural substrates of spontaneous musical performance: An fMRI study of jazz improvisation." *PLoS ONE* 3(2): e1679.

Lindauer, R. J., J. Booij, et al. (2008). "Effects of psychotherapy on regional cerebral blood flow during trauma imagery in patients with post-traumatic stress disorder: A randomized clinical trial." *Psychol Med* 38(4): 543–54.

Lindauer, R. J., M. Olff, et al. (2006). "Cortisol, learning, memory, and attention in relation to smaller hippocampal volume in police officers with posttraumatic stress disorder." *Biol Psychiatry* 59(2): 171–7.

Lindsay, S., P. Bellaby, et al. (2008). "Enabling healthy choices: Is

ICT the highway to health improvement?" *Health (London)* 12(3): 313–31.

List, A., and A. Landau (2006). "Attention and intention, decoded!" *J Neurosci* 26(26): 6907–8.

Livingston, R. W., and B. B. Drwecki (2007). "Why are some individuals not racially biased? Susceptibility to affective conditioning predicts nonprejudice toward blacks." *Psychol Sci* 18(9): 816–23.

Lobaugh, N. J., E. Gibson, et al. (2006). "Children recruit distinct neural systems for implicit emotional face processing." *Neuroreport* 17(2): 215–9.

Long, W., and C. A. Millsap (2008). "Fear of AIDS and Homophobia Scales in an ethnic population of university students." *J Soc Psychol* 148(5): 637–40.

Lorberbaum, J. P., S. Kose, et al. (2004). "Neural correlates of speech anticipatory anxiety in generalized social phobia." *Neuroreport* 15(18): 2701–5.

Lowery, B. S., E. D. Knowles, et al. (2007). "Framing inequity safely: Whites' motivated perceptions of racial privilege." *Pers Soc Psychol Bull* 33(9): 1237–50.

Lubetzky, O., and I. Gilat (2002). "The impact of premature birth on fear of personal death and attachment of styles in adolescence." *Death Stud* 26(7): 523–43.

Lungu, O. V., T. Liu, et al. (2007). "Strategic modulation of cognitive control." *J Cogn Neurosci* 19(8): 1302–15.

Lunt, A. (2004). "The implications for the clinician of adopting a recovery model: The role of choice in assertive treatment." *Psychiatr Rehabil J* 28(1): 93–7.

Lustig, A. (2004). "Immortality." *Commonweal* 131(3): 7–8.

Lutz, A., J. Brefczynski-Lewis, et al. (2008). "Regulation of the neural circuitry of emotion by compassion meditation: Effects of meditative expertise." *PLoS ONE* 3(3): e1897.

Lutz, A., H. A. Slagter, et al. (2008). "Attention regulation and monitoring in meditation." *Trends Cogn Sci* 12(4): 163–9.

MacDonald, H. B. (1991). "Meat and its place in the diet." *Can J Public Health* 82(5): 331–4.

Magill, M. K., and W. J. Kane (2001). "What opportunities have we missed, and what bad deals have we made?" *Fam Med* 33(4): 268–72.

Mahaffey, A. L., A. Bryan, et al. (2005). "Sex differences in affective responses to homoerotic stimuli: Evidence for an unconscious bias among heterosexual men, but not heterosexual women." *Arch Sex Behav* 34(5): 537–45.

Maier, S. F., K. T. Nguyen, et al. (1999). "Stress, learned helplessness, and brain interleukin-1 beta." *Adv Exp Med Biol* 461: 235–49.

Mallinger, J. B., and S. J. Lamberti (2007). "Racial differences in the use of adjunctive psychotropic medications for patients with schizophrenia." *J Ment Health Policy Econ* 10(1): 15–22.

Mangurian, G. E. (2007). "Realizing what you're made of." *Harv Bus Rev* 85(3): 125–30, 144.

Marill, I. H., and E. R. Siegel (2004). "Success and succession." *J Am Psychoanal Assoc* 52(3): 673–88.

Mathews, A., J. Yiend, et al. (2004). "Individual differences in the modulation of fear-related brain activation by attentional control." *J Cogn Neurosci* 16(10): 1683–94.

Mayhew, P. J. (2001). "Herbivore host choice and optimal bad motherhood." *Trends Ecol Evol* 16(4): 165–167.

McVeagh, P. (2000). "Eating and nutritional problems in children." *Aust Fam Physician* 29(8): 735–40.

Mehner, A., U. Lindblad, et al. (2008). "Cholesterol in women at high cardiovascular risk is less successfully treated than in corresponding men. The Skaraborg Hypertension and Diabetes Project." *Eur J Clin Pharmacol* 64(8): 815–20.

Meili, T., and J. Kabat-Zinn (2004). "The power of the human heart: A story of trauma and recovery and its implications for rehabilitation and healing." *Adv Mind Body Med* 20(1): 6–16.

Menges, T., J. Boldt, et al. (1993). "[The effect of different autotransfusion procedures on the antibiotic picture: A study on cephalosporin cefamandole]." *Anaesthesist* 42(8): 509–15.

Meredith, P. J., J. Strong, et al. (2006). "The relationship of adult attachment to emotion, catastrophizing, control, threshold and tolerance, in experimentally-induced pain." *Pain* 120(1–2): 44–52.

Meriau, K., I. Wartenburger, et al. (2006). "A neural network reflecting individual differences in cognitive processing of emotions during perceptual decision making." *Neuroimage* 33(3): 1016–27.

Meyer-Lindenberg, A. (2008). "Impact of prosocial neuropeptides on human brain function." *Prog Brain Res* 170: 463–70.

Midgley, N., and M. S. Abrams (1974). "Fear of success and locus of control in young women." *J Consult Clin Psychol* 42(5): 737.

Miedema, B. B., J. Easley, et al. (2006). "Young adults' experiences with cancer: Comments from patients and survivors." *Can Fam Physician* 52(11): 1446–7.

Miller, R. H. (1996). "Competition in the health system: Good news and bad news." *Health Aff (Millwood)* 15(2): 107–20.

Milne, E., and J. Grafman (2001). "Ventromedial prefrontal cortex lesions in humans eliminate implicit gender stereotyping." *J Neurosci* 21(12): RC150.

Minore, B., M. Boone, et al. (2004). "How clients choices influence cancer care in northern Aboriginal communities." *Int J Circumpolar Health* 63 Suppl 2: 129–32.

Mogg, K., M. Garner, et al. (2007). "Anxiety and orienting of gaze to angry and fearful faces." *Biol Psychol* 76(3): 163–9.

Mojzisch, A., and S. Schulz-Hardt (2007). "Being fed up: A social cognitive neuroscience approach to mental satiation." *Ann N Y Acad Sci* 1118: 186–205.

Monk, C., K. L. Leight, et al. (2008). "The relationship between women's attachment style and perinatal mood disturbance: Implications for screening and treatment." *Arch Womens Ment Health* 11(2): 117–29.

Monk, C. S., E. B. McClure, et al. (2003). "Adolescent immaturity in attention-related brain engagement to emotional facial expressions." *Neuroimage* 20(1): 420–8.

Moores, K. A., C. R. Clark, et al. (2008). "Abnormal recruitment of working memory updating networks during maintenance of trauma-neutral information in post-traumatic stress disorder." *Psychiatry Res* 163(2): 156–70.

Morey, R. A., F. Dolcos, et al. (2009). "The role of trauma-related distractors on neural systems for working memory and emotion processing in posttraumatic stress disorder." *J Psychiatr Res* 43(8): 809–17.

Morey, R. A., C. M. Petty, et al. (2008). "Neural systems for executive and emotional processing are modulated by symptoms of posttraumatic stress disorder in Iraq War veterans." *Psychiatry Res* 162(1): 59–72.

Moriguchi, Y., T. Ohnishi, et al. (2005). "Specific brain activation in Japanese and Caucasian people to fearful faces." *Neuroreport* 16(2): 133–6.

Morris, J. S., C. Buchel, et al. (2001). "Parallel neural responses in amygdala subregions and sensory cortex during implicit fear conditioning." *Neuroimage* 13(6 Pt 1): 1044–52.

Morris, J. S., M. deBonis, et al. (2002). "Human amygdala responses to fearful eyes." *Neuroimage* 17(1): 214–22.

Morris, J. S., B. DeGelder, et al. (2001). "Differential extrageniculostriate and amygdala responses to presentation of emotional faces in a cortically blind field." *Brain* 124(Pt 6): 1241–52.

Morris, J. S., and R. J. Dolan (2004). "Dissociable amygdala and orbitofrontal responses during reversal fear conditioning." *Neuroimage* 22(1): 372–80.

Morse, G. (2006). "Decisions and desire." *Harv Bus Rev* 84(1): 42, 44–51, 132.

Murphy, S. E., C. Longhitano, et al. (2009). "The role of serotonin in nonnormative risky choice: The effects of tryptophan supplements on the 'reflection effect' in healthy adult volunteers." *J Cogn Neurosci* 21(9): 1709–19.

Myers, H. F. (2009). "Ethnicity- and socio-economic status-related stresses in context: An integrative review and conceptual model." *J Behav Med* 32(1): 9–19.

Nair, C., H. Colburn, et al. (1989). "Cardiovascular disease in Canada." *Health Rep* 1(1): 1–22.

Najstrom, M., and B. Jansson (2006). "Unconscious responses to threatening pictures: Interactive effect of trait anxiety and social desirability on skin conductance responses." *Cogn Behav Ther* 35(1): 11–8.

Namima, M., K. Sugihara, et al. (1999). "Quantitative analysis of the effects of lithium on the reverse tolerance and the c-Fos expression induced by methamphetamine in mice." *Brain Res Brain Res Protoc* 4(1): 11–8.

Nash, L., and H. Stevenson (2004). "Success that lasts." *Harv Bus Rev* 82(2): 102–9, 124.

Nausheen, B., Y. Gidron, et al. (2007). "Loneliness, social support and cardiovascular reactivity to laboratory stress." *Stress* 10(1): 37–44.

Nguyen, J. T., A. K. Berger, et al. (2008). "Gender disparity in cardiac procedures and medication use for acute myocardial infarction." *Am Heart J* 155(5): 862–8.

Nisan, M. (1975). "Children's evaluations of temporally distant outcomes." *J Genet Psychol* 126(1st Half): 53–60.

Nitschke, J. B., E. E. Nelson, et al. (2004). "Orbitofrontal cortex tracks positive mood in mothers viewing pictures of their newborn infants." *Neuroimage* 21(2): 583–92.

Nitzke, S., and J. Freeland-Graves (2007). "Position of the American Dietetic Association: Total diet approach to communicating food and nutrition information." *J Am Diet Assoc* 107(7): 1224–32.

Noriuchi, M., Y. Kikuchi, et al. (2008). "The functional neuroanatomy of maternal love: Mother's response to infant's attachment behaviors." *Biol Psychiatry* 63(4): 415–23.

Nutt, D. J., and A. L. Malizia (2004). "Structural and functional brain changes in posttraumatic stress disorder." *J Clin Psychiatry* 65 Suppl 1: 11–7.

O'Brien, K. S., J. D. Latner, et al. (2008). "Do antifat attitudes predict antifat behaviors?" *Obesity (Silver Spring)* 16 Suppl 2: S87–92.

O'Brien, T. (1993). "Palliative care and taboos within motor neurone disease." *Palliat Med* 7(4 Suppl): 69–72.

Ogden, T. H. (1988). "Misrecognitions and the fear of not knowing." *Psychoanal Q* 57(4): 643–66.

Ohman, A., and J. J. Soares (1994). "'Unconscious anxiety': Phobic responses to masked stimuli." *J Abnorm Psychol* 103(2): 231–40.

Olff, M., W. Langeland, et al. (2007). "Gender differences in posttraumatic stress disorder." *Psychol Bull* 133(2): 183–204.

Olsen, N. J., and E. W. Willemsen (1978). "Fear of success—Fact or artifact?" *J Psychol* 98(1st Half): 65–70.

Orsini, M. G., G. J. Huang, et al. (2006). "Methods to evaluate profile preferences for the anteroposterior position of the mandible." *Am J Orthod Dentofacial Orthop* 130(3): 283–91.

Overmier, J. B., and R. Murison (2000). "Anxiety and helplessness in the face of stress predisposes, precipitates, and sustains gastric ulceration." *Behav Brain Res* 110(1–2): 161–74.

Overmier, J. B., and R. Murison (2005). "Trauma and resulting sensitization effects are modulated by psychological factors." *Psychoneuroendocrinology* 30(10): 965–73.

Pachankis, J. E., M. R. Goldfried, et al. (2008). "Extension of the rejection sensitivity construct to the interpersonal functioning of gay men." *J Consult Clin Psychol* 76(2): 306–17.

Pagnoni, G., M. Cekic, et al. (2008). "'Thinking about not-thinking': Neural correlates of conceptual processing during Zen meditation." *PLoS ONE* 3(9): e3083.

Pais-Ribeiro, J., A. M. da Silva, et al. (2007). "Relationship between optimism, disease variables, and health perception and quality of life in individuals with epilepsy." *Epilepsy Behav* 11(1): 33–8.

Paluck, E. L., and D. P. Green (2009). "Prejudice reduction: What works? A review and assessment of research and practice." *Annu Rev Psychol* 60: 339–67.

Paquette, V., J. Levesque, et al. (2003). "'Change the mind and you change the brain': Effects of cognitive-behavioral therapy on the neural correlates of spider phobia." *Neuroimage* 18(2): 401–9.

Paradies, Y. (2006). "A review of psychosocial stress and chronic disease for 4th world indigenous peoples and African Americans." *Ethn Dis* 16(1): 295–308.

Pedersen, C. A. (2004). "Biological aspects of social bonding and the roots of human violence." *Ann N Y Acad Sci* 1036: 106–27.

Peng, C. K., I. C. Henry, et al. (2004). "Heart rate dynamics during three forms of meditation." *Int J Cardiol* 95(1): 19–27.

Peres, J. F., A. B. Newberg, et al. (2007). "Cerebral blood flow changes during retrieval of traumatic memories before and after psychotherapy: A SPECT study." *Psychol Med* 37(10): 1481–91.

Pessoa, L., S. Japee, et al. (2006). "Target visibility and visual awareness modulate amygdala responses to fearful faces." *Cereb Cortex* 16(3): 366–75.

Pessoa, L., and S. Padmala (2005). "Quantitative prediction of perceptual decisions during near-threshold fear detection." *Proc Natl Acad Sci U S A* 102(15): 5612–7.

Pessoa, L., S. Padmala, et al. (2005). "Fate of unattended fearful faces in the amygdala is determined by both attentional resources and cognitive modulation." *Neuroimage* 28(1): 249–55.

Peters, E., N. F. Dieckmann, et al. (2009). "Bringing meaning to numbers: The impact of evaluative categories on decisions." *J Exp Psychol Appl* 15(3): 213–27.

Peters, T. J. (1979). "Leadership: Sad facts and silver linings." *Harv Bus Rev* 57(6): 164–72.

Petrovic, P., R. Kalisch, et al. (2008). "Oxytocin attenuates affective evaluations of conditioned faces and amygdala activity." *J Neurosci* 28(26): 6607–15.

Pettijohn, T. F., 2nd, and T. F. Pettijohn (1996). "Perceived happiness of college students measured by Maslow's hierarchy of needs." *Psychol Rep* 79(3 Pt 1): 759–62.

Petty, F., and A. D. Sherman (1979). "Reversal of learned helplessness by imipramine." *Commun Psychopharmacol* 3(5): 371–3.

Phelps, E. A., C. J. Cannistraci, et al. (2003). "Intact performance on an indirect measure of race bias following amygdala damage." *Neuropsychologia* 41(2): 203–8.

Phelps, E. A., M. R. Delgado, et al. (2004). "Extinction learning in humans: Role of the amygdala and vmPFC." *Neuron* 43(6): 897–905.

Phelps, E. A., K. J. O'Connor, et al. (2000). "Performance on indirect measures of race evaluation predicts amygdala activation." *J Cogn Neurosci* 12(5): 729–38.

Phillips, M. L., L. M. Williams, et al. (2004). "Differential neural responses to overt and covert presentations of facial expressions of fear and disgust." *Neuroimage* 21(4): 1484–96.

Piefke, M., M. Pestinger, et al. (2007). "The neurofunctional mechanisms of traumatic and non-traumatic memory in patients with acute PTSD following accident trauma." *Neurocase* 13(5): 342–57.

Pillay, S. S., S. A. Gruber, et al. (2006). "fMRI of fearful facial affect recognition in panic disorder: the cingulate gyrus-amygdala connection." *J Affect Disord* 94(1–3): 173–81.

Polit, D. F., and C. T. Beck (2008). "Is there gender bias in nursing research?" *Res Nurs Health* 31(5): 417–27.

Porter, M. E., and E. O. Teisberg (2004). "Redefining competition in health care." *Harv Bus Rev* 82(6): 64–76, 136.

Praamstra, P., L. Boutsen, et al. (2005). "Frontoparietal control of spatial attention and motor intention in human EEG." *J Neurophysiol* 94(1): 764–74.

Price, K. (2006). "Health promotion and some implications of consumer choice." *J Nurs Manag* 14(6): 494–501.

Pujol, J., A. Lopez, et al. (2002). "Anatomical variability of the anterior cingulate gyrus and basic dimensions of human personality." *Neuroimage* 15(4): 847–55.

Rakowski, E. (2002). "Who should pay for bad genes?" *Calif Law Rev* 90(5): 1345–414.

Ramacciotti, A., M. Sorbello, et al. (2001). "Attachment processes in eating disorders." *Eat Weight Disord* 6(3): 166–70.

Ramasubbu, R., S. Masalovich, et al. (2007). "Neural representation of maternal face processing: A functional magnetic resonance imaging study." *Can J Psychiatry* 52(11): 726–34.

Ranote, S., R. Elliott, et al. (2004). "The neural basis of maternal responsiveness to infants: An fMRI study." *Neuroreport* 15(11): 1825–9.

Rauch, A. V., P. Ohrmann, et al. (2007). "Cognitive copying style modulates neural responses to emotional faces in healthy humans: a 3-T FMRI study." *Cereb Cortex* 17(11): 2526–35.

Rauch, S. L., P. J. Whalen, et al. (2000). "Exaggerated amygdala response to masked facial stimuli in post-traumatic stress disorder: a functional MRI study." *Biol Psychiatry* 47(9): 769–76.

Rice, T. (1987). "An economic assessment of health care coverage for the elderly." *Milbank Q* 65(4): 488–520.

Richeson, J. A., and J. N. Shelton (2003). "When prejudice does not pay: Effects of interracial contact on executive function." *Psychol Sci* 14(3): 287–90.

Rigsby, C. S., W. E. Cannady, et al. (2005). "Aldosterone: Good guy or bad guy in cerebrovascular disease?" *Trends Endocrinol Metab* 16(9): 401–6.

Ristkari, T., A. Sourander, et al. (2008). "Life events, self-reported psychopathology and sense of coherence among young men—A population-based study." *Nord J Psychiatry* 62(6): 464–71.

Risvas, G., D. B. Panagiotakos, et al. (2008). "Factors associated with food choices among Greek primary school students: A cluster analysis in the ELPYDES study." *J Public Health* (Oxf) 30(3): 266–73.

Robertson, B., L. Wang, et al. (2007). "Effect of bupropion extended release on negative emotion processing in major depressive disorder:

A pilot functional magnetic resonance imaging study." *J Clin Psychiatry* 68(2): 261–7.

Rondahl, G., S. Innala, et al. (2004). "Nursing staff and nursing students' emotions towards homosexual patients and their wish to refrain from nursing, if the option existed." *Scand J Caring Sci* 18(1): 19–26.

Rothman, E. F., E. M. Edwards, et al. (2008). "Adverse childhood experiences predict earlier age of drinking onset: Results from a representative US sample of current or former drinkers." *Pediatrics* 122(2): e298–304.

Rothman, M. (1996). "Fear of success among business students." *Psychol Rep* 78(3 Pt 1): 863–9.

Rousseau, C. M., G. N. Ioannou, et al. (2008). "Racial differences in the evaluation and treatment of hepatitis C among veterans: A retrospective cohort study." *Am J Public Health* 98(5): 846–52.

Rushworth, M. F. (2008). "Intention, choice, and the medial frontal cortex." *Ann N Y Acad Sci* 1124: 181–207.

Ryniker, M. R. (2008). "Lesbians still face job discrimination." *J Lesbian Stud* 12(1): 7–15.

Saarela, M. V., Y. Hlushchuk, et al. (2007). "The compassionate brain: Humans detect intensity of pain from another's face." *Cereb Cortex* 17: 230–7.

Sabatinelli, D., M. M. Bradley, et al. (2005). "Parallel amygdala and inferotemporal activation reflect emotional intensity and fear relevance." *Neuroimage* 24(4): 1265–70.

Saclarides, T. J. (2006). "Current choices—good or bad—for the proactive management of postoperative ileus: A surgeon's view." *J Perianesth Nurs* 21(2A Suppl): S7–15.

Saewyc, E. M., Y. Homma, et al. (2009). "Protective factors in the lives of bisexual adolescents in North America." *Am J Public Health* 99(1): 110–7.

Samwel, H. J., A. W. Evers, et al. (2006). "The role of helplessness, fear of pain, and passive pain-coping in chronic pain patients." *Clin J Pain* 22(3): 245–51.

Saulis, A. S., T. A. Mustoe, et al. (2007). "A retrospective analysis of patient satisfaction with immediate postmastectomy breast reconstruction: Comparison of three common procedures." *Plast Reconstr Surg* 119(6): 1669–76; discussion 1677–8.

Schecter, D. E. (1979). "Fear of success in women: A psychodynamic reconstruction." *J Am Acad Psychoanal* 7(1): 33–43.

Schienle, A., A. Schafer, et al. (2005). "Gender differences in the processing of disgust- and fear-inducing pictures: An fMRI study." *Neuroreport* 16(3): 277–80.

Schwartz, C. E., C. I. Wright, et al. (2003). "Differential amygdalar response to novel versus newly familiar neutral faces: A functional MRI probe developed for studying inhibited temperament." *Biol Psychiatry* 53(10): 854–62.

Segerstrom, S. C. (2007). "Optimism and resources: Effects on each other and on health over 10 years." *J Res Pers* 41(4): 772–86.

Selye, H. (1975). "Stress and distress." *Compr Ther* 1(8): 9–13.

Severijnen, R., I. Hulstijn-Dirkmaat, et al. (2003). "Acute loss of the small bowel in a school-age boy. Difficult choices: To sustain life or to stop treatment?" *Eur J Pediatr* 162(11): 794–8.

Sewards, T. V., and M. A. Sewards (2002). "Fear and power-dominance drive motivation: Neural representations and pathways mediating sensory and mnemonic inputs, and outputs to premotor structures." *Neurosci Biobehav Rev* 26(5): 553–79.

Shannahoff-Khalsa, D. S. (2004). "An introduction to Kundalini yoga meditation techniques that are specific for the treatment of psychiatric disorders." *J Altern Complement Med* 10(1): 91–101.

Shapiro, J. P. (1979). "'Fear of success' imagery as a reaction to sex-role inappropriate behavior." *J Pers Assess* 43(1): 33–8.

Shapiro, S. L., D. Oman, et al. (2008). "Cultivating mindfulness: Effects on well-being." *J Clin Psychol* 64(7): 840–62.

Sharabany, R., and E. Israeli (2008). "The dual process of adolescent immigration and relocation: From country to country and from childhood to adolescence—Its reflection in psychodynamic psychotherapy." *Psychoanal Study Child* 63: 137–62.

Sharot, T., A. M. Riccardi, et al. (2007). "Neural mechanisms mediating optimism bias." *Nature* 450(7166): 102–5.

Sheese, B. E., M. K. Rothbart, et al. (2008). "Executive attention and self-regulation in infancy." *Infant Behav Dev* 31(3): 501–10.

Sheline, Y. I., D. M. Barch, et al. (2001). "Increased amygdala response to masked emotional faces in depressed subjects resolves with antidepressant treatment: An fMRI study." *Biol Psychiatry* 50(9): 651–8.

Shelton, J. N., J. A. Richeson, et al. (2005). "Ironic effects of racial bias during interracial interactions." *Psychol Sci* 16(5): 397–402.

Sherman, A. D., and G. L. Allers (1980). "Relationship between regional distribution of imipramine and its effect on learned helplessness in the rat." *Neuropharmacology* 19(2): 159–62.

Shin, L. M., S. L. Rauch, et al. (2006). "Amygdala, medial prefrontal cortex, and hippocampal function in PTSD." *Ann N Y Acad Sci* 1071: 67–79.

Shin, L. M., C. I. Wright, et al. (2005). "A functional magnetic resonance imaging study of amygdala and medial prefrontal cortex responses to overtly presented fearful faces in posttraumatic stress disorder." *Arch Gen Psychiatry* 62(3): 273–81.

Shors, T. J. (2004). "Learning during stressful times." *Learn Mem* 11(2): 137–44.

Shumake, J., D. Barrett, et al. (2005). "Behavioral characteristics of rats predisposed to learned helplessness: Reduced reward sensitivity, increased novelty seeking, and persistent fear memories." *Behav Brain Res* 164(2): 222–30.

Simmons, A. N., M. P. Paulus, et al. (2008). "Functional activation and neural networks in women with posttraumatic stress disorder related to intimate partner violence." *Biol Psychiatry* 64(8): 681–90.

Sinding, C., P. Grassau, et al. (2006). "Community support, community values: The experiences of lesbians diagnosed with cancer." *Women Health* 44(2): 59–79.

Singh, N. N., G. E. Lancioni, et al. (2008). "Clinical and benefit-cost outcomes of teaching a mindfulness-based procedure to adult offenders with intellectual disabilities." *Behav Modif* 32(5): 622–37.

Son Hing, L. S., G. A. Chung-Yan, et al. (2008). "A two-dimensional model that employs explicit and implicit attitudes to characterize prejudice." *J Pers Soc Psychol* 94(6): 971–87.

Song, S., and S. A. Burgard (2008). "Does son preference influence children's growth in height? A comparative study of Chinese and Filipino children." *Popul Stud (Camb)* 62(3): 305–20.

Spitzer, C., M. Vogel, et al. (2007). "Psychopathology and alexithymia in severe mental illness: The impact of trauma and posttraumatic stress symptoms." *Eur Arch Psychiatry Clin Neurosci* 257(4): 191–6.

Stewart, B. D., and B. K. Payne (2008). "Bringing automatic stereotyping under control: Implementation intentions as efficient means of thought control." *Pers Soc Psychol Bull* 34(10): 1332–45.

Stotts, N. A., and H. W. Hopf (2005). "Facilitating positive outcomes in older adults with wounds." *Nurs Clin North Am* 40(2): 267–79.

Strathearn, L., J. Li, et al. (2008). "What's in a smile? Maternal brain responses to infant facial cues." *Pediatrics* 122(1): 40–51.

Stremel, K. (1991). "Communicating with people who have multiple sensory impairments." *ASHA* 33(11): 30–1, 60.

Sue, D. W., J. Bucceri, et al. (2007). "Racial microaggressions and the Asian American experience." *Cultur Divers Ethnic Minor Psychol* 13(1): 72–81.

Surguladze, S. A., M. J. Brammer, et al. (2003). "A preferential increase in the extrastriate response to signals of danger." *Neuroimage* 19(4): 1317–28.

Swain, J. E., J. P. Lorberbaum, et al. (2007). "Brain basis of early parent-infant interactions: Psychology, physiology, and in vivo functional neuroimaging studies." *J Child Psychol Psychiatry* 48(3–4): 262–87.

Swain, J. E., E. Tasgin, et al. (2008). "Maternal brain response to own baby-cry is affected by cesarean section delivery." *J Child Psychol Psychiatry* 49(10): 1042–52.

Szubert, S., A. Florkowski, et al. (2008). "[Impact of stress on plasticity of brain structures and development of chosen psychiatric disorders]." *Pol Merkur Lekarski* 24(140): 162–5.

Tabbert, K., R. Stark, et al. (2005). "Hemodynamic responses of the amygdala, the orbitofrontal cortex and the visual cortex during a fear conditioning paradigm." *Int J Psychophysiol* 57(1): 15–23.

Takabayashi, K., M. Numazaki, et al. (2008). "[Women's activated self-representations influence their stereotyping and prejudice toward other traditional and nontraditional women]." *Shinrigaku Kenkyu* 79(4): 372–8.

Tamietto, M., and B. de Gelder (2008). "Affective blindsight in the intact brain: Neural interhemispheric summation for unseen fearful expressions." *Neuropsychologia* 46(3): 820–8.

Tamir, M. (2005). "Don't worry, be happy? Neuroticism, trait-consistent affect regulation, and performance." *J Pers Soc Psychol* 89(3): 449–61.

Tanev, K. (2003). "Neuroimaging and neurocircuitry in post-traumatic stress disorder: What is currently known?" *Curr Psychiatry Rep* 5(5): 369–83.

Thomas, K. M., W. C. Drevets, et al. (2001). "Amygdala response to facial expressions in children and adults." *Biol Psychiatry* 49(4): 309–16.

Tomkiewicz, J., and K. Bass (1999). "Changes in women's fear of success and fear of appearing incompetent in business." *Psychol Rep* 85(3 Pt 1): 1003–10.

Travis, F., and A. Arenander (2006). "Cross-sectional and longitudinal study of effects of transcendental meditation practice on interhemispheric frontal asymmetry and frontal coherence." *Int J Neurosci* 116(12): 1519–38.

Travis, F., D. A. Haaga, et al. (2009). "Effects of Transcendental

Meditation practice on brain functioning and stress reactivity in college students." *Int J Psychophysiol* 71(2): 170–6.

Turner, de S. (2005). "Hope seen through the eyes of 10 Australian young people." *J Adv Nurs* 52(5): 508–15.

Turner, R. N., M. Hewstone, et al. (2007). "Reducing explicit and implicit outgroup prejudice via direct and extended contact: The mediating role of self-disclosure and intergroup anxiety." *J Pers Soc Psychol* 93(3): 369–88.

Tyler, R. S., M. W. Lowder, et al. (1984). "Initial Iowa results with the multichannel cochlear implant from Melbourne." *J Speech Hear Res* 27(4): 596–604.

Ubel, P. A. (2002). "Is information always a good thing? Helping patients make 'good' decisions." *Med Care* 40(9 Suppl): V39–44.

Ullsperger, M., H. Nittono, et al. (2007). "When goals are missed: Dealing with self-generated and externally induced failure." *Neuroimage* 35(3): 1356–64.

Vahtera, J., M. Kivimaki, et al. (2007). "Liability to anxiety and severe life events as predictors of new-onset sleep disturbances." *Sleep* 30(11): 1537–46.

Vallevand, A. L., D. M. Paskevich, et al. (2007). "Use of simulations to assess the injury evaluation and management skills of advanced student athletic therapists at a Canadian university." *J Allied Health* 36(3): e244–56.

van der Werf, S. P., A. Evers, et al. (2003). "The role of helplessness as mediator between neurological disability, emotional instability, experienced fatigue and depression in patients with multiple sclerosis." *Mult Scler* 9(1): 89–94.

van Dijk, S., M. S. van Roosmalen, et al. (2008). "Decision making regarding prophylactic mastectomy: Stability of preferences and the impact of anticipated feelings of regret." *J Clin Oncol* 26(14): 2358–63.

van Honk, J., J. S. Peper, et al. (2005). "Testosterone reduces unconscious fear but not consciously experienced anxiety: Implications for the disorders of fear and anxiety." *Biol Psychiatry* 58(3): 218–25.

van Honk, J., A. Tuiten, et al. (1998). "Baseline salivary cortisol levels and preconscious selective attention for threat. A pilot study." *Psychoneuroendocrinology* 23(7): 741–7.

Vanman, E. J., J. L. Saltz, et al. (2004). "Racial discrimination by low-prejudiced whites. Facial movements as implicit measures of attitudes related to behavior." *Psychol Sci* 15(11): 711–4.

Vastfjall, D., and T. Garling (2007). "Validation of a Swedish short self-report measure of core affect." *Scand J Psychol* 48(3): 233–8.

Vaughan, K. B., and J. T. Lanzetta (1980). "Vicarious instigation and conditioning of facial expressive and autonomic responses to a model's expressive display of pain." *J Pers Soc Psychol* 38(6): 909–23.

Verweij, K. J., S. N. Shekar, et al. (2008). "Genetic and environmental influences on individual differences in attitudes toward homosexuality: An Australian twin study." *Behav Genet* 38(3): 257–65.

Vig, E. K., N. A. Davenport, et al. (2002). "Good deaths, bad deaths, and preferences for the end of life: A qualitative study of geriatric outpatients." *J Am Geriatr Soc* 50(9): 1541–8.

Vinkovic, D., and A. Kirman (2006). "A physical analogue of the Schelling model." *Proc Natl Acad Sci U S A* 103(51): 19261–5.

Volker, D. L., D. Kahn, et al. (2004). "Patient control and end-of-life care part I: The advanced practice nurse perspective." *Oncol Nurs Forum* 31(5): 945–53.

Volkow, N. D., and T. K. Li (2004). "Drug addiction: The neurobiology of behaviour gone awry." *Nat Rev Neurosci* 5(12): 963–70.

Volz, K. G., and D. Y. von Cramon (2006). "What neuroscience can tell about intuitive processes in the context of perceptual discovery." *J Cogn Neurosci* 18(12): 2077–87.

Vrticka, P., F. Andersson, et al. (2008). "Individual attachment style modulates human amygdala and striatum activation during social appraisal." *PLoS ONE* 3(8): e2868.

Vuilleumier, P., J. L. Armony, et al. (2001). "Effects of attention and emotion on face processing in the human brain: An event-related fMRI study." *Neuron* 30(3): 829–41.

Vuilleumier, P., and G. Pourtois (2007). "Distributed and interactive brain mechanisms during emotion face perception: Evidence from functional neuroimaging." *Neuropsychologia* 45: 174–94.

Vuilleumier, P., and S. Schwartz (2001). "Beware and be aware: Capture of spatial attention by fear-related stimuli in neglect." *Neuroreport* 12(6): 1119–22.

Waelde, L. C., M. Uddo, et al. (2008). "A pilot study of meditation for mental health workers following Hurricane Katrina." *J Trauma Stress* 21(5): 497–500.

Wangchuk, P., D. Wangchuk, et al. (2007). "Traditional Bhutanese medicine (gSo-BA Rig-PA): An integrated part of the formal health care services." *Southeast Asian J Trop Med Public Health* 38(1): 161–7.

Ward, A. (2007). "The social epidemiologic concept of fundamental cause." *Theor Med Bioeth* 28(6): 465–85.

Waschbusch, D. A., D. P. Sellers, et al. (2003). "Helpless attributions and depression in adolescents: The roles of anxiety, event valence, and demographics." *J Adolesc* 26(2): 169–83.

Weaver, L. A., and K. Andrutis (2004). "IACUC replacement parts: What are the requirements? Bad choices." *Lab Anim (NY)* 33(10): 17–8.

Wegner, D. M., and L. Smart (1997). "Deep cognitive activation: A new approach to the unconscious." *J Consult Clin Psychol* 65(6): 984–95.

Weiner, C. L., M. Primeau, et al. (2004). "Androgens and mood dysfunction in women: Comparison of women with polycystic ovarian syndrome to healthy controls." *Psychosom Med* 66(3): 356–62.

Weinreich-Haste, H. (1978). "Sex differences in 'fear of success' among British students." *Br J Soc Clin Psychol* 17(1): 37–42.

Weisberg, E. (1986). "The practical aspects of clinical trials of contraceptive methods." *Clin Reprod Fertil* 4(2): 139–47.

Weiskrantz, L., J. L. Barbur, et al. (1995). "Parameters affecting conscious versus unconscious visual discrimination with damage to the visual cortex (V1)." *Proc Natl Acad Sci U S A* 92(13): 6122–6.

Weiss, H., and H. Lang (2000). "Object relations and intersubjectivity in depression." *Am J Psychother* 54(3): 317–28.

Wessa, M., and H. Flor (2007). "Failure of extinction of fear responses in posttraumatic stress disorder: Evidence from second-order conditioning." *Am J Psychiatry* 164(11): 1684–92.

Whalen, P. J., J. Kagan, et al. (2004). "Human amygdala responsivity to masked fearful eye whites." *Science* 306(5704): 2061.

Whalen, P. J., S. L. Rauch, et al. (1998). "Masked presentations of emotional facial expressions modulate amygdala activity without explicit knowledge." *J Neurosci* 18(1): 411–8.

Whitney, P., J. M. Hinson, et al. (2007). "Somatic responses in behavioral inhibition." *Cogn Affect Behav Neurosci* 7(1): 37–43.

Wild, B., M. Erb, et al. (2001). "Are emotions contagious? Evoked emotions while viewing emotionally expressive faces: Quality, quantity, time course and gender differences." *Psychiatry Res* 102(2): 109–24.

Wild, J., and R. C. Gur (2008). "Verbal memory and treatment response in post-traumatic stress disorder." *Br J Psychiatry* 193(3): 254–5.

Williams, L. M., P. Das, et al. (2005). "BOLD, sweat and fears: fMRI and skin conductance distinguish facial fear signals." *Neuroreport* 16(1): 49–52.

Williams, L. M., P. Das, et al. (2006). "Mode of functional connectivity in amygdala pathways dissociates level of awareness for signals of fear." *J Neurosci* 26(36): 9264–71.

Williams, L. M., A. H. Kemp, et al. (2006). "Trauma modulates amygdala and medial prefrontal responses to consciously attended fear." *Neuroimage* 29(2): 347–57.

Williams, L. M., B. J. Liddell, et al. (2006). "Amygdala-prefrontal dissociation of subliminal and supraliminal fear." *Hum Brain Mapp* 27(8): 652–61.

Williams, L. M., B. J. Liddell, et al. (2004). "Mapping the time course of nonconscious and conscious perception of fear: An integration of central and peripheral measures." *Hum Brain Mapp* 21(2): 64–74.

Williams, L. M., M. L. Phillips, et al. (2001). "Arousal dissociates amygdala and hippocampal fear responses: Evidence from simultaneous fMRI and skin conductance recording." *Neuroimage* 14(5): 1070–9.

Williams, M. A., and J. B. Mattingley (2004). "Unconscious perception of non-threatening facial emotion in parietal extinction." *Exp Brain Res* 154(4): 403–6.

Williams, M. A., F. McGlone, et al. (2005). "Differential amygdala responses to happy and fearful facial expressions depend on selective attention." *Neuroimage* 24(2): 417–25.

Williams, M. A., A. P. Morris, et al. (2004). "Amygdala responses to fearful and happy facial expressions under conditions of binocular suppression." *J Neurosci* 24(12): 2898–904.

Windmann, S., and T. Kruger (1998). "Subconscious detection of threat as reflected by an enhanced response bias." *Conscious Cogn* 7(4): 603–33.

Winston, J. S., J. O'Doherty, et al. (2003). "Common and distinct neural responses during direct and incidental processing of multiple facial emotions." *Neuroimage* 20(1): 84–97.

Woodward, S. H., D. G. Kaloupek, et al. (2006). "Decreased anterior cingulate volume in combat-related PTSD." *Biol Psychiatry* 59(7): 582–7.

Woon, F. L., and D. W. Hedges (2008). "Hippocampal and amygdala volumes in children and adults with childhood maltreatment-related posttraumatic stress disorder: A meta-analysis." *Hippocampus* 18(8): 729–36.

Wright, C. I., M. M. Wedig, et al. (2006). "Novel fearful faces activate the amygdala in healthy young and elderly adults." *Neurobiol Aging* 27(2): 361–74.

Wu, J. (1992). "Masochism and fear of success in Asian women: Psychoanalytic mechanisms and problems in therapy." *Am J Psychoanal* 52(1): 1–12.

Wu, W. L., and W. Zhang (2005). "[Relationship between the adult attachment styles of social anxiety disorder (SAD) and its cognitive mode and behavior mode]." *Sichuan Da Xue Xue Bao Yi Xue Ban* 36(2): 271–3.

Yamasue, H., K. Kasai, et al. (2003). "Voxel-based analysis of MRI reveals anterior cingulate gray-matter volume reduction in posttraumatic stress disorder due to terrorism." *Proc Natl Acad Sci U S A* 100(15): 9039–43.

Yoshida, W., and S. Ishii (2006). "Resolution of uncertainty in prefrontal cortex." *Neuron* 50(5): 781–9.

Zak, P. J., R. Kurzban, et al. (2005). "Oxytocin is associated with human trustworthiness." *Horm Behav* 48(5): 522–7.

Zamora-Munoz, P. M., and C. Orellana-Reta (2007). "[Treatment of the tibial bone defects by traumatic sequels with the Ilizarov method in children]." *Acta Ortop Mex* 21(6): 318–22.

Zanni, G. R. (2008). "Optimism and health." *Consult Pharm* 23(2): 112–6, 119, 121, 124, 126.

Zikmund-Fisher, B. J., A. Fagerlin, et al. (2004). "'Is 28% good or bad?' Evaluability and preference reversals in health care decisions." *Med Decis Making* 24(2): 142–8.

Zinn, J. S., W. E. Aaronson, et al. (1993). "The use of standardized indicators as quality improvement tools: An application in Pennsylvania nursing homes." *Am J Med Qual* 8(2): 72–8.

Zuckerman, M., and S. N. Allison (1976). "An objective measure of fear of success: Construction and validation." *J Pers Assess* 40(4): 422–30.

Index

Boldface page references indicate illustrations and graphs. Underscored references indicate charts.

B

D

N

O

P

S

W

X

Y

Z